THE APPLAUSE SCREENPLAY SERIES

TERMINATOR 2
JUDGMENT DAY

The Book of the Film

An Illustrated Screenplay

by
James Cameron
&
William Wisher

OVER 700
photographs and storyboards
and including
a selection of omitted sequences
and the complete credits

Introduction by James Cameron

Annotations by Van Ling
Creative Supervisor

D1127610

An Applause Original
TERMINATOR 2: JUDGMENT DAY

Library of Congress Cataloging-in-Publication Data:

Cameron, James, 1954-
        Terminator 2: judgment day : the book of the film / by James Cameron & William Wisher ;
introduction by James Cameron.
                p.   cm. - - (The Applause screenplay series)
        "With over 700 photographs from the film and the original storyboards."
         "An Applause original" - - T.p. verso.
          ISBN 1-55783-097-5 : $17.95
          I. Wisher, William.   II. Terminator 2.   III. Title.   IV. Series.
        PN1997.T397   1991
        791.43'72 - - dc20

APPLAUSE BOOKS
211 West 71st Street
New York, NY 10023
Phone (212) 595-4735
Fax (212) 721-2856

First Applause Printing, 1991.

ACKNOWLEDGEMENTS

In the almost five years that I've worked for Jim Cameron, there has rarely been a quiet moment. From the first time Jim outlined the story of *Terminator 2* to me back in 1986 to its spectacular release five years later, I have watched it grow and evolve, become heavy with the weight of a hundred great ideas and then slim down to fighting weight, lean and trim; I've seen its characters develop, flare briefly in the light of the narrative and then fade into the ether, only to rise again like phoenixes from the ashes of early concepts. It was like being caught in a brainstorm without an umbrella. There is nothing more exciting and educational than to watch a vision coalesce into celluloid reality, and to help make it happen. It is my intention in the notes and annotations to chronicle that narrative creation and to convey the fascination of story evolution, to share in the wonder of watching a film grow from its beginnings on the page into full-blown motion.

This is not a book about production; it is a book about creation. The foundations of any film are its story and characters, and the way they develop and mature is the story behind the story.

A book of this magnitude is not taken on lightly. There was a lot of faith invoked on all sides, from the folks at Carolco licensing and Applause Books who made the agreement to publish the screenplay in the first place, to the non-stop work of those of us who cared enough about the project to put in an extraordinary amount of hours into putting it together, to Jim Cameron himself, who agreed that a chronicle of the evolution of the narrative was much more fascinating and valuable than a mere transcript of the film.

My eternal thanks to: Geoff Burdick and Steve Quale at Lightstorm Entertainment, whose unconditional support and tireless work in gathering materials, sorting photos and artwork, making layouts, and much more on too many an all-nighter have made this book possible; Don Shay of Cinefex magazine, whose invaluable experience and encouragement helped me to organize my thoughts; designer/illustrators Steve Burg and Duncan Kennedy, the artists at Stan Winston Studios and Industrial Light and Magic, and storyboard artists Phill Norwood, George Jensen, and Sherman Labby, whose work is represented in this book; Clarinda Wong and rest of the editorial staff on the production, for their assistance in getting us the film we needed to make the frame blowups; Nila Fields, Gary Sanden, and the folks at Select Color for making the frame blowups happen; Steve Newman, our T2 unit publicist who liaisoned with a multitude of parties to get us our clearances; all my other coworkers at Lightstorm Entertainment for their help and encouragement; Brian Keeney, Charles de Lauzirika, Jay Shepard, Chris Manson, and Wendy and Joseph Grossberg of the USC FX Club, and Larry Herbst for volunteering many hours of service in sorting and trimming the photos; Glenn Young at Applause Books in New York for his patience; Mark Mixson and his wife Farryl from Applause, who flew out to Los Angeles to hold it all together; my girlfriend Carolyn for still recognizing and welcoming me on those increasingly infrequent occasions when I managed to see her; and of course Jim Cameron, whose vision has been a great source of inspiration --and perspiration-- to me.
Anytime, anywhere...

Van Ling
Creative Technical Supervisor,
Lightstorm Entertainment
Los Angeles
July 1991

CONTENTS

INTRODUCTION

In the years since *The Terminator*, *Terminator 2* has been like a Great White shark circling slowly out in the black ocean of my subconscious, waiting patiently for its time to return and strike. In those years the story existed for me as a vague sketch, almost like a dream dimly remembered on awakening. It had no detail, but it had the beating heart of an idea that I knew would work.

Despite occasional temptations, however, I never sat down to flesh out this idea.
Perhaps superstitiously, I must have believed that by wanting the film to happen, by investing in it emotionally as one must to write a screenplay, I would condemn it to oblivion. My paranoia was based on the fact that I did not control the rights to a *Terminator* sequel, and therefore no amount of wishing on my part could bring the film into existence.

The rights to a second *Terminator* film were held by a number of entities who were involved in the first picture, and could not see eye to eye. It took a mighty swordstroke from an Alexander the Great, a.k.a. Mario Kassar of Carolco, to hack through this Gordian Knot and get the project moving, six years after the release of *The Terminator*. Just as it was foretold that whoever solved the mystery of the Gordian Knot would conquer the world, Mario Kassar has boldly brought into existence a film which has conquered all competition. As I write this, *T2* has been in release for a little less than a week and has ground all the other summer films under its treads. It has made more money in six days than *The Abyss* made in its entire domestic theatrical run. So here I am, trying to cast my mind back to the days of writing this script, that innocent time when we had no idea where all this would lead... when the future was, as it always is, a black highway at night.

When Mario called to say he was collecting the rights and that he had a deal with Arnold, I agreed readily to do the film. For years I had shunned the idea, wanting to explore other realms and make other films. But the gestation period was right, at six years, (the same time between *Alien* and the start of *Aliens*) and it was an opportunity I couldn't pass up. My one proviso was that I would not write one word of the script until a deal had been made with Linda Hamilton, because the return of her character was as essential to me as that of Arnold's. After not speaking with her in years, I tracked her down and broached the subject of another *Terminator* film. My call came out of the blue for her, on a day when she was about to take a role in another science fiction film which would have been a direct conflict. Fate was on our side; she was positive about my rough verbal outline, which was little more than "your son is the target and you're in a mental hospital. The kid teams up with a "good" terminator and comes to break you out. Then you save the world." She said only "I want to be crazy." I said, "I can do that." On the strength of that conversation, she turned down the other film.

An agonizing month went by before Linda's deal could be closed, but with her finally on board, there remained no obstacles to writing the best damn sequel possible, except...
Writing.
My old bête noir.
I hate writing. It is the most tedious, solitary, terrifying part of making a film. It is the moment when the creative die is cast, although it will take months, maybe years, and millions of dollars to find out if the throw was lucky or unlucky.
In the horrible heat of battle, on the set, when the crew is tired and the set is taking too long to be lit which means you won't have enough time to get the shots you need, the script is your bible, your map through the jungle. There is no time to question it then, or all will dissolve into chaos. It must be right. You must have unquestioning faith in it.

The problem is that when you're writing, you can't think of that awesome responsibility or you won't ever get a single word down on paper. You have to divorce yourself mentally from the director-self which will be sweating months later under the yoke your writer-self is creating. And to take responsibility for the financial success of a multi-million dollar project at that fragile stage of creation is the death of art. This makes the writing process also slightly schizophrenic, at least for writer-director-producer mutant hyphenates like myself.

Equally, it's pure strangulation to try to think in advance of how the images are going to actually get done. With a kind of abandon I pre-absolve myself from the responsibility of creating stunts and special effects in the real world, and plunge into the story as if I am writing a novel, rather than a screenplay which is only a means to an end. Later there will be enough negative voices, enough nay-sayers and bean-counters to provide the crushing weight of gravity which will pull these flights of fancy back to earth. When I'm writing, I just put on some loud music and put the throttle down hard.

So the moment of truth was finally at hand. The Great White had finished circling. It was time to put something on paper and call it *Terminator 2*. In the face of that terrifying prospect, I did what I always do when I have a problem. I make my problem someone else's problem.

Bill Wisher was remarkably calm when I proposed to him that he co-write the script with me. He was just finishing up another screenplay and was available to start immediately, which was almost soon enough. Bill had done a little writing on *The Terminator* (for an "Additional Dialogue" credit) and knew the characters and all the dramatic intentions of that piece in his sleep. He jumped in with both feet and we spent an intensive couple of weeks pacing around the tiny writing office at my house, batting around ideas, acting out scenes and bits of dialogue, pushing each other out of the way at the word processor to get our thoughts down in words. It was an intensely creative period and when the dust settled we had a treatment. It was wild and woolly and had way too many scenes and would have cost more than Operation Desert Storm to produce, but we were rolling.

We divided up the treatment into sections and started writing separately. We traded pages and talked on the phone a lot. We kept the hammer down, forcing ourselves to produce. Just make scenes, I told him... keep it flowing. If it's shit, we'll throw it out later. I had set myself the somewhat arbitrary target of completing the script in time for my flight to Cannes in four weeks, knowing that Carolco would be announcing the project there at their legendary party and subsequent press conference. I was determined to put the rough draft into Arnold's hands on that flight to France, as I had promised him months earlier.

As the deadline loomed, the nights got longer. Family and friends knew from experience not to call. I became like a wounded, pregnant wolverine holed up in a cave. I wrote every night in a frenzy and crashed at dawn. I took Bill's scenes and pasted them into the "thing" that was growing in my hard drive. When I finally gave my computer the print command to spit out the entire script, the limo was waiting in the driveway to take me to the airport and we had been up for 36 hours straight. The last 25 pages had written themselves in a non-stop pounding of keys. My fingers were sore. I grabbed the script out of the laser printer tray, stuffed it in my briefcase and headed for the airport. I was booed as I boarded the Carolco charter jet, since I was the last of a hundred people to arrive and had delayed the flight. I slept, coma-like, as Arnold read. Somehow I sensed whenever he would stop reading, and would crack one eye open to watch him. As he read on I would sink back into sleep. It was a night flight and very turbulent. Arnold read as the aircraft bucked and plummetted. Later he would tell me that he was riveted, that it was all he had hoped for.
We had a movie.

We announced the film at Cannes, calmly stating that it would be ready for a July 4 1991 release. 13 months to deliver the completed film. And we had nothing but a very rough script. Not even a producer. This was madness. But summer was the right time to release, so we just had to pull it off somehow.

Returning to L.A., I plunged into a whirlwind of activity, bringing aboard not one but two co-producers to share the burden with me. Budgeting, storyboarding, and special effects contract bidding were the primary areas of concern, with little time to rewrite the bloated first draft script from which we were all working. Sensing an imminent train wreck, I finally called time out and by pushing the start date back one week, carved out a little time to do the much-needed rewrite.

The opening was pared down drastically, both for budget and running-time considerations. A sub-plot involving a character named Gant was removed, although a narrative residue of those scenes remains with the visit to Salceda's compound in the desert.

This first revision essentially became the shooting script. There were additional revision pages, but the subsequent changes were trivial. A shot here, a line there.

We started shooting on October 8th, 1990, and wrapped in April of 1991. During that time there were only microscopic revisions. Two of Terminator's best lines were actually made up on the set: "Trust me" and "I need a vacation". The latter is actually in the prose description of the scene, and Arnold and I thought it might be fun to have him say it.

The next major wave of changes did not occur until the editing room, in the spring of '91. Here, in what I always think of as the last step in the writing process, a few scenes that I was certain in the fall I could not live without were removed. And the film improved. This is the point at which a film truly comes to life. I think of it as the film slowly revealing itself to me. Only in the pressure cooker of the cutting room, with the spectre of a three-hour film looming, do the real priorities become clear. You find out what the film is really about. With a gesture or a word, a good actor can evoke a sense of the character which the writer was certain would require pages of dialogue and intricate backstory. I pared down the writer's flourishes, trusting in the work of my cast... leaning and honing. It's dangerous to do too much of this in the original writing, because often the moments and the ideas which ultimately wind up on the cutting room floor are a necessary part of the actor's creation of the character, and have informed them as they went along in the creation of the other, more important moments which remain in the film.

We removed the first of Sarah's two nuclear nightmares, which seemed to make the one remaining even more powerful. Since this second dream propels the narrative for the latter half of the film, anything which made it more dramatically potent could only help. Also taken out was a beautiful little scene in which Dyson discusses his work with his wife, Tarissa. It was acted with great warmth and intelligence by Joe Morton and Epatha Merkerson, but it slowed the relentless forward pace of the story at a critical point when the audience is waiting for the film to declare its dramatic intentions, where every second of delay hurt. We also removed the surgery scene, where Sarah and John take out Terminator's CPU and switch it to 'write mode'. Although a fascinating and compelling scene, magnificently acted, it was one of the few narrative chunks that could be taken out seamlessly without compromising story or character. By suggesting instead, through off-camera dialogue recorded in post-production, that Terminator's neural net "learning computer" mind was already capable of absorbing human behavior, we were able to save 4 minutes of screen time in a critical "soft" section of the film.

The last significant change of course was the removal of the final scene, which we always called the "Future Park" or the "Coda Park". This was a classic example of something which worked perfectly on paper but which didn't work on the screen. We all felt that something was wrong, that there was a slightly sour note at the end of the symphony. Perhaps, after the 40 miles of bad road preceding the coda, the film just couldn't go on that much longer... perhaps we just sensed that everything that needed to be said had already been said. Perhaps emerging from the dark industrial inferno of the steel mill into the bright idyllic sunshine of a world delivered from peril was too dislocating, and seemed to be a scene from another film. I had always thought that it was important to show that their efforts, the sacrifices made by Terminator and by Miles Dyson, were not in vain and that history was changed. But I began to think that the message of the film might be better served by not letting the audience off the hook so easily. We decided to not tie it all up with a bow, but to suggest that the struggle was ongoing, and in fact might even be an unending one for us flawed creatures trying to come to terms with technology and our own violent demons.

So my final writing on T2 came less than a month before release, with the voice-over narration which ends the film.

The writing for me is always a means to an end, a transitional phase between the mind and the final work, which is the film. I do not allow myself to fall in love with the words. I fall in love with performances, with images, and protect them through the cutting process when they are worthy. The script is nothing more than a means of communicating with my cast, my crew, and with the people who are putting up the dough. It is not a thing in itself, in the way that a story or a novel is. My writing style is informal, for that reason, because evoking an image or a feeling with the words is the only important thing, not the rigid adherence to proper script form.

So as you read this book and compare it in your mind to the film, you will see that the script was marking out a path, which was sometimes followed and sometimes strayed from. As a result, even the very last umpteenth revision does not accurately represent the movie, but is still merely a sketch from which the film became the finished painting. The joy of creation for me is not in exactly reproducing the script on film, but in going beyond it... allowing it to inspire the actors to performances which in turn will inspire me. Still, it all begins with the written word, even in this age of computer-generated imagery where the only remaining limitations are imagination and money.

Which is why whenever I begin a film, I will always sit down in that solitary and terrifying place, and confront that empty page (or computer screen).
Even though I hate writing.

Jim Cameron
July 9, 1991

FOREWORD

Filmmaking is a collaborative art, and storytelling is by nature an evolutionary process. A screenplay is only a blueprint from which a motion picture is constructed; the final film is a product of both creative give-and-take and the exigencies of shooting: scenes are altered because a crucial prop or set or stunt was not ready as scheduled; lines of dialogue are tried, thrown out, and improvised; a walkthrough of a location brings out new and better ideas; a juxtaposition of two shots in editing or one look in a performance can convey in one moment the essence of a scene that originally comprised three pages of dialogue. Through all three phases of filmmaking --preproduction, principal photography, and postproduction-- things that don't work (sometimes readily apparent, other times unnoticed until a crucial point) get sifted out; the stuff that works comes to the fore. Scenes written into the script are deleted before they are shot when it is realized that they are not necessary to the narrative; other scenes are shot as scripted and then found to be redundant in the editing process, while new scenes are added to address certain points not covered in the script. The emphasis and pacing of a scene can change with blocking, with performance, with camera position. Transposition of scenes can make a world of difference in the unfolding of the plot; revelations in one scene can change the meaning of another. Running time is also a consideration; the longer the film, the fewer number of screenings per day, the greater the risk of tiring the audience. (This is why most films have a running time of around two hours; the longest generally acceptable film length today is around 140 minutes, and is only done with trepidation.) All of these factors contribute to rather than detract from the storytelling process, for they are indicative of the filmmaking dynamic in action.

This book is meant as a study of presentation, covering both the broad strokes of narrative and many of the little details that mark the evolutionary progress of a story from script to screen. The annotations, by no means exhaustive, are written to illuminate the differences between the screenplay and the finished film and to illustrate the process by which scenes and narrative elements are developed, revised, reevaluated, and prioritized within the context of production.

DRAFT HISTORY

The first draft of *Terminator 2: Judgment Day* was completed on 5/10/90 and was considered a work-in-progress; the first distributed shooting script, significantly streamlined from the first draft, was issued on 7/18/90, as the film went into preproduction; a major revision of 65+ pages was issued on 9/10/90, based upon various departmental discussions, preliminary location scouts, actors' meetings, and general streamlining; a set of 5 revision pages was issued on 9/13/90 to address a series of minor changes in location and action; another series of revisions was issued on 10/1/90, a few days prior to the start of principal photography, to scale down and delete a pair of major effects scenes; more minor revisions appeared on 1/3/91 to streamline the dialogue at the climax of the story; and on 2/19/91, a final set of revision pages was issued to accommodate the shooting schedule and simplify the action while keeping the essence of the story intact. The script published in this book is the final revised shooting script that incorporates all of the revision pages issued before and during production; in several instances, changes that were incorporated into shooting had never made it to a revision page, even though they were always planned to be shot that way. In comparing the final film to the script, it is interesting to note how some scenes are captured shot for shot as they are written in the script, while others have evolved in completely different directions but yet convey the same meaning and purpose.

STORYBOARDS

Storyboards are an invaluable tool in the visualization of a film and, like the written word, can be either rough sketches or finished renderings, to be rigidly adhered to or thrown out completely as the visuals of the narrative evolve. These pages include only a very small sampling of the hundreds of drawings created to assist in the production process.

TERMINATOR 2
JUDGMENT DAY

LOS ANGELES 2029A.D.

1   EXT. CITY STREET - DAY

Downtown L.A. Noon on a hot summer day. On an EXTREME LONG LENS the lunchtime crowd
stacks up into a wall of humanity. In SLOW MOTION they move in herds among the glittering
rows of cars jammed bumper to bumper. Heat ripples distort the torrent of faces. The image is
surreal, dreamy... and like a dream it begins very slowly to

DISSOLVE TO:

2   EXT. CITY RUINS - NIGHT

Same spot as the last shot, but now it is a landscape in Hell. The cars are stopped in rusted rows,
still bumper to bumper. The skyline of buildings beyond has been shattered by some
unimaginable force like a row of kicked-down sandcastles.
Wind blows through the desolation, keening with the sound of ten million dead souls. It scurries
the ashes into drifts, stark white in the moonlight against the charred rubble.
A TITLE CARD FADES IN:

LOS ANGELES, July 11, 2029

3   ANGLE ON a heap of fire-blackened human bones. Beyond the mound is a vast tundra of skulls
and shattered concrete.   The rush hour crowds burned down in their tracks.

4   WE DISSOLVE TO a playground... where intense heat has half-melted the jungle gym, the blast
has warped the swing set, the merry-go-round has sagged in the firestorm. Small skulls look
accusingly from the ash-drifts. WE HEAR the distant echo of children's voices... playing and
laughing in the sun. A silly, sing-songy rhyme as WE TRACK SLOWLY over seared asphalt
where the faint hieroglyphs of hopscotch lines are still visible.

CAMERA comes to rest on a burnt and rusted tricycle... next to the tiny skull of its owner. HOLD
ON THIS IMAGE as a female VOICE speaks:

                    VOICE
          3 billion human lives ended on August 29th, 1997. The survivors
          of the nuclear fire called the war Judgment Day. They lived
          only to face a new nightmare, the war against the Machines...

A metal foot crushes the skull like china.

TILT UP, revealing a humanoid machine holding a massive battle rifle. It looks like a
CHROME SKELETON... a high-tech Death figure. It is the endoskeleton of a Series 800
terminator.   Its glowing red eyes compassionlessly sweep the dead terrain, hunting.

In the 5/10/90 draft, this expository voiceover is given by the adult John Connor, not Sarah; in the 7/18/90
draft, it has been substantially tightened and is presented on title cards rather than voiceover, much like the
expository cards at the head of the first film; with the main portion of the Future War sequence cut, there
seemed to be no justification for having John Connor narrate the story, and therefore the film. The question
of main narrative voice determines to a great extent the primary or central character of any story, and with
the 9/10/90 revision, the emphasis on Sarah's story became prominent. By making Sarah the narrator, it not
only echoes the "Sarah as historian" motif established at the end of the first film, but gives a logical vantage
point to the story that sets the tone for the use of voiceover exposition later in the film.

The SOUND of ROARING TURBINES. Searchlights blaze down as a formation of flying HK
(Hunter-Killer) patrol machines passes overhead.   PAN WITH THEM toward the jagged
horizon, beyond which we see flashes, and hear the distant thunder of a pitched battle in progress.

The final Future War sequence was substantially reduced in both narrative and scope from the version in the original 5/10/90 draft --which included Skynet's defeat by the human Resistance and the time-displacement scene with Reese-- for a variety of reasons, not only due to the enormous cost of designing, building, and shooting the battle sequences, but also because the original longer version delayed the process of getting into the main plot, which begins with the arrival of the two terminators. Through the course of production, the sequence was scaled down and simplified into a short documentary-style prologue, which actually enhanced its narrative value, for although it was not strictly necessary to the plot to show the war, its inclusion in the film serves as both a visceral illustration of what the characters in the film are fighting to prevent, and a narrative reminder to the audience of the world postulated by the first film. It is interesting to note that this sequence is in fact Sarah's vision of the impending future, as imparted to her by Kyle Reese in the first film; Sarah has not experienced the war directly, but only through the eyes of another. Refer to the appendix of omitted sequences for the original full-length Future War sequence from the 5/10/90 draft.

5   EXT. BATTLEFIELD - NIGHT

       THE BATTLE. Human troops in desperate combat with the machines for possession of the dead Earth. The humans are a ragtag guerrilla army. Skynet's weapons consist of the Ground HKs (tank-like robot gun-platforms), flying Aerial HKs, four-legged gun-pods called Centurions, and the humanoid terminators in various forms.

       SEQUENCE OF RAPID CUTS:
5A   Explosions! Beam-weapons firing like searing strobe-lights.
5B   A gunner in an armored personnel carrier fires a LAW rocket at a pursuing Aerial HK, bringing it down in a fiery explosion.
5C   Another APC is crushed under the treads of a massive Ground HK.

5D   A TEAM OF GUERRILLAS in an intense fire-fight with terminator
5E   endoskeletons in the ruins of a building. Three terminator endoskeletons
5F   advance, firing rapidly. Another (complete cyborg), with flesh ripped open and back broken, gropes for a rifle on the ground.

5G   A Centurion overruns a human firing position. Soldiers are cut down as they run. Fiery explosions light the ranks of advancing machines.

6   IN A BLASTED GUN EMPLACEMENT at the edge of battle, a man watches the combat with night-vision binoculars. He wears the uniform of a guerrilla general, and a black beret. He is still amid running, shouting techs and officers.

       C.U. MAN, pushing slowly in as the battle rages O.S. He lowers the binoculars. He is forty-five years old. Features severe. The left side of his face is heavily scarred. A patch covers that eye. An impressive man, forged in the furnace of a lifetime of war. The name stitched on the band of his beret is CONNOR. We push in until his eyes fill frame, then...

                                                              DISSOLVE TO:

FIRE. SLOW, ROILING, ENORMOUS. FILLING FRAME.

                         VOICE (SARAH CONNOR)
                 Skynet, the computer which controlled the Machines, sent two
                 terminators back through time. Their mission: to destroy the
                 leader of the human Resistance... John Connor. My son.

                 The first terminator was programmed to strike at me, in the
                 year 1984... before John was born.
                 It failed.

TERMINATOR 2
JUDGMENT DAY

The second was set to strike at John himself, when he was still a child. As before, the Resistance was able to send a lone warrior. A protector for John. It was just a question of which one of them would reach him first...

DISSOLVE TO:

The main title sequence in the film, which takes place between the end of Sarah's narration and the arrival of Terminator, depicts a burning playground that ominously contrasts the carefree city and playground shots at the very head of the film; key images include the emergence of the terminator endoskeleton from the fire and what was dubbed "the seahorse, rocking-horse, turtle, and chipmunk of the Apocalypse."

7   EXT. TRUCKSTOP - NIGHT

Wild fingers of BLUE-WHITE ELECTRIC ARCS dance in a steel canyon formed by two TRACTOR TRAILERS, parked side by side in the back lot of an all-night truck stop. Then...

The strange lightning forms a circular opening in mid-air, and in the sudden flare of light we see a FIGURE in a SPHERE OF ENERGY. Then the FRAME WHITES OUT with an explosive THUNDERCLAP!

Through the clearing vapor we see the figure clearly... a naked man. TERMINATOR has come through. Physique: massive, perfect. Face: devoid of emotion. Terminator stands and impassively surveys its surroundings.

8   INT. TRUCK STOP DINER - NIGHT

On a back route north of L.A.   A handful of local TRUCKERS hunch over chili-sizes, CAT hats pushed back on their heads. Three BIKERS are playing a game of pool in the back, their Miller empties lining the table's rail. The dive's owner, LLOYD, a fat, aging biker-type in a soiled apron, stands behind the bar. Nothing much going on...

Then the front door opens and a big naked guy strolls in-- that doesn't happen here every night. All eyes simultaneously swivel toward Terminator. Its emotionless gaze passes over the customers as it walks calmly through the room. Everyone freezes, not sure how to react.

8A   TERMINATOR POV. A digitized electronic scan of the room, overlaid with alphanumeric readouts which change faster than the human eye can follow. In POV we move past the staring truckers, past the owner and the awestruck WAITRESS, and approach a large nasty-looking biker puffing on a cigar. His body is outlined, or "selected", and thousands of estimated measurements appear. His clothing has been analyzed and deemed suitable...

8B   TERMINATOR
             I need your clothes, your boots, and your motorcycle.

The big biker's eyes narrow. He takes a long draw on his cigar, getting the tip cherry-red hot.

                          CIGAR BIKER
             You forgot to say please.

He grinds the cigar out on Terminator's chest. Which produces not the slightest reaction of pain. Terminator calmly, and without expression, grabs Cigar by his meaty upper arm...
Cigar screams from the hydraulic grip.

Terminator doesn't see Cigar's friend, behind him, holding his pool cue by the narrow end like a Louisville Slugger. The heavy end whistles in a powerful swing and CRACKS IN TWO across the back of Terminator's head.

Terminator seems not to notice. Doesn't even blink. Without releasing his grip on Cigar, he snaps his arm straight back and grabs Pool Cue by the front of his jacket. Suddenly the heavyset biker finds himself flying through the nearest window. CRAASSH!

Terminator hurls Cigar, all 230 pounds of him, clear over the bar, through the serving window into the kitchen, where he lands on the big flat GRILL. We hear a SOUND like SIZZLING BACON as Cigar screams, flopping and jerking. He rolls off in a smoking heap.

The third biker whips out a knife with an eight-inch blade and slashes at Terminator's face.

Terminator grabs the arcing blade with his bare hand. Holding it by the razor-sharp blade he jerks it from the guy's hand.
Ultra-fast here: He flips it. Grabs the handle like you're supposed to hold a knife. Grabs the biker and slams him face-down over the bar. Then brings the knife whistling down, pinning the biker's shoulder to the bar top with his own steel.

9   INT. KITCHEN

The door BANGS OPEN and Terminator strides in.
The Mexican cook does a fast fade as Terminator walks toward Cigar, who is cursing in pain on the floor.

With his deep-fried fingers he struggles to get out the .45 auto tucked under his leather jacket. But he can't even hold onto it. Terminator takes it from him. Instead of pointing it at him, Terminator carefully examines the weapon, analyzing its caliber and operating condition. Terminator never threatens... that's a human thing. He just takes.

Cigar senses what he must do when the emotionless eyes come back to him. He slides the keys to his bike across the floor to Terminator's foot. Then painfully starts getting out of his jacket.

10   INT. TRUCK STOP

Terminator strides from the kitchen, fully clothed now in a black leather jacket, leather riding pants, and heavy, cleated boots. He moves toward the moaning biker pinned to the pool table. Without slowing his stride he jerks the knife out. The guy slumps to the floor, groaning, behind him.

Terminator continues toward the front of the diner, passing Lloyd, the owner. At the door, he comes abreast of two truckers who sit frozen like a snapshot in mid-bite. One of the truckers finally nods.

10   TRUCKER
        Evening...

Terminator impassively stares back. Then moves on out the door.

Terminator's exit from biker bar was omitted in the final film. After having established that Terminator is taking whatever he wants, there is no need to illustrate this further; in fact, the direct cut to Terminator standing outside --fully clothed and armed-- to the accompanying track of the song "Bad to the Bone," conveys the scene in a humorous visual shorthand.

11   EXT. TRUCK STOP

Terminator walks out, surveying the parked Harleys. Sticks the .45 in his belt and swings one leg over a massive CUSTOM ELECTRO-GLIDE. He slips the dagger in his boot and the key in the ignition. Kicks over the engine. It catches with a roar and he slams the heavy iron into gear with a KLUNK.

Lloyd appears at the diner's door with a sawed-off 10-GAUGE WINCHESTER LEVER-ACTION SHOTGUN. He fires into the air and jacks another round in fast, aiming at Terminator's back.

                         LLOYD
            I can't let you take the man's bike, son. Now get off or I'll put
            you down!

Terminator turns and considers him coldly. He eases the shifter up into neutral. Rocks the bike onto its kickstand. Swings his leg over and walks calmly toward the guy.

Terminator strides right up to Lloyd, staring straight into the shotgun's muzzle. Lloyd starts sweating, trying to decide if he's going to kill a man in cold blood. He's still trying to decide when Terminator's hand blurs out like a striking cobra and is somehow suddenly holding the shotgun.

Lloyd gapes, knowing he is screwed.   Then...
Terminator reaches toward him. Oh shit...
And slips the sunglasses out of Lloyd's shirt pocket. Puts them on. Strides back to the Harley and roars off in a shower of gravel.

12   EXT. FREEWAY - NIGHT

Terminator roars down the freeway, heading into L.A. Cold neon flares across the chrome of the big bike. The 10-gauge is jammed through the clutch and brake cables, across the handlebars. The lights flow over Terminator's wrap-around sunglasses like the tracks of tracer rounds.

                                          CUT TO:

13   EXT. OVERPASS - NIGHT

The First Street Bridge. Rusting chain-link fences and graffiti-covered walls. An L.A.P.D. BLACK-AND-WHITE cruises the empty street.

A TREMENDOUS BLUE-WHITE GLARE suddenly spills out between the columns of the overpass. The young UNIFORMED COP in the car whips his head around at the source of the light. He pulls over quickly, in time to see...

13A   The powerfully arcing electrical discharge reaches its peak between the columns. Lightning climbs the chain-link fences and light standards, lighting up the night, and papers swirl in a blasting whirlwind.

13B   The cop climbs from his cruiser as the glow fades.
        He sees vapor dissipating as he approaches the spot where he saw the strange light. He draws his revolver and cautiously moves into the shadows between the rows of pillars.

        A NAKED MAN glides from a shadowed doorway behind the cop. Nothing special about him. Certainly not built like a terminator. The flash of light and the fact that he is naked are pretty good clues that he just arrived from the future. His features are handsome bordering on severe. His eyes are gray ice. Penetrating. Intelligent.

THE COP spins at a sound. Too late. Mr. X is already on him. The blow is lightning fast and the cop drops like a bag of sand.

LOW ANGLE as the unconscious cop hits the deck, his BERETTA 9mm AUTOMATIC clattering next to him. A hand ENTERS FRAME and picks up the pistol.

                                                                    CUT TO:

13C   HIGHLY POLISHED BLACK SHOES rounding the rear tire of the police cruiser. FOLLOW THE SHOES to the cruiser's door then MOVE UP as Mr. X, dressed now in LAPD blue, climbs behind the wheel. He looks and acts exactly like a cop. Cool, alert, confident in his power, his expression emotionless and judgmental.
Mr. X, now Officer X, puts the car in gear and drives into the night.

──

The insert shot of the police computer screen showing John's police record and location was moved up to this point from Scene 26 not only to clarify the mysterious new arrival's mission, but also to provide a natural segue to the introduction of young John Connor in the next scene.

──

                                                                    CUT TO:

14   INT. SUBURBAN HOUSE / GARAGE - DAY

TIGHT ON YOUNG JOHN CONNOR, who at this moment is ten years old and busy reassembling the carburetor on his Honda 125 dirtbike. He has ripped Levi's and long stringy hair. A sullen mouth. Eyes which reveal an intelligence as sharp as a scalpel. The Ramones' "I Wanna Be Sedated" blasts from a boom box next to him.

A WOMAN, JANELLE VOIGHT, stands in the doorway of the garage, yelling over the music.

                        WOMAN
            ...John? John! Get in here right now and clean up that pigsty of
            yours.

John's friend TIM, a thirteen-year-old Hispanic kid, watches as John replies by turning up the volume on the boom box.
Janelle gives up with a SLAM of the house's back door.

                        TIM
            Your foster parents are kinda dicks, huh?

                        JOHN
            Gimme that Phillips right there.

15   INT. HOUSE - LIVING ROOM

Janelle storms into the room. TODD VOIGHT, her husband, watches sports on the TV. They're both in their thirties. Middle-class working stiffs.

                        JANELLE
            I swear I've had it with that goddamn kid. He won't even
            answer me.
                        (neither does he)
            Todd? Are you gonna sit there or are you gonna do something?

He sighs. Throws down the TV's remote and heads for the garage.

24

```
NAME:  CONNOR, JOHN
ARREST RECORD: J 66455705

415 PC: TRESPASS    DR 91-17530
484 PC: SHOPLIFT    DR 92-20008
415 PC: DIST. PEACE DR 92-17111
594 PC: VANDALISM   DR 93-12986
        602 WIC
```

16   INT. GARAGE

John hops on the bike. Kick-starts it. Tim picks up John's nylon bag, then climbs on the back.
Todd ENTERS and shouts over the engine, which John revs louder and louder.

                         TODD
              John! Get your ass inside right now and do what your mother
              says!

John pins Todd with a defiant glare.

                         JOHN
              She's <u>not</u> my mother, *Todd*!

He revs the engine and peels out of the garage, with Tim almost falling off the back. They take off
down the street.

17   EXT. VACANT LOT/ DRAINAGE CANAL

John cuts through a vacant lot to a trail running beside a fenced-in drainage canal.   He guns the
bike through a hole in the retaining fence.   Tim's eyes go wide as they roar down the concrete
embankment.

===

Originally intended as a narrative segue to the introduction of Sarah Connor in the next scene, Scene 17A
was omitted because there is no need for it; John's line "She's not my mother, Todd" works as enough of a
segue to the next scene at Pescadero, where we meet his real mother. Scene 17, which establishes the
boys riding in the flood control canals, was moved to later in the film, just after Scene 38.

===

17A   IN THE DRAINAGE CANAL John zig-zags along, throwing up a roostertail of muddy water. Tim
        shouts, pretending he didn't just see his life flash before his eyes. He slaps John on the back.

                         TIM
              Major moves, homes! So... where is your real mom, anyway?
                    (John doesn't answer)
              She <u>dead</u> or something?

It's hard to read John's expression.

                         JOHN
              She might as well be.

John twists the throttle angrily and the bike lunges forward.

                                                        CUT TO:

18   EXT. PESCADERO STATE HOSPITAL - DAY

A SIGN on a chain link fence topped with concertina wire reads: PESCADERO STATE
HOSPITAL FOR THE CRIMINALLY INSANE. Beyond it squats an imposing four-story
building. Institutional brick. Barred windows. About as inviting as KGB headquarters.
Security cars patrol the manicured grounds.

19   INT. HOSPITAL - MAXIMUM SECURITY WING

Sunlight is a barred slash on the bare institutional wall. The room is empty of all furnishings
save the bed, a stainless steel sink, toilet, and a dented metal mirror. WE HEAR a rhythmic
grunting, small explosions of breath in perfectly-metered time.

PAN TO a bedframe leaned upright against the wall, legs facing outward. A pair of sweaty hands grip one leg. Tendons knot and release as SOMEONE does pull-ups. A mane of tangled hair hides the face that comes INTO FRAME, dips out, comes back.

WIDER. A WOMAN in a tank top and hospital pants is hanging from the top leg of the vertical bedframe. Her body is straight and taut. Knees bent so the feet clear the ground. The arms are lean and muscular. The inmate, face hidden, pulls up, dips, pulls up. Like a machine. No change in rhythm.

20   INT. HOSPITAL / CORRIDOR

FIGURES MOVE TOWARD US down a corridor of polished tile and two-tone walls. DR. PETER SILBERMAN, a smug criminal psychologist, leads a group of young INTERNS. Following, laconically, are THREE BURLY ATTENDANTS.

                    SILBERMAN
          The next patient is a 29-year-old female diagnosed as acute
          schizo-affective disorder. The usual indicators... depression,
          anxiety, violent acting-out, delusions of persecution.
                    (the interns nod judiciously)
          Here we are.

Silberman stops at one of the SOUNDPROOF STEEL DOORS. There is a two-way speaker beneath a tiny window. Silberman flips the intercom switch.

21   INT. CELL

Silberman's scrubbed and cheerful face at cell window. HIS VOICE comes over the tinny speaker.

                    SILBERMAN
          'Morning, Sarah.

REVERSE ANGLE as she turns slowly into CLOSE UP.
SARAH CONNOR is not the same woman we remember from last time. Her eyes peer out through a wild tangle of hair like those of a cornered animal. Defiant and intense, but skittering around looking for escape at the same time. Fight or flight. Down one cheek is a long scar, from just below the eye to her upper lip.
Her VOICE is a low and chilling monotone.

                    SARAH
          Good morning, Dr. Silberman.   How's the knee?

22   INT. CORRIDOR

Silberman's smug composure drops a second. Then returns.

                    SILBERMAN
          Fine, Sarah.
                    (he switches off, speaks to the interns)
          She, uh... stabbed me in the kneecap with a screwdriver a few
          weeks ago.

Sarah watches them talking about her through the glass, but can't hear them. She feels like a lab animal. The interns look in at her through the glass as Silberman talks. With her face drawn, eyes haggard and hair wild, she looks like she belongs where she is.

                    SILBERMAN
The delusional architecture is interesting. She believes a
machine called a "terminator", which looks human of course,
was sent back through time to kill her. And also that the father
of her child was a soldier, sent to protect her... he was from the
future too...
                    (he smiles)
The year 2029, if I remember correctly.
                    (the interns chuckle)
Let's move on, shall we?

As the interns walk on, Silberman steps close to DOUGLAS, the head attendant, and speaks low.

                    SILBERMAN
Douglas, I don't like the patients disrupting their rooms like
this. See that she takes her thorazine, would you?

DOUGLAS is 6'4", 250 pounds and warm-hearted as a rattlesnake. He nods, catching
Silberman's meaning, and gestures for the other attendants to hang back as Silberman moves on
in his rounds.

23   INT. CELL

Sarah looks up as the cell door opens.   Douglas walks in slow, idly tapping his POLICE BATON
against the door in an ominous rhythm.   The other two orderlies ease in behind him.   One of them
carries a STUN BATON (like a sawed-off cattle prod). The other has a tray with cups of red
liquid-thorazine.

                    DOUGLAS
Time to take your meds, Connor.

Sarah faces him, weight centered. Feral eyes darting from one to the other.

                    SARAH
You take it.

Douglas grins, casual--

                    DOUGLAS
Now you know you got to be good 'cause you up for review this
afternoon...

                    SARAH
I'm not taking it. Now I don't want any trouble...

                    DOUGLAS
Ain't no trouble at all--

He whips the baton in a whistling backhand which--
WHAP! Takes her square in the stomach. She doubles over and drops to her knees, unable to
breathe. Douglas tips the bed and it slams down with a crash, right next to her. He takes the stun
wand from the other attendant and walks forward.

TIGHT ON SARAH, grimacing and struggling to breathe.

                    SARAH
You... son of a... AAARRGH!!

The stun wand hits her between the shoulder blades as she tries to rise. It drives her to the floor, pinning her like a bug. Little ELECTRIC ARCS CRACKLE as the baton makes her writhe in pain.

Douglas grabs her by the hair and jerks her up to her knees. Holds the cup of thorazine in front of her lips.

> DOUGLAS
> Last call, sugar.

Gasping, she chokes the zombie juice down.

Scene 23 was shot as scripted but omitted from the final film due to both time considerations and to the fact that it was deemed unnecessary to show further that Pescadero's not a nice place to live. The loss of the set-up of Douglas' sadistic cruelty here so he can get his come-uppance later in Sarah's escape is well covered by his slimy performance in Scene 60. This omitted scene also stacks the audience's sympathy toward Sarah --which is something she is supposed to earn in the course of the story-- too early; by intentionally keeping Sarah appropriately harsh in the hospital, it gives her a point of departure for the development of her character.

                                                              CUT TO:

24   EXT. BANK PARKING LOT- DAY

John furtively hunches before a Ready-Teller machine at the rear of a local bank while his friend Tim stands lookout. John slips a stolen ATM card into the machine's slot. It is something he's rigged up, because trailing from the card is a ribbon-wire which goes to some kind of black-box electronics unit he's got in his ever-present knapsack. He holds the pack between his knees and pulls out a little lap-top keyboard, which is also connected to the black-box.

John enters a few commands and the plasma-screen displays the PIN number for that account. He quickly enters the number on the Ready-Teller's keypad and asks it for 300 bucks. The machine whirs then begins dispensing twenty-dollar bills. Tim looks back over his shoulder, amazed.

> JOHN
> Easy money!

> TIM
> Where'd you learn all this stuff?

John collects the twenties as the machine kicks them out. A cool and professional electronic-age thief at ten years old.

> JOHN
> From my mom. My real mom, I mean. Come on baby...
>   (he grabs the last bills)
> Let's go!

They sprint around the corner to an--

25   EXT. ALLEY BEHIND BANK

They huddle behind the building as John counts out Tim's share.
He folds five twenties and palms them to the other kid. When John opens his wallet to put in his money, Tim notices a picture in a plastic sleeve.

> TIM
> That her?

John reluctantly shows his friend the Polaroid. It is a shot of Sarah. Pregnant, in a jeep near the Mexican border. John doesn't know it now, but he will carry that photo with him for over 30 years, and give it to a young man named Kyle Reese, who will travel back in time to become his father. Yes, *that* photo.

                         TIM
          So she's pretty cool, huh?

                         JOHN
          Actually, no, she's a complete psycho. That's why she's up at
          Pescadero. She tried to blow up a computer factory, but she got
          shot and arrested.

                         TIM
          No shit?

                         JOHN
          Yeah, she's a total loser. C'mon, let's check out the 7-Eleven,
          whatya say?

John has tried to sound macho casual, but we see in his eyes that it really hurts. He slaps Tim on the shoulder and they jump onto his Honda. John fires up and they whine off down the alley.

                                        CUT TO:

26   INT. POLICE CRUISER - DAY

      CLOSE ON COMPUTER TERMINAL, attached to the dash. A Juvenile Division file. Subject:
      John Connor. Below his ARREST RECORD are his vital stats. Mother: Sarah Connor. Legal
      Guardians: Todd and Janelle Voight. And below their names, an address: 523 S. Almond.
      Reseda, Ca.

      OFFICER X stares at the screen a moment. Then gets out of the car.

27   INT./EXT. VOIGHT HOUSE - DAY

      TIGHT ON FRONT DOOR as Todd Voight opens it, revealing the unsmiling face of Officer X
      beyond the screen door. Todd greets him with a weary sigh.

                         OFFICER X
          Are you the legal guardian of John Connor?

                         TODD
          That's right, officer. What's he done now?

      Officer X ignores the question. He casually scans the living room.

                         OFFICER X
          Could I speak with him, please?

      Todd shrugs, showing the cop he's past his patience with the boy.

                         TODD
          Well, you could if he was here. But he took off on his bike this
          morning. Could be anywhere. You gonna tell me what this is
          about?

                         OFFICER X
          I just need to ask him a few questions.

Janelle appears in the doorway behind Todd, concerned.

> JANELLE
> There was a guy here this morning asking about him, too.

> TODD
> Yeah, big guy. On a bike. Has that got something to do with it?

Officer X registers the significance of that. He realizes who the big guy must be. He smiles. Reassuringly shakes his head no.

> OFFICER X
> I wouldn't worry. Do you have a photograph of John?

Todd stares unhappily at the cop. Turns to Janelle.

> TODD
> Get the album, Janelle.

In the final film, T-1000's questioning of Todd and Janelle takes place prior to John's robbing of the ATM, which is then followed by Terminator's searching for John; this creates a better sense of convergence and narrative flow. John's line "Please insert your stolen card here" --added in postproduction-- not only clarifies that John is robbing the ATM but also shows his sense of humor and the flippancy with which he breaks the rules to get what he wants --like he's been doing it all his young life.

CUT TO:

28   EXT. STREET

ANGLE THROUGH AN ALLEY from the main street. We see John and Tim flash by on the Honda a block away. Hold a beat. Then...

A BIG CHROME WHEEL ENTERS FRAME. BOOM UP a leather-clad leg to Terminator's implacable face. It surveys the area slowly as the bike idles, then kicks it into gear and moves on, scanning in a slow shark-like manner, not aware that it missed its prey by seconds.

CUT TO:

29   INT. SARAH'S CELL - DAY

CLOSE ON SARAH. She is shackled, hands and feet, to the bed. Sunlight falls across her pale face. A hand enters frame, gently stroking her cheek. She wakes up to see--

KYLE REESE. Sitting on the edge of her bed, looking exactly the same as we last saw him in 1984. Scruffy blond hair and a long raincoat.

> SARAH
> Kyle..? You're dead.

He gives her a gentle smile.

> REESE
> I know. This is a dream, Sarah.

> SARAH
> Oh. Yeah. They... make me take this stuff...

He puts a finger to her lips. Then silently unfastens her restraints. They gaze into each other's eyes. And in that look we see that his death and the horror she has been through since hasn't touched their love at all.

                          SARAH
            Hold me.

She melts into Reese's arms. Pulls him to her.

                          REESE
            I love you. I always will.

                          SARAH
            Oh, God... Kyle. I need you so much.

She kisses him passionately. They are locked together in a timeless moment. PUSH IN TIGHT on Sarah as she buries her face in his shoulder. She shuts her eyes tight. Stay on Sarah as Reese speaks. His voice strangely cold.

                        REESE (O.S.)
            Where's John, Sarah?

Sarah opens her eyes and he is no longer in her arms. He is standing across the room. Pinning her with an accusing gaze.

                          SARAH
            They took him away from me.

                          REESE
            It's John who's the target now. You have to protect him. He's
            wide open.

                          SARAH
            I know!

                          REESE
            Don't quit, Sarah. Our son needs you.

                          SARAH
               (struggling not to cry)
            I know, but I'm not as strong as I'm supposed to be. I can't do it.
            I'm screwing up the mission.

                          REESE
            Remember the message... the future is not set. There is no fate
            but what we make for ourselves.

He turns toward the door.

                          SARAH
            Kyle, don't go!

                          REESE
               (turning back to her)
            There's not much time left in the world, Sarah.

Reese goes out the door. Sarah jumps from the bed, frantic. Yanks the door open. Follow her out.

30   INT. CORRIDOR

Sarah staggers from her cell. Reese is already, impossibly, a hundred feet away, striding down
the dim corridor. A silhouette in a long coat, disappearing around a corner.

Sarah runs after him, her bare feet slapping the cold linoleum. Her hospital gown floats out behind
her as she dream-runs along the seemingly infinite corridor. She reaches the corner, slides
around it, and...

30A   Slams right into the arms of Douglas and his three helpers. They grab her as she struggles and
screams. Then Silberman is there, smiling soothingly. They force her down and she is pinned to
the floor, screaming. A new figure approaches... one even more menacing.

TERMINATOR walks toward her, with heavy, measured steps. Backlit, eyes concealed by the
sunglasses, it stands over her like the angel of death itself. It reaches down and...
Takes her hand. Lifts her up. Leads her to a door. They go through together. Emerging into...

30B   A BEAUTIFUL SUNLIT MORNING. CHILDREN are playing nearby... sliding down slides,
clambering through a jungle gym. Sarah knows this dream now... it is the worst of all her
nightmares. She starts to scream but no sound comes out.

30C   THE SKY EXPLODES into WHITE LIGHT. Everything is seared by the unholy glare, hotter than
a thousand suns. The children ignite like match heads. Sarah is burning, screaming silently,
everything silent and overexposed. Terminator's flesh and clothing are burning, silently. It
grips her hand, Virgil to her Dante in this tour of the nuclear-age Inferno.

30D   THE BLAST WAVE HITS... a near-solid wall of compressed air followed by 250-mph winds. The
children, charcoal statues frozen in positions of play, explode into black leaves of ash and swirl
away. SOUND hits now, with a thunderous roar. Sarah's scream merges with the howl of the wind
as the blast hits her, exploding the flesh from her bones. Beside her, Terminator is stripped of its
burnt flesh, becoming a smoking skeleton of steel.

30E   Then she wakes up... in her cell, shackled to the bed. Sunlight hurts her eyes. She looks desperate
and defeated. She knows the war is coming. It visits her every time she closes her eyes. Lost and
alone, Sarah feels all hope recede for herself and for humanity.

Sarah's first nuclear nightmare was first pared down during production by the elimination of Terminator from
the dream due to both scheduling conflicts and to a desire to simplify the amount of puppet work in the
dream imagery. The portions involving Michael Biehn as Kyle Reese were filmed but subsequently cut due
to time considerations, for although the Reese sequence provides resonance with the first film, reinforces
the crucial line (paraphrased from the first film) "The future is not set. There is no fate but what we make for
ourselves," and personifies Sarah's own guilt over her inability to protect John in her current condition, it was
ultimately deemed unnecessary to the main message of the nightmare, namely, Sarah's persistent vision of
the imminent nuclear war. In fact, this essential point of the dream was originally repeated three times --
twice visually in Sarah's nightmares and·once verbally in her description of it to Silberman on videotape in
the following scene. In the end, the whole first nightmare was excised due to time and to the fact that Sarah
describes it so vividly in the next scene, making the dream itself unnecessary. In the 5/10/90 draft version of
the nightmare, Silberman and attendants turn out to be terminators themselves, which is revealed as Sarah
struggles with them and claws at their faces, tearing them open and exposing metal endoskeletons under
their flesh.

CUT TO:

31   INT. PESCADERO STATE HOSPITAL - INTERVIEW ROOM

TIGHT ON VIDEO SCREEN, playing a previously-recorded session.
Sarah is in a strait-jacket, talking softly.

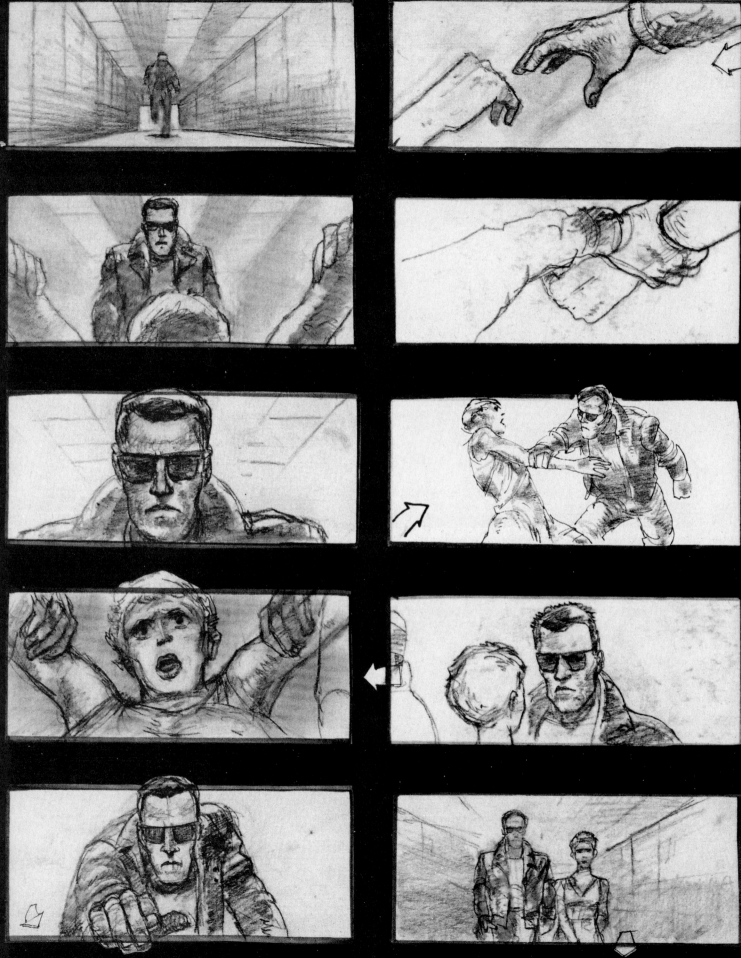

WHITE
OUT
FRAME

VIDEO SARAH

... it's... like a giant strobe light, burning right through my
eyes... but somehow I can still see. Look, you know the dream's
the same every night, why do I have to--

VIDEO SILBERMAN

Please continue...

31A   The REAL SARAH dispassionately watches herself on the screen. Her expression is controlled.
Silberman watches her watching. They are in a brightly-lit interview room. TWO
ATTENDANTS stand nearby.

31B   **VIDEO SARAH**

The children look like burnt paper... black, not moving. Then
the blast wave hits them and they fly apart like leaves..."

Video Sarah can't go on. Real Sarah watches herself cry on tape, her expression cold. We hear
Silberman speak on the tape.

VIDEO SILBERMAN

Dreams about cataclysm, or the end of the world, are very
common, Sarah...

Video Sarah cuts him off, her mood shifting to sudden rage.

VIDEO SARAH

It 's not just a dream. It's real, you moron! I know the date it
happens!!

VIDEO SILBERMAN

I'm sure it feels very real to you--

VIDEO SARAH

On August 29th 1997 it's going to *feel* pretty fucking real to you,
too!   Anybody not wearing number two million sunblock is
gonna have a real bad day, get it?!

VIDEO SILBERMAN

Relax now, Sarah--

VIDEO SARAH

You think you're alive and safe, but you're already dead.
Everybody, you, him...
        (she gestures at the attendant)
everybody... you're all fucking dead!

She is raving, half out of her chair. The orderly moves to inject her with
something.

VIDEO SARAH

You're the one living in a dream, Silberman, not me! <u>Because I
know it happens.</u> *It happens!*

31C   Silberman pauses the tape... freezing Sarah's contorted face.
Real Sarah turns away from the screen, her expression stony.

SARAH
I was afraid... and confused. I feel much better, now. Clearer.

In the final film, Sarah's first line after the videotape has been freeze-framed is simply, "I feel much better now," which plays as a big tension-relieving laugh after the morbid, angry hysterics of her outburst on the tape.

Silberman gives a calculated paternal smile.

SILBERMAN
Yes. Your attitude has been very positive lately.

Sarah looks up at him. Her voice is hopeful.

SARAH
It has helped me a lot to have a goal, something to look forward
to.

SILBERMAN
And what is that?

As she answers, WE PULL BACK, revealing that we have been looking through a one-way mirror from an adjacent OBSERVATION ROOM. In the shadows of the observation room we see the interns from the earlier rounds, and a couple of STAFF PSYCHOLOGISTS. They smoke and make the occasional note.

SARAH
You said I could be transferred to the minimum security wing
and have visitors if I showed improvement in six months.
Well, it's been six months, and I was looking forward to seeing
my son.

SILBERMAN
I see. Let's go back to what you were saying about these
terminator machines. Now you think they don't exist?

CLOSE ON SARAH. Her voice sounds hollow.

SARAH
They don't exist. I see that now.

Silberman leans back, studying her. Toying with her.

SILBERMAN
But you've told me on many occasions about how you crushed
one in a hydraulic press.

SARAH
If I had, there would have been some evidence. They would have
found something at the factory.

SILBERMAN
I see. So you don't believe anymore that the company covered it
up?

Sarah shakes her head no.

CUT TO:

32   EXT. CYBERDYNE SYSTEMS - DAY

The corporate headquarters of a mega-electronics corporation. An imposing cubist castle of black glass.

33   INT. SECOND FLOOR/ ELEVATORS

The elevator doors slide open with a whisper and MILES DYSON strides out. Black. In his early thirties. The star of the Special Projects Division. He's brilliant, aggressive, driven. Dyson walks down the corridor, swinging his arms... a man in a hurry. A man with much to do.

He reaches a solid security door and zips his ELECTRONIC KEY-CARD through the scanner. The door unlocks with a clunk.
The sign next to the door reads: SPECIAL PROJECTS DIVISION: AUTHORIZED PERSONNEL ONLY.

34   INT. SECURITY STATION

He nods to the guards as he passes through the security checkpoint. They can see all activities on the floor on their bank of video monitors.
He unlocks another secure door with his card and enters--

35   INT. ARTIFICIAL INTELLIGENCE (A.I.) LAB

The lab is quite large, comprising banks of processors, disk drives, test bays, prototype assembly areas. Extremely high tech.

                    DYSON
          Greetings, troops.

He is jokingly saluted by fellow workers. Not a lab coat in sight. This is a strictly jeans and sneakers crowd. All young and bright. They sit at their consoles drinking Cokes and changing technology as we know it.   A young LAB ASSISTANT rushes over to Dyson. Name tag says he's BRYANT.

                    BRYANT
          Mr. Dyson? The materials team wants to run another test on the
          uh... on *it*.

                    DYSON
          Yup. Come on. I'll get it.

Dyson produces an unusual-looking KEY from his pocket as they stride through the lab. Bryant has to hustle to keep up.

                    BRYANT
          Listen, Mr. Dyson, I know I haven't been here that long, but I
          was wondering if you could tell me... I mean, if you know...

                    DYSON
          Know what?

                    BRYANT
          Well... where *it* came from.

DYSON
I asked them that question once. Know what they told me? Don't
ask.

In light of scheduling and production considerations, the Cyberdyne introduction sequence was simplified to basically one single long Steadicam shot, centering on and following Dyson as he goes into the vault to check out the artifacts from the first terminator. The scenes showing the elaborate security measures at Cyberdyne and establishing the geography of the lab area were deemed unnecessary, as was the greater emphasis on Dyson's character; the sense of the computer lab working excitedly on the development of the new technology and Dyson's blind fascination with the chip and metal endoskeleton arm in the vault are retained in the final film through actor Joe Morton's performance.

---

36   INT. VAULT ROOM

Dyson enters with Bryant. Dyson and a GUARD stand together before what looks like a high-tech bank vault. It requires two keys to open, like the launch controls in a nuclear silo. The guard and Dyson insert their keys and turn them simultaneously. Dyson then enters a passcode at a console and the vault unlocks itself with a sequence of clunks. The door swings open and Dyson enters. Bryant stays outside with the guard, who notes Dyson's name and the time on a clipboard.

37   INT. VAULT

Dyson walks to a stainless steel cabinet and opens it. Inside is a small artifact in a sealed container of inert gas. IT --a ceramic rectangle, about the size of a domino, the color of liver. It has been shattered, painstakingly reconstructed and mounted on a metal frame.

Dyson removes the artifact, in its inert-gas flask, and sets it on a specially-designed cart. He handles it like the Turin Shroud.
Dyson closes the cabinet. Turns to the one next to it. Opens its door. In this cabinet is a larger object... an intricate METAL HAND AND FOREARM.

At the elbow, the metal is twisted and crushed. But the forearm and hand are intact. Its metal surface scorched and discolored, it stands upright in a vacuum flask, as if saluting.   This is all that remains of the terminator Sarah destroyed. Dyson stares at it, lost in thought. Then he closes the cabinet, BLACKING OUT FRAME.

CUT TO:

38   INT. INTERVIEW ROOM/ OBSERVATION ROOM

We can see through the one-way mirror into the interview room where Sarah is still talking with Silberman. The OTHER PSYCHOLOGISTS are still watching through the mirror. Reviewing Sarah's condition.

SARAH
So what do you think, Doctor? I've shown a lot of improvement,
haven't I?

SILBERMAN
You see, Sarah... here's the problem. I know how smart you are,
and I think you're just telling me what I want to hear. I don't
think you really believe what you've been telling me today.

We go tight on Sarah's reaction. And we see that Silberman is right. She was playing him and it didn't work. And she knows she's fucked. Her tone becomes quietly pleading.

> SARAH
> You have to let me see my son. Please. It's very important.
> He's in danger. At least let me call him--

Silberman pins her with his sweet reptilian gaze.

> SILBERMAN
> I'm afraid not. Not for a while. I don't see any choice but to recommend to the review board that you stay here another six months.

Sarah's eyes turn cold and lethal in one second. She knows she's lost. She knows this guy is just playing with her, and she--
LEAPS ACROSS THE TABLE AT HIM.

> SARAH
> YOU SON OF BITCH!!

Silberman jumps back and the attendants dive on her. She is writhing and twisting like a bobcat. Silberman whips open a drawer and pulls out a syringe. He jabs it into her as she yells--

> SARAH
> Goddammit. Let me go!! Silberman! You don't know what you're doing! You fuck! You're dead! You hear me!!

Silberman signals and the attendants drag her out.
He looks at the doctors behind the glass. Shrugs.

> SILBERMAN
> Model citizen.

> CUT TO:

39   EXT. 7-ELEVEN STORE - DAY

Officer X has stopped two young girls in front of a 7-Eleven. He is leaning out the cruiser window and showing them the picture of John. The first girl nods.

> FIRST GIRL
> Yeah, he was here about fifteen minutes ago. I think he said he was going to the Galleria.

> OFFICER X
> The what?

The second girl points toward a massive complex visible above the houses several blocks away. Officer X stares at it.

Scenes 39 and 40 were transposed in the final film to allow Terminator to acquire John first. The juxtaposition of these two scenes also illustrates the two terminators' different search methodologies: Terminator's brute-force searching for John, riding around on his motorcycle and just looking, versus T-1000's more stealthy and gregarious inquiries. An added beat in Scene 39 of the two girls giggling hysterically in disbelief after T-1000 earnestly asks for directions to the Galleria ("i'm kinda new around here...") was filmed but did not make the final cut.

SCAN LEVELS:

234654 453 30
654334 450 16
245261 865 26
453665 766 46
382856 863 09
356876 544 04
634217 986 89
234346 956 32

SEARCH CRITERIA
MATCH MODE 5496

ALL LEVELS OPERATIVE

NW N NE

SPEED
ONT
RRECT 11
ATION 328
E COMP 305

CODE:
23 4654
65 4334

MATCH CRITERIA

NETFILE 342–589
MISSION PROFILE

CONNOR, JOHN

HGHT 234654 453 30
WGHT 654334 450 16
HAIR 245261 865 26
EYES 453665 766 46
GEND 382856 863 09
DIST 356878 544 04

IDENT POSITIVE

40   EXT. STREET

Terminator cruises slowly on the bike. Scanning. He crosses an overpass above a drainage
canal and whips his head around at the sound of a dirt-bike engine.

40A   TERMINATOR POV-- OF TWO KIDS ON A BIKE DOWN IN THE CANAL.
THE IMAGE SNAP-ZOOMS IN. FREEZES ON THE DRIVER'S FACE.
IDENT POS FLASHES NEXT TO THE BLURRY IMAGE OF JOHN.

40B   Terminator wheels the Harley around, cutting onto a street which runs parallel to the canal.
Terminator hauls ass to keep John in sight. He catches glimpses of the kid through trees and
houses. Loses him. Catches one last glimpse of him heading into the parking garage of a large
SHOPPING MALL.

41   INT. GALLERIA - DAY

John works his way through a crowded video arcade. Sees some guys he knows. Stops to talk,
striking a pose. Mall rats in their element. We don't hear the dialogue.

42   INT. GALLERIA PARKING GARAGE

TERMINATOR'S idling Harley shakes the parking garage walls.   He stops at a row of bikes
near the escalators. John's little Honda sits proudly with the big street bikes. Terminator parks.

43   INT. GALLERIA

OFFICER X is moving through the flow of shoppers. The place is a zoo. He stops some kids and
shows them the picture. They shrug.

The intercutting between John's videogame playing and the converging of the two terminators on his tail
builds the tension and suspense of the scene. The irony of John playing Missile Command --in which the
player must stop the nuking of cities-- is fully intentional.

43A   IN A CROWDED VIDEO ARCADE JOHN is lost in an intense battle, going for a new high score at
"Missile Command".   He parries deftly as the enemy ICBMs deploy their MIRVs... the warheads
stream down... it's more than he can deal with. The world gets nuked. Game over. He slouches
away from the game, looking for another. Bored.

RACK FOCUS to Officer X passing the entrance of the store behind him.
The cop moves on, down the concourse, out of sight.
John gets into an "Afterburner" simulator game.

43B   ON TERMINATOR, walking through the crowd in slow motion. Scanning.
He moves with methodical purpose, knowing the target is close. We see that he is, incredibly,
carrying a box of LONG-STEM ROSES. Like some hopeful guy with a hot date.

43C   THE COP is pointed toward the arcade by some kids hanging out at the multi-cinema. He walks
into the maze of kids engaged in synthesized conflict. Cheap electronic sound effects blare above
the crowd noise.

43D   JOHN is shooting down MiGs at Mach 2. His friend Tim slides up next to him. Taps him on the
shoulder, trying to play it cool.

                                    TIM
                    Some cop is scoping for you, dude.

John looks around the corner of the "Afterburner" ride. Sees the cop showing a picture to some of the kids. The kids point his way.

John ducks just as the cop glances over. He slinks out the other side of the ride and heads for the back of the store, instinctively retreating. Sarah has taught him that cops are bad news.

THE COP scans the crowded arcade. Glimpses John, looking back as he moves around a row of machines. Starts toward him.

JOHN sees the cop homing in and starts walking fast. Looks back.
THE COP is shoving through clots of kids. One of them is slammed to the floor. An eddy of outrage behind the cop as he gains speed.
John breaks into a run. So does the cop.
Kids scatter like ten-pins as the cop charges after John.
John sprints through the arcade's back office and store-rooms.

44   INT. SERVICE CORRIDOR

John emerges through a firedoor into a long corridor which connects to the parking garage. He's running full out, when around the corner ahead of him comes...

TERMINATOR. Time stretches to nightmarish crawl as John tries to brake to a stop. Terminator reaches into the box of roses.

SLOW MOTION. The cold black steel of the SHOTGUN emerges as the box falls open, the roses spilling to the floor. TERMINATOR'S BOOT crushes the flowers as it moves forward.

JOHN, transfixed by terror, is trapped in the narrow featureless shooting gallery of the corridor. THE SHOTGUN COMES UP. Terminator expressionlessly strides forward. Jacks a round into the chamber, slow and fluid.

John looks behind him for a place to run. Sees the cop coming toward him, pulling his Beretta pistol. Incredibly, John realizes the cop is aiming his gun at <u>him</u>!
John looks back at Terminator. He is staring into the black muzzle of the 10-gauge now. Aimed right at his head. He realizes he's screwed. Then something crazy happens...

                              TERMINATOR
          Get down.

John instinctively ducks. Terminator pulls the trigger. KABOOM!

THE COP catches the SHOTGUN'S BLAST square in the chest just as he fires his pistol. The pistol's shot goes wild.

TERMINATOR pumps another round into him. Then another. And another. And another. Advancing a step each time he fires, he empties the shotgun into the cop, blowing him backward down the corridor. The sound is DEAFENING. Then silence.

THE COP lies still on his back.

44A   Terminator is now standing right over John. They both watch as the cop, incredibly, sits up unharmed and gets to its feet. Terminator grabs John roughly by his jacket. Clutches the kid to his chest then spins around as the cop opens fire with the Beretta.

44B   The "cop", who not only isn't a cop, he clearly isn't even *human*, pulls the trigger so fast it almost seems like a machine-pistol.

ON TERMINATOR'S BACK, as the 9mm slugs slam into it, punching bloody holes in the motorcycle jacket.

JOHN is bug-eyed with fear, but completely unscratched. Terminator's body has blocked the bullets.

The original intention was to mislead the audience into believing that Terminator is once again the killer and that T-1000 --intentionally Reese-like in many respects-- is a human protector, culminating in the revelation in the mall service corridor that the mysterious "cop" is a terminator assassin and that Terminator is the good guy. It was thus important to subtly show that Terminator does not kill anybody without tipping the hand; by the same token, T-1000 had to be shown doing nothing extraordinary that would give him away as being a liquid metal terminator. In the final analysis, it was determined that the existence of two terminators and Terminator's status as protector would be revealed as marketing points in the theatrical trailers and advertising campaign prior to the film's release; thus, there was less incentive to play the "bait and switch" idea out. In its place, a slight transposition of action sequencing in this scene --Terminator shields John first, then blows T-1000 away-- draws out the revelation of T-1000's pseudomorphic capabilities and portrays Terminator's protector role in action.

The Beretta CLACKS empty. Terminator turns at the sound.
Shoves John behind a Coke machine. Drops the empty shotgun, Starts walking toward the "cop".
The empty magazine clatters to the floor.
The cop inserts another one.   Snaps back the slide.
Terminator still has twenty feet to go.
He doesn't break his purposeful stride.

The cop opens fire. Bullets rake Terminator's chest. He doesn't even flinch.
Ten feet to go. BLAM BLAM BLAM BLAM! Neither the cop nor Terminator show the slightest change in expression as the gun rips Terminator's wardrobe to shreds.

CLACK. The pistol empties again. Terminator stops two feet in front of the cop.   They appraise each other for a second.

We realize now that the cop is a terminator too. We don't know the details yet, but let's call him the T-1000 (since that's what he is). A newer model than the one we've come to know so well (the 800 Series "Arnold"). This guy's an advanced prototype... and he's got quite a few surprises.

T-1000 AND TERMINATOR size each other up. Terminator moves first. He grabs the T-1000 in his massive hands but the T-1000 snaps back with a counter-grip. After about two seconds of intense slamming, the walls on both sides of the corridor have all the plaster smashed in, and the two battling machines have blasted through the wall and disappeared.

JOHN, totally stunned by all of this, remembers to move. He staggers to his feet. Stumble-runs toward the parking garage.

44C   THIRD LEVEL CONCOURSE. A plate glass window EXPLODES and Terminator crashes through to the tile floor like a sack of cement amid the screaming crowd.

44D   T-1000 turns without a word and heads back through the store after John, accelerating slowly into a loping, predatory run.

44E   Terminator is totally still. A JAPANESE TOURIST cautiously steps forward and takes a picture of the body. Suddenly, Terminator's eyes snap open. The stunned tourist backs away.

He sits up and looks around. Gets his bearings. Rises smoothly to his feet. All servos seem to be working fine. The tourist's camera whirs as the motor-drive runs on by itself, taking shot after shot. The owner isn't even looking through the eyepiece, he's so shocked.

45   INT. PARKING GARAGE

John is frantically pumping the kick-starter of his bike, scared shitless and the damned thing won't start. His hands are shaking so badly he can't find the choke. He looks up to see--
The T-1000 running down the corridor toward him.
John fumbles with the choke. The bike catches. He slams it in gear and spins the bike out into the main aisle of the garage.

John looks back... the T-1000 is behind him, running. He twists the throttle and guns the little bike forward. Incredibly, the T-1000 is gaining. This nightmare isn't happening. John races out the exit ramp, and charges right into the street.

46   EXT. STREET

John shoots into the busy traffic. Cuts off a BIG-RIG TOW TRUCK.
The DRIVER swears. Hits his air horn. What the driver doesn't see is the cop, running faster than O.J. Simpson at the airport, who emerges onto the street and runs right at his truck.

46A   IN THE TRUCK. The driver hears a thump as something slams against his door, then feels himself pulled right out. T-1000 slides in and takes his place. The truck is still rolling along about 25 mph. T-1000 accelerates after John without missing a beat. It can see him, up ahead, weaving through traffic.

46B   Out of the garage entrance, Terminator roars onto the street on the Harley.
He accelerates after the others.

47   EXT. FLOOD CONTROL CHANNEL

John slides his bike down the service ramp faster than he's ever done it before. He races along the bottom of the canal, turning into a narrower tributary which has vertical sides.

He looks back. No sign of pursuit.
47A   Suddenly he sees the sun blocked out by a great shadow.
The Kenworth tow-truck... big as a house, all chrome and roaring diesel engine... crashes through the fence and launches itself right into the center of the canal.

It crashes down, 15 feet to the ground, going about 60, hits at an angle and tears into the concrete wall with a hideous grinding of metal. It ricochets back and forth between the walls then, bellowing like a gutshot stegosaurus, it just keeps on plowing forward, gathering speed.

47B   John looks back and sees this wall of metal almost filling the narrow concrete canal and he milks every last bit of throttle the little bike has. The Kenworth is all muscle, tearing along the canal like a train in a tunnel. Its big tires send up huge sheets of muddy spray, backlit in the setting sun. It looks like some kind of demon. And... it's gaining.

47C   ABOVE THEM, on the service road running parallel, Terminator is fighting to overtake them. He looks down and sees John with the tow-truck from Hell catching up to him. It is only about twenty feet behind him and still gaining.

47D   ANGLE IN THE CANAL, looking back past a desperate John, at the wall of metal filling frame behind him.

47E   ABOVE, Terminator cuts the bike suddenly hard to the left, leaving the road. Hitting an earth embankment just right, he jumps the bike into the air like Steve McQueen in "The Great Escape" and vaults the fence bordering the canal. It slams down at the edge of the canal and tears along, inches from the drop-off on a dirt path, accelerating past the truck in the channel below.

47F   John hits some water and slews momentarily, losing speed. The massive push-plate on the front of the truck slams his back fender. Panicked, he pulls a little ahead. All this is happening at about sixty miles an hour. Top speed for the little dirt bike.

47G   SLOW MOTION as Terminator jumps the bike again. This time the 700-pound Harley sails out into space and drops into the canal. It arcs down between the truck and John, hitting on its wheels. It bottoms out, an explosion of sparks from under the frame. Only the ultra-fast reflexes of a machine could keep the bike upright. Terminator fights for control.

47H   He guns the throttle and the powerful bike roars up beside John's tiny Honda. Terminator sweeps the kid off his machine with one arm and swings him onto the Harley, in front of him. John's Honda weaves and falls, smashed instantly under thundering tires.

The Harley roars ahead. It hits eighty. Ahead is an overpass, and supporting it is an abutment which bisects the canal into two channels. The Harley thunders into one channel, which is essentially a short tunnel.

47I   The truck can't fit on either side. Neither can it stop, at that speed. Tires locked, it slides on the muddy concrete and piles into the concreted abutment at seventy.

47J   Terminator and John emerge from the tunnel, looking back to see a fireball blasting through behind them as the truck's side-tanks explode.

Terminator stops the Harley. John peers around his body to see the destruction. A burning wheel wobbles out of the tunnel and flops in the mud. Terminator revs the bike and they roar away, down the canal, disappearing around a bend.

Although much of the canal chase was shot verbatim to the script, there were various changes of specific actions in the script based on the production's location scouts of the canals; the physical features of the canals precluded certain stunts (like the "Great Escape" fence jump) but gave ideas for several new gags. The "convertible" tow-truck gag, where the top of the tow-truck is sheared off by a low overpass, came about when it was realized that in one prime shooting location in the canal, the overpass was too low for the truck to fit under, necessitating a practical and cinematic way to make it fit. The insert of the battery cable spark igniting the fumes from the ruptured gas tank was added for the sake of accuracy, as vehicles do not just explode upon impact with things, contrary to much movie lore. Other logical additions to the sequence include Terminator shooting at the tow-truck and his various overpass gate crossings.

47K   ANGLE ON THE FIRE, as a column of black smoke rises from the overpass.
Smoke boils from the tunnel as well, and inside it is a solid wall of flame. A figure appears in the fire.
Just an outline. Walking slowly... calmly.
The figure emerges from the flames.

It is human-shaped but far from human. A smooth chrome man. Not a servo-mechanism like Terminator is underneath, with its complex hydraulics and cables... this thing is a featureless, liquid chrome surface, bending seamlessly at knees and elbows as it walks. It reminds us of mercury. A mercury man. Its face is simple, unformed.
Unruffled by thousand-degree heat, it walks toward us.

With each step detail returns.
First the shapes and lines of its clothing emerge from the liquid chrome surface, then finer details... buttons, facial features, ears...

47K   But it's still all chrome. With its last step, the color returns to everything. It is the cop again... handsome young face, blond hair, moustache. Icy eyes. It stops and looks around.

It is a perfect chameleon. A liquid metal robot. A killing machine with the ultimate skills of mimicry for infiltration of human society.

47L   ANGLE NEARBY, as several police cruisers and a fire truck pull up.
T-1000 climbs out of the canal behind them. More cops arrive. T-1000 blends in perfectly. There are always cops at disasters and scenes of violence. We now see why its choice of protective mimicry is so perfect.
It walks among the other cops unnoticed.
Gets into one of the squad cars. Starts it and drives away.

T-1000's acquisition of a new police car at the scene of the tow-truck crash was filmed but ultimately deemed unnecessary to the plot; we can assume that T-1000 still has its earlier police car. The question of why T-1000 maintains the same face and general wardrobe has both a narrative and dramatic answer: the cop outfit is the perfect disguise (who dares question or look suspiciously at a cop?) and has been taken on as its default camouflage; and, obviously, the audience has to be able to recognize the character through both looks and performance continuity.

---

48   EXT. SIDE STREET - DUSK

Terminator, with John in front of him on the Harley, roars down the empty street. John cranes his neck around to get a look at the person/thing he is riding with. The image is strangely reminiscent of father/son, out for an evening ride.

John is still shaking from the experience of what just happened and he's just a ten-year-old kid, but he's also the John Connor who will someday rise to greatness, and we see a bit of that in him even now.

                          JOHN
             Whoa... time out. Stop the bike!

Terminator immediately complies. He leans the bike into a turn. They head into a nearby alley.

49   EXT. ALLEY

Terminator and John roll into the alley and come to a stop. John slides off the gas tank.
Terminator impassively stares at him. John checks him out. Tentatively speaks.

                    JOHN
          Now don't take this the wrong way, but you are a <u>terminator</u>,
          right?

                    TERMINATOR
          Yes. Cyberdyne Systems, Model 101.

                    JOHN
               No way!

John touches Terminator's skin. Then the blood on his jacket.
His mind overloads as the reality of it hits him.

                    JOHN
          Holy shit... you're really real! I mean... whoah!
               (stepping back)
          You're, uh... like a machine underneath, right... but sort of
          alive outside?

                    TERMINATOR
          I'm a cybernetic organism. Living tissue over a metal
          endoskeleton.

                    JOHN
          This is <u>intense</u>. Get a grip, John.   Okay, uh... you're not here to
          kill me... I figured that part out for myself. So what's the deal?

                    TERMINATOR
          My mission is to protect you.

                    JOHN
          Yeah?. Who sent you?

                    TERMINATOR
          You did. Thirty five years from now you reprogrammed me to
          be your protector here, in this time.

John gives him an amazed look.

                    JOHN
               This is *deep*.

50   EXT. STREET - NIGHT

John and Terminator on the bike again, weaving through the side streets.   They blend into the
evening traffic. In the darkness, Terminator's wounds are not readily visible.   John cranes his
head up and back.

                    JOHN
          So this other guy? He's a terminator too, right, like you?

                    TERMINATOR
          Not like me. A T-1000. Advanced prototype.   A mimetic
          polyalloy.

                    JOHN
          What's that mean?

                         TERMINATOR
          Liquid metal.

                         JOHN
          Radical.

                         TERMINATOR
          You are targeted for termination. The T-1000 will not stop until
          it completes its mission. Ever.

John mulls that over.

                         JOHN
          Where we going?

                         TERMINATOR
          We have to leave the city, immediately. And avoid the
          authorities.

                         JOHN
          Can I stop by my house?

                         TERMINATOR
          Negative. The T-1000 will definitely try to reacquire you there.

                         JOHN
          You sure?

                         TERMINATOR
          I would.
                                                      CUT TO:

51   EXT. PAYPHONE

   John is quickly going through his pockets for change.   He has plenty of bills but no quarters.

                         JOHN
          Look, Todd and Janelle are dicks but I gotta warn them. Shit!
          You got a quarter?

Terminator reaches past John and smashes the cover plate off the phone's cash box with the heel of
his hand. A shower of change tumbles out. Terminator hands one to John. John dials.

52   INT. VOIGHT HOUSE - KITCHEN - NIGHT

Janelle Voight picks up the kitchen phone and cradles it with her shoulder while she continues to
chop vegetables with a large knife.   She answers sweetly.

                         JANELLE
          Hello?

                         JOHN
                    (filtered through phone)
          Janelle? It's me.

In the backyard, John's German Shepherd is going bonkers, barking at something.

70

                    JANELLE
        John? Where are you, honey? It's late. You should come home,
        dear. I'm making a casserole.

AT THE PAYPHONE. John listens, an odd look on his face. He covers the phone's mouthpiece
and turns to Terminator.

                    JOHN
                (whispering)
        Something's wrong. She's never this nice.

IN THE VOIGHTS' KITCHEN. Todd comes in through the kitchen's back door. Just home from
work. He ignores Janelle and opens the fridge. Grabs a carton of milk. Takes a sip. Frowns at
the dog's barking.

                    TODD
        What the hell's the goddamn dog barking at? SHUT UP, YOU
        MUTT!

TIGHT ON JANELLE as Todd growls around the kitchen behind her. He passes OUT OF FRAME
next to her. Janelle switches the phone to her other hand then... THUNK! Her free hand seems to
do something out of frame. There is a gurgling, and the sound of liquid dribbling onto the floor.
(Don't go away. We'll found out what happened in a moment)

AT THE PAYPHONE. John cups the phone again. Turns to Terminator.

                    JOHN
        The dog's really barking. Maybe it's already there. What
        should I do?

Terminator takes the phone from John's hand. Janelle's voice is floating through the receiver.

                    JANELLE
                (filtered)
        John? John, are you okay?

Terminator speaks into the phone in a perfect imitation of John's voice...

                    TERMINATOR
                (in John's voice)
        I'm right here. I'm fine.
                (to John, a whisper)
        What is the dog's name?

                    JOHN
        Max.

Terminator nods. Speaks into the phone.

                    TERMINATOR
        Hey Janelle, what's wrong with Wolfy? I can hear him
        barking. Is he okay?

                    JANELLE
                (filtered)
        Wolfy's fine, honey. Where are you?

Terminator unceremoniously hangs up the phone. Turns to John.

> TERMINATOR
> Your foster parents are dead. Let's go.

Terminator heads for the bike. John, shocked, stares after him.

53   INT. VOIGHT HOUSE / KITCHEN

Janelle hangs up the phone. Her expression is neutral. Calm.

PAN OVER along her arm, which is stretched out straight from the shoulder. Partway along its length her arm has turned smoothly into something else-- a metal cylinder which tapers into a sword-like spike. Now we see Todd Voight PINNED TO A KITCHEN CABINET by the spike which has punched through his milk carton, through his mouth and exits the back of his head into the cabinet door. His eyes are glassy and lifeless.

The spike is withdrawn-- SWIISHHTT!-- so rapidly, Todd is actually standing there a second before he slumps out of sight. THUMP.

53A Janelle doesn't bat an eye as the spike smoothly changes shape and color, transforming back into a hand, and then...

53B JANELLE CHANGES rapidly into the COP we now know as the T-1000. The change has a liquid quality. T-1000 opens the back door.

54   EXT. VOIGHT HOUSE/ BACKYARD - NIGHT

T-1000 approaches the big German Shepherd, which slinks away from it, barking in fear. T-1000 walks right into CLOSE UP. Reaches down, OUT OF FRAME. We hear that sickening THUNK followed by a shrill YELP. Then T-1000's hand snaps up INTO FRAME holding a bloody dog collar.
The tag reads "MAX".
T-1000 nods thoughtfully. Heads back to the house.

The short scene in which T-1000 goes out to the Voight backyard and silences the family dog was filmed but again was ultimately omitted from the film as unnecessary. Much of T-1000's tracking of John is implied by Terminator's own tracking of John; as stated by Terminator in the film, each terminator can roughly anticipate each other's moves based upon his own information and actions. "Wolfy" is the nickname (short for Beowulf) of a German Shepherd that Jim Cameron used to own; it can be assumed that Terminator acquired the dog's name from hearing it in passing during his earlier search for John on the streets.

---

55   EXT. PARKING LOT - NIGHT

Dark. Off a quiet street. Terminator stands near the Harley, watching John pace before him. John's brain is calling time-out. This is all too weird.

> JOHN
> I need a minute here, okay? You're telling me it can imitate anything it touches?

> TERMINATOR
> Anything it samples by physical contact.

John thinks about that, trying to grasp their opponent's parameters.

> JOHN
> Like it could disguise itself as anything... a pack of cigarettes?

                    TERMINATOR
            No. Only an object of equal size.

John's still reeling from meeting one terminator, which now seems downright conventional next
to the exotic new model.

                    JOHN
            Well, why didn't it just become a bomb or something to get me?

                    TERMINATOR
            It can't form complex machines. Guns and explosives have
            chemicals, moving parts. It doesn't work that way. But it can
            form solid metal shapes.

The addition during shooting of John's line "Like what?" and Terminator's response "Knives and stabbing weapons" further clarifies the T-1000's metier. An intended but not crucial implication is that T-1000 has no default "weapons" in its memory but acquires their forms through the tactile sampling of objects; hence, T-1000's sword-blade arm used at the Voight house is a sampled and augmented version of Janelle's kitchen knife.

---

56   INT. VOIGHT HOUSE - NIGHT

T-1000 walks down the dark hall. It passes the bathroom and we see the real Janelle's legs through
the half-open door. The shower is running. Her blood mixes with water on the white tile floor.

56A   In John's bedroom the T-1000 begins searching methodically in the dark.
        Calmly and dispassionately ripping the room apart for any clues that could lead it to its target.
        T-1000 finds a box of audio cassettes marked "Messages from Mom". In it are some letters, and
        envelopes filled with snapshots. It begins looking through some of the photos...

        SHOTS OF JOHN AND SARAH during the missing years. Sarah in olive cammos with an RPG 7
        grenade launcher, teaching John how to aim. Sarah with a group of military-clad Guatemalan
        men, standing next to cases of Stinger missiles. John and Sarah in a Contra camp, deep in the
        mountains.

Scenes of T-1000 searching John's room at the Voight house for clues were filmed but not used in the final cut, since the scenes were deemed not necessary early on. The inserts of pictures of Sarah and John in South America were never shot, for both time considerations and the fact that John gives much of this exposition in his dialogue in later scenes. The reveal of Janelle's body in the shower was implied and likewise unnecessary to show.

---

57   EXT. PARKING LOT - NIGHT

John is now sitting on the curb, lost in stunned thought. Terminator stands above him, watching
the street like a Doberman. He glances down at John.

                    JOHN
            We spent a lot of time in Nicaragua... places like that. For a
            while she was with this crazy ex-Green Beret guy, running
            guns. Then there were some other guys.

                    JOHN
She'd shack up with anybody she could learn from. So then she
could teach me how to be this great military leader. Then she
gets busted and it's like... sorry kid, your mom's a psycho.
Didn't you know?   It's like... everything I'd been brought up to
believe was just made-up fantasy, right? I hated her for that.
          (he looks up)
But everything she said was true.
          (he stands)
We gotta get her out of there.

                    TERMINATOR
Negative. The T-1000's highest probability for success now
would be to copy Sarah Connor and wait for you to make contact
with her.

                    JOHN
Oh, great. And what happens to her?

Terminator's reply is matter-of-fact.

                    TERMINATOR
Typically, the subject being copied is terminated.

                    JOHN
TERMINATED!? Shit! Why didn't you tell me? We gotta go
right now!

                    TERMINATOR
Negative. She is not a mission priority.

                    JOHN
Yeah, well fuck you, she's a priority to me!

John strides away. Terminator goes after him and grabs his arm. John struggles against the
grip. Which doesn't do him much good.

                    JOHN
Hey, goddammit! What's your problem?

Starts dragging John back to the bike. John spots a couple of college-age slab-o-meat JOCK-TYPES
across the street and starts yelling to them.

                    JOHN
Help! HELP!! I'm being kidnapped! Get this psycho off of me!

The TWO JOCKS start toward them. John yells in outrage at Terminator.

                    JOHN
Let go of me!!

To his surprise, Terminator's hand opens so fast John falls right on his butt.
He looks up at the open hand.

                    JOHN
Oww! Why'd you do that?

TERMINATOR

You told me to.

John stares at him in amazement as he realizes...

JOHN

You have to do what I say?!

TERMINATOR

That is one of the mission parameters.

JOHN

Prove it.... stand on one foot.

Terminator expressionlessly lifts one leg.
John grins. He's the first on his block...

JOHN

Cool! My own terminator. This is great!

The two guys get there and look at Terminator standing there calmly with one leg up in the air.
This big guy in black leather and dark glasses, standing like a statue.

FIRST JOCK

Hey, kid. You okay?

John turns to him. No longer needing to be rescued.

JOHN

Take a hike, bozo.

FIRST JOCK

Yeah? Fuck you, you little dipshit.

JOHN

Dipshit? Did you say <u>dipshit</u>?!
            (to Terminator)
Grab this guy.

John's improvised throwaway line to Terminator ("Put your leg down") adds some humor to the scene, in contrast to the sobering seriousness of the next moment, in which John realizes that he's got a truly deadly weapon --a terminator-- on his hands. John's line change during production to "And I <u>order</u> you to help me" both clarifies and exemplifies John's first major exercise of his newly-found responsibility/authority.

Terminator complies instantly, hoisting him one-handed by the collar. The guy's legs are pinwheeling.

JOHN

Now who's a dipshit, you jock douchebag?

Immediately, things get out of hand. The guy's friend jumps behind Terminator and tries to grab him in a full nelson--
Terminator throws the first guy across the hood of a car--
Grabs the second by the hair, whips out his .45 in a quick blur, and aims the muzzle at the guy's forehead.

John grabs Terminator's arm with a yell as he pulls the trigger-- John's weight is just enough to deflect the gun a few inches. The guy flinches, stunned by the K-<u>BOOM</u> next to his ear. He stares, shocked. Pissing himself. John is freaking out, too.
He screams at Terminator.

                    JOHN
              <u>Put the gun down! NOW!!</u>

Terminator sets the .45 on the sidewalk. John scoops it up fast then turns to the shocked civilians, who can't believe what just happened.

                    JOHN
              Walk away.

They do. Fast. John grabs Terminator by the arm and tugs him toward the bike. John still holds the gun, reluctant to give it back.

                    JOHN
              Jesus... you were gonna kill that guy!

                    TERMINATOR
              Of course. I'm a terminator.

John stares at him. Having your own terminator just became a little bit less fun to him.

                    JOHN
              Listen to me, <u>very carefully</u>, okay? You're not a terminator
              anymore. Alright? You got that? You can't just go around
              killing people!

                    TERMINATOR
              Why?

                    JOHN
              Whattaya mean, why? 'Cause you can't!

                    TERMINATOR
              Why?

                    JOHN
              You just can't, okay? Trust me on this.

Terminator doesn't get it. John just stares at him. Frightened at what just almost happened. He gets a glimpse of the responsibility that comes with power. Finally he hands the .45 back to Terminator, who puts it away.

                    JOHN
              Look, I'm gonna go get my mom. You wanna come along, that's
              fine with me.

                                        CUT TO:

58   INT. VOIGHT HOUSE / BEDROOM - NIGHT

T-1000 finds an envelope... a letter from Sarah to John sent since she's been at Pescadero State Hospital. It reads the return address on the envelope. It has what it needs. It picks up a tape player and the battered shoebox full of Sarah's tapes and exits.

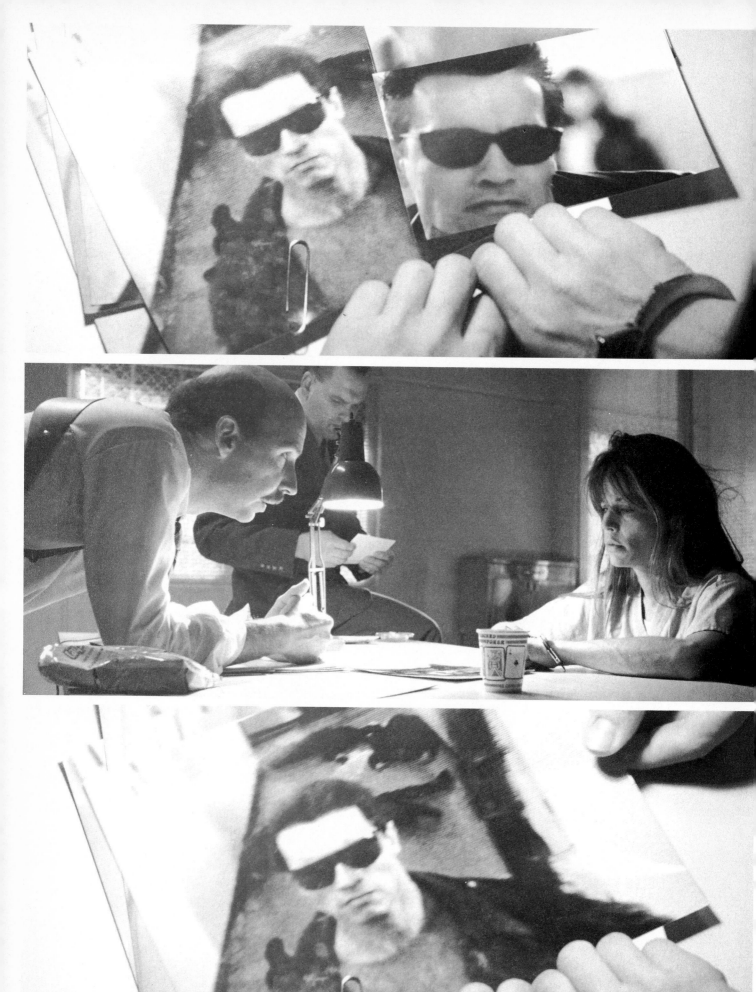

CUT TO:

59 CLOSE ON A BLACK & WHITE PHOTOGRAPH. The image is a nightmare from the past. It is a surveillance camera still-frame from the L.A. police station where the first terminator made such an impression in 1984. We see the blurry forms of cops frozen in the emergency lights of a burning corridor.

A black-clad figure stands at the end of the corridor. The guy has short-cropped hair and dark glasses. An AR-180 assault rifle in one hand, and a 12-gauge in the other --holding them both like toy pistols.
ANOTHER PHOTO is slapped on top of the first. Another still-frame blow-up is placed over the last. Terminator looms in CLOSEUP.

                    DETECTIVE WEATHERBY (O.S.)
          These were taken at the West Highland police station in 1984.
          You were there.

WIDER. We're in--

59A INT. INTERVIEW ROOM / PESCADERO - NIGHT

The photos are lying on the table in front of Sarah, placed there by DETECTIVE WEATHERBY. His partner DET. MOSSBERG, and Dr. Silberman, sit at the table as well. Two uniformed cops, plus Douglas, stand by the door. Sarah stares listlessly at the top photo. She's withdrawn, haggard... drugged-looking.

                    MOSSBERG
          He killed seventeen police officers that night. Recognize him?

Weatherby slaps another black-and-white eight-by-ten on the table. A closeup of Terminator taken by the Japanese tourist at the mall. It's the same face.

                    MOSSBERG
          This one was taken by a Japanese tourist today.

Sarah doesn't react. It's hard to tell she's thinking. Whether she's given up hope or is just in a drugged stupor.

                    WEATHERBY
          Ms. Connor, you've been told your son's missing. His foster
          parents have been murdered, and we know this guy's involved.
          Talk to us. Don't you care?

Sarah looks up at him. A cold and empty stare. He glances at Silberman.
Then at his partner.

                    MOSSBERG
          We're wasting our time.

One of the uniformed cops opens the door and Mossberg strides into the hall. Weatherby and the two uniforms follow him out, with Silberman right behind.

SILBERMAN
Sorry, gentleman...

TIGHT ON SARAH, slumped under the bright lights. Totally out of it. Then we see her hand, creeping along the edge of the table toward the stack of photos. She slips off the paper clip binding the stills together, and hides it between her fingers. Douglas jerks her up by the arm and leads her out.

In the 5/10/90 original draft there is an earlier scene at the mall garage after the canal chase, in which detectives Mossberg and Weatherby find the fully-clothed body of the policeman from Scene 13 in the stolen police car's trunk, to clarify the concept that T-1000 sampled the first victim's clothing rather than actually taking the clothes; the tourist who took the pictures of Terminator in the mall then came running up to the policemen, excitedly waving his camera. Written as a set-up for this hospital interview scene with Sarah, it was not vital to the telling of the story and was omitted from later versions of the script.

CUT TO:

60   INT. SARAH'S CELL

Douglas cinches up the last of Sarah's restraints. Then leans over her... looking down. Even wrecked as she is, we see the beauty in her face. He bends down. We think he's going to kiss her. Instead he runs his tongue across her face like a dog would. She seems not to even see him. Her dull eyes see past him. He can't provoke a reaction. Even here, strapped down, the two of them alone, she gives him no superiority. He smirks and leaves. We hear the sound of his night-stick tapping its way down the corridor, growing fainter.

Sarah's eyes snap suddenly alert. There is intensity and resolve in them. She slips the paper clip out from between her fingers and awkwardly spreads it open into a straight piece of wire. With slow, painful concentration she moves it toward the lock of the restraints that bind her wrists to the bed at her sides.

CUT TO:

61   EXT. ROAD - NIGHT

Terminator and John charge through the night on the Harley. Streetlights flare past them like comets. Two serious guys with a mission. One a ten-year-old kid, the other a half-man/half-machine cyborg killer from the post-Apocalyptic future.

CUT TO:

62   INT. SARAH'S CELL

TIGHT ON RESTRAINT LOCK as it unlatches... successfully picked by Sarah's paper clip. This is not an easy thing to do. But Sarah taught herself a lot of things in her years of hiding.

SARAH, her hands free, sits up and releases the Velcro straps on her feet. She rolls off the bed and we see her in a whole new light. She is totally alert, almost feral in her movements.

CUT TO:

63   EXT. HOSPITAL ENTRANCE

GUARD SHACK. A bored security guard glances up as an LAPD black-and-white pulls up. He raises the barricade and nods at the T-1000/cop as it passes.

THE CRUISER pulls in next to the other police vehicles. The T-1000 walks toward the main entrance.

CUT TO:

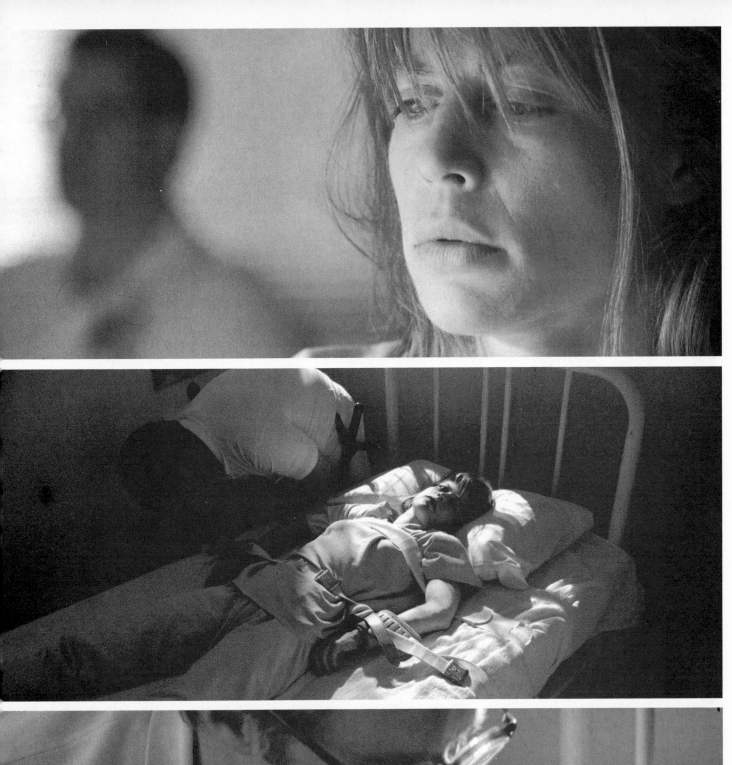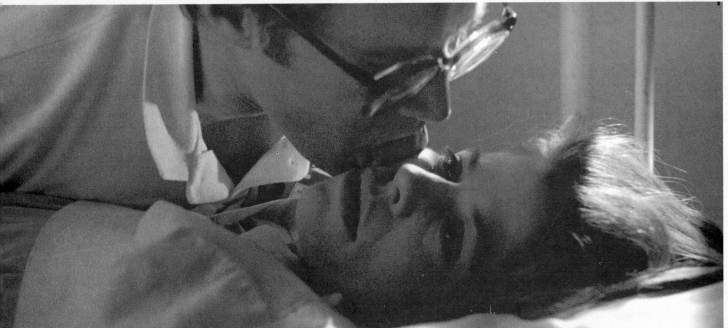

64   INT. SARAH'S CELL / CORRIDOR

        Sarah is using the paper clip on the door lock.   She hears an echoing tapping sound. It's getting louder, coming her way. She goes back to work on the lock.

65   IN THE CORRIDOR. Douglas the attendant is tapping his stick along the wall like he does every night on his rounds. It is dark. He shines a little mag-light in the windows of the cells as he passes, barely slowing.

65A   He rounds the corner. His footsteps echo in the dark hallway.
        The tip of the stick hits the wall.
        Tap, tap, tap... getting closer to Sarah's cell. He stops at her door. He is about to shine his light in when he notices that a utility closet across the hall is open. He goes to shut it, absently flicking his light into the dark closet. He notices something strange among the buckets and cleaning supplies. A mop lies on the floor, with its handle snapped off about halfway up. The other half is missing.

        Douglas ponders that for half a second, then hears a SOUND behind him and spins around. The sound he heard was Sarah's cell door.
        The missing two feet of MOP HANDLE fills his vision as it CRACKS viciously across the bridge of his nose.

        250 pounds of doughy attendant hit the floor like a sack of cement. Sarah slams the makeshift baton down expertly across the back of his head, bouncing him off the linoleum. Lights out, Douglas.
        She drags him into her cell and locks him in with his own keys. Then swaps her mop-handle for his nice heavy night-stick.

65B   Sarah moves down the dark corridor, cat-stepping in her bare feet. She holds the baton like a pro, laid back along her forearm, police-style. She looks *dangerous*.

                                         CUT TO:

66   INT. HOSPITAL ENTRANCE / CORRIDOR

        A long corridor ends at a reception area, which is closed, and a NIGHT RECEIVING DESK, which is a glass window where they can buzz you in through a heavy door. A NIGHT NURSE types at a desk nearby. She looks up at the sound of footsteps and sees a young cop (T-1000) walking toward her.

                        T-1000
              You have a Sarah Connor here?

        She assumes he's with the other cops. Smiles.

                    NIGHT NURSE
              Running late, aren't you?

        She turns to the inner door to buzz him in and sees Silberman and the cops coming toward the door from the other side.

                    NIGHT NURSE
           Your friends are on their way out now...

        When she turns back to the window, T-1000's no longer there. She goes to the counter and leans out to see if he's at the drinking fountain or someplace. No. Reception is empty. And so is the long corridor beyond. She frowns. Too weird.

Several of the hospital scenes have been transposed and reordered in the film for better pacing and greater suspense: T-1000's arrives at the hospital prior to the reveal of Sarah's determination to escape, and the two actions are intercut for tension as Sarah struggles to escape her cell while T-1000 kills and imitates Lewis the Guard, closing in on her; Sarah does not escape her cell until after T-1000 has made it into the ward and is roaming the halls; and Terminator and John are not shown on their way to Pescadero until after T-1000 and Sarah are both free in the halls of the hospital.

66A   Silberman comes through the solenoid door with Mossberg and Weatherby, the two uniform cops, and the hospital security guard. The guard retrieves his 9mm pistol from a lock-out box behind the night desk. Silberman faces him.

                                    SILBERMAN
                Lewis, see these gentleman out and then lock up for the night.

The security guard nods. Silberman goes back into the secure area of the hospital and the cops walk down the long corridor to the main doors. No sign of T-1000. Mossberg and the other cops exit, and the guard locks the door behind them.

66B   The guard walks slowly back along the long corridor. The hall is dark, with the light at the night desk far ahead like a sanctuary. His footsteps ring hollowly on the tile floor. His keys jingle.

66C   ANGLE ON FLOOR as the guard's feet pass through FRAME. An instant later *the floor starts to move.*
        It shivers and bulges upward like a liquid mass, still retaining the two-tone checkerboard of the tile. It hunches up silently into a quivering shadow in the darkness behind the guard.

66D   Up ahead we hear typing. The night nurse has her back to us, working. The guard stops at the drinking fountain. Bends to take a sip. Behind him the fluid mass has reached six feet of height and begins to resolve rapidly into a human figure. It loses the color and texture of the tile and becomes... THE GUARD.

        T-1000's mass had been spread out a quarter of an inch thick over several square yards of floor. The guard walked over the T-1000, and his structure was sampled in that instant. Now we see it drawing in and pulling up to form the figure of the guard.

        The T-1000/Guard's feet are the last to form, the last of the "liquid floor" pulling in to form shiny black guard shoes. The shoes detach with a faint sucking sound from the real floor as the T-1000/Guard takes its first step.

66E   The real guard spins at the sound of footsteps to see... *himself.*
        He has one deeply disturbing moment to consider the ramifications of that. Then he sees his double calmly raise its hand and, inexplicably, point its right index finger directly at the real guard's face, about a foot away. In a split second, the finger spears out, elongating into a thin steel rod which snaps out like a stiletto, slamming into the guard's eye.
        It punches into the corner of the eye, past the eyeball like a trans-orbital lobotomy tool, and emerges from the back of the guard's skull.

        Life quietly empties from the guard's face. He is dead weight now, hanging from the rod/finger, which suddenly retracts-- SSSNICK. As the guard slumps, the T-1000 takes his weight easily with one hand and walks him, like it's carrying a suit on a hanger, back toward the night desk. The wounds are so tiny, no blood drips onto the floor.

66F   ON THE NURSE, glancing up as the T-1000/Guard walks past, dragging something casually which she can't see because it's below the countertop.

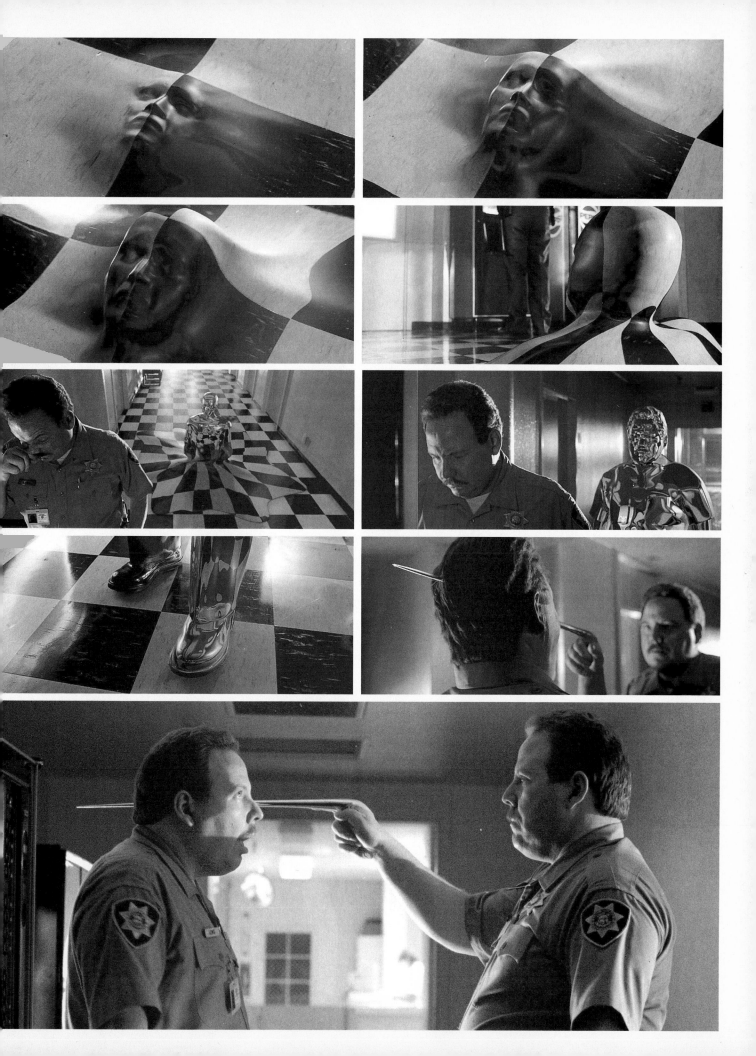

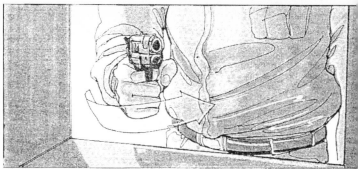

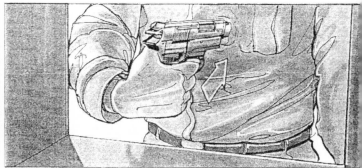

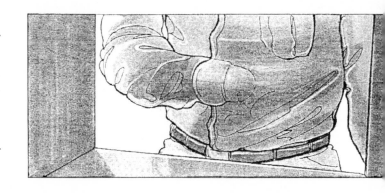

In the final film, it was only necessary to show that T-1000 takes the guard's gun, so the business of T-1000 concealing the weapon from the night nurse by secreting it within its own body was dropped before it was to be filmed.

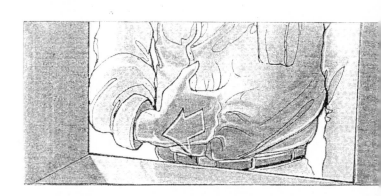

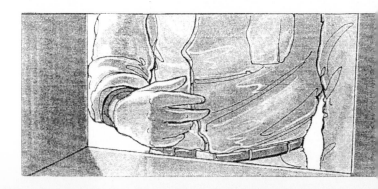

                    NIGHT NURSE
          Whatcha got, Lewis?

                    T-1000/GUARD
          Just some trash.

She nods, uninterested. Keeps typing. T-1000 moves past, dragging the unseen guard toward a closet down the hall from the night receiving station. T-1000/Guard removes the Browning High-Power pistol and the keys from the real guard's belt, then stuffs his body into the utility closet.

66G   INT. CORRIDOR / NIGHT RECEIVING DESK

T-1000/Guard comes back out and glances at the nurse.

                    T-1000/GUARD
          All set.

She glances toward it. Sees the Beretta in its holster.

                    NIGHT NURSE
          Gotta to check the gun first, Lewis.

                    T-1000/GUARD
          Yeah, sorry.

T-1000 opens the locker and blocks it from her view with its body as it mimes putting the gun in.

66H   CLOSE ANGLE ON T-1000'S CHEST, from inside the locker. Instead of setting the gun in the locker, it inserts the pistol *into its own chest*, where it disappears inside like it was dropped into a pot of hot fudge. It withdraws its hand. The chest is once again a surface that looks like cloth, buttons, name-tag etc. You'd never guess it was really an intelligent liquid metal.

The visual effect of T-1000/Lewis hiding the gun in its chest was omitted during production prior to the hospital location shoot for both technical and production scheduling conflicts in shooting the plate for the computer graphics; it was a neat but unnecessary detail that was going to cost a great deal of time and money to shoot. The whole idea of the guards having to check in their guns when in the patient areas, although technically accurate, took time to establish and unnecessarily slowed the pacing of this and other scenes. The irony of the night nurse not noticing Lewis getting killed by T-1000 plays adequately in the spiking scene itself, so the "Just some trash" bit of business, although filmed, was cut as unnecessary. The important point showing T-1000/Lewis taking the dead Lewis' gun is retained.

T-1000 slams the locker door and waits as the nurse hits the button unlocking the door with a BUZZ-CLACK. T-1000/Guard goes through.

                                                            CUT TO:

67   INT. ISOLATION SECURITY CHECKPOINT

A small room before a short SALLY-PORT corridor designed to prevent violent inmates from making a run for it. There are doors at each end. The first one is barred like a jail-cell door, and the second is a steel fire door.   The attendants have a video monitor with which they can see the corridor on the other side of the doors.

The two bored attendants barely notice the T-1000/Guard as it approaches. Looks briefly at a chart next to the door, seeing SARAH CONNOR is in #19.
T-1000/Guard goes into the Isolation Ward through the two doors, which lock behind it.

67A   IN THE ISOLATION WARD, the T-1000 passes a nurses' station which looks like a cage, walled in by heavy metal mesh. Silberman, leaning in the open doorway, is talking to an attendant in the cage. He doesn't glance twice at Lewis the Guard passing by.

This bridging scene establishing Silberman in the night attendant's station and showing T-1000/Lewis the Guard's unnoticed walkby was also omitted as unnecessary.

---

68   SARAH, moving like a ghost in the darkened corridor, hears footsteps coming and quietly but quickly unlocks a cell next to her with Douglas's master key.
68A   She slips into the cell and waits as the footsteps pass.
We glimpse the T-1000/Guard pass the window.
She waits as the footsteps fade away. She looks over. A female inmate, strapped to a bed, watches her with bird-like eyes. She puts a finger to her lips-- SSHHH. The inmate nods. Sarah exits.

Sarah's ducking into a fellow inmate's cell was never filmed; it was an unnecessary beat of action that would have required a redressed cell and an additional actress, taking valuable production time away from the filming of more crucial scenes.

68B   POV MOVING TOWARD nurse's station. We hear Silberman's voice, reviewing medication with the night attendant.

ON SILBERMAN yawning, looking at his watch.
He turns to go... <u>Sarah is there</u>.
She slams into him, hurling him through the door into the cage and following him in. The orderly jumps up, going for his stunner, but she nails him with Douglas's baton. WHAP-WHAP-WHAP! You can barely see the thing she's swinging it so fast. The guy goes down.

Silberman lunges for the alarm button and she cracks down hard on his arm. He cries out and grabs his wrist.
She grabs him by the hair and slams him face down on the desk, smacking him behind the knees expertly with the baton.
His legs buckle and he drops to his knees with his chin on the desk.
She pins him with one hand. His face is full of outraged disbelief.

> SILBERMAN
> You broke my arm!

> SARAH
> There's 215 bones in the human body, motherfucker. That's
> <u>one</u>. Now don't move!

68B   Moving rapidly, she whips open a medication drawer and grabs a syringe.
They keep a few of these handy for tranking unruly patients. She jams it into the orderly's butt and fires the whole shot. Still holding the empty syringe, she sees what she needs next.
They keep the toxic cleaning supplies in here to keep the inmates from drinking the Drano. She grabs a plastic jug of LIQUID PLUM'R and slams it down on the desk inches from Silberman's eyes.

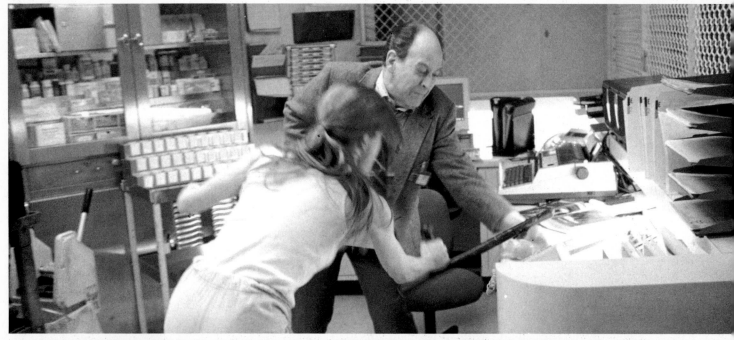

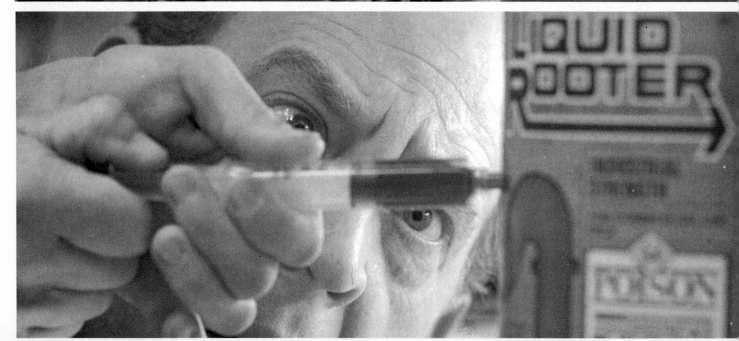

She jabs the empty syringe into the plastic jug.
Draws back the plunger. The syringe fills with blue liquid.
She whips it out of the jug and jams the needle into Silberman's neck. His horrified eyes rack toward it. 10 cc's of blue death fill the cylinder.
Her thumb hovers over the plunger.
She jerks him to his feet by the collar and gets a tight grip on him, then hauls him through the door.

In the final film, Silberman's added line."What are you going to do?" as Sarah is drawing the chemical into the syringe marks the end of the scene, avoiding the unpleasant visual of watching Sarah jab it into his neck and creating more suspense as to whether or not Sarah is going to kill him outright by saving the reveal of what she's doing until Scene 71. There were of course legal reasons for the change to "Liquid Rooter" in the film, as Liquid Plum'r would not appreciate such an imaginative use of their product.

---

69   IN THE CORRIDOR outside cell #19 the T-1000 stops and looks in the window. Douglas, his face a bloody mess, yells to be heard.

DOUGLAS
Open the door! The goddamn bitch is loose in the halls!

To Douglas's amazement, Lewis the Guard turns impassively and walks away, leaving him shouting soundlessly at the window.

T-1000/Lewis' ignoring of the battered Douglas in Sarah's cell was filmed but not used in the film; this scene not only softens Sarah's vicious beating of Douglas by showing that he's still alive but also plays one last trick on him by leaving him locked in the cell. This was a nice bit of icing to his come-uppance but was unnecessary to the story's accelerating forward momentum, and was replaced by the offscreen morph of T-1000 back to its default cop form. In the script, T-1000 stays in its Lewis the Guard form until it reforms in the elevator in Scene 76, but it was decided to have it revert back to the more familiar and menacing form of actor Robert Patrick sooner in order to maintain both a simpler continuity and the recognition of the character.

CUT TO:

70   EXT. HOSPITAL

Terminator and John are approaching the guard gate on the Harley. They can see the guard inside look up at the sound of the engine.

JOHN
Now remember, you're not gonna kill anyone, right?

TERMINATOR
Right.

John looks at him. He's not convinced.

JOHN
Swear.

TERMINATOR
What?

JOHN
Just say "I swear I won't kill anyone."

John holds his hand up, like he's being sworn in. Terminator stares at John a beat. Then mimics the gesture.

> TERMINATOR
> I swear I will not kill anybody.

Terminator stops the bike and gets off.
The guard, sensing trouble, has his gun drawn as he comes out of the shack. Terminator walks toward him drawing his .45 smoothly. <u>BLAM</u>!
He shoots the guard accurately in the thigh.
The guy drops, screaming and clutching his leg.
Terminator kicks the guard's gun away, then smashes the phone in the shack with his fist. He pushes the button to raise the gate and walks back to the bike.

> TERMINATOR
> He'll live.

Terminator climbs on the bike. They drive toward the hospital, heading down an ambulance ramp to an underground receiving area.

71   INT. ISOLATION FLOOR

The attendants at the security checkpoint look up at the monitor as someone enters the corridor.
They see Sarah, holding Silberman at syringe-point.
Sarah speaks to them through an intercom on the wall. Her voice comes through the speaker.

> SARAH
> Open it or he'll be dead before he hits the floor.

The attendants' adrenalin levels just went off the scale. The first attendant adamantly shakes his head no. The amperage here is really high. The second attendant keys the intercom mike.

> 2ND ATTENDANT
> There's no way, Connor. Let him go.

Silberman's face is the color of suet.

> SILBERMAN
> It won't work, Sarah. You're no killer. I don't believe you'd do
> it.

Her voice is a deadly cold hiss.

> SARAH
> You're already dead, Silberman. Everybody here dies. You
> know I believe that. <u>So don't fuck with me!</u>

> SILBERMAN
> Open the goddamn door!

The attendants look at one another. One of them finally hits the solenoid button. The far door unlocks.

71A   IN THE LOCKOUT CORRIDOR. Sarah pushes Silberman ahead of her.
The nearer, barred door must be unlocked manually.
One of the attendants cautiously approaches. Nervously unlocks it.

SARAH

Step back!

He does. She faces both of them.

SARAH

Down on the floor! *Now!*

They comply. She comes through with Silberman, giving them a wide berth. Starts backing down the hall away from them, still holding her hostage. She's actually pulling this off.

71B   ANGLE FROM BEHIND HER. What we can see, but she can't, is a third orderly waiting just around the corner. He's poised, ready to jump her when she comes abreast of him.

ON SARAH backing up. She reaches the corner.
The third attendant lunges, grabbing her syringe-hand.
Sarah spins on the orderly and catches him across the throat with the nightstick. He loses interest fast, dropping to his knees and gagging. Silberman pulls away, screaming at the top of his lungs.

SILBERMAN

Get her!

They scramble up as Sarah takes off like a shot around the corner.
One of them hits the panic button and ALARMS begin to sound.

72   IN THE ISOLATION WARD, the T-1000 is looking in at a very stoned attendant inside the nurses' station when the alarms shriek through the halls. It reaches into its chest and pulls out the 9mm pistol. Heads for the security entrance.

73   IN ANOTHER CORRIDOR in the maze of the vast hospital, Sarah flies past us, her bare feet slapping on the cold tiles. The orderlies charge after her.
She's like an animal in a maze. She turns a corner, glancing off the wall, and sprints on without slowing. She reaches a steel door. Tries it. Locked.
Footsteps like a drum solo behind her.

She fumbles with Douglas's keys, breathing hard. Jams the master in.
The orderlies are bearing down on her at full tilt.
Sarah gets the door open. Dives through. Slams it.
She turns a deadbolt knob just as the first orderly grabs the latch on the other side. He's too late.

Sarah sees them beyond the window, fumbling with their keys.

73A   Sarah is in another sally-port corridor. A jail-cell type barred door is between her and the corridors of the ward beyond.
She sprints to the wall of bars, jams her key into the door.
She unlocks and pulls open this door just as she hears the latch of the one she just came through being unlocked.

She flings herself frantically through the barred door as the first orderly comes through behind her.
She slams the bars shut. CLANG.
Her keys are dangling from the lock on the other side from her.
The orderly is racing at her, white-lipped with rage.

She reaches back through the bars, turns the key, and *purposefully snaps it off in the lock*. An instant later the big orderly slams against the door, grabbing through the bars for her as she dances back just out of reach.
He lunges against the steel bars, unbelievably pissed off.

Sarah takes off running, looking back at the frustrated orderlies. They're shouting at each other, unable to fit their keys into the lock--
The broken-off key tip makes it impossible to get their keys in.
Silberman shouts at them.

> SILBERMAN
> Go around, goddammit! Go around!!

The orderlies run back the way they came, and along a cross-corridor to another set of doors.

73B ON SARAH as she rounds a corner and sees the elevators ahead.
Now she's home-free. At a full-tilt sprint, she's nearly there when the elevator doors part...

TERMINATOR steps out... his head swiveling to face her.
Sarah reacts, stricken by the image from her worst nightmares.
Her eyes go wide as momentum carries her forward.
Her bare feet slip on the slick tile. She slams to the floor, staring up at the leather-clad figure with the shotgun.

She loses all semblance of courage and some of her sanity.
She's not even aware that she is screaming, or what would be screaming if she could get the breath to do it.
In slowed-down dream-time, Sarah scrambles back along the floor like a crab, spinning and clawing her way to her feet along the wall.

She runs like the wind, like in her nightmare. If she looked back she would have seen John step warily out of the corridor behind Terminator. John, however, catches a glimpse of the fleeing Sarah and figures out instantly what happened.

> JOHN
> <u>Mom</u>!! Wait!

Sarah doesn't hear. She has clicked fully into her own nightmare.
They take off running after Sarah.

73C She is pelting down the long corridor, back the way she came. As she reaches an intersection with a cross-corridor a white-clad figure blurs from that corridor. The orderly hits her in a flying tackle. She skids across the floor, shrieking and struggling. The other two orderlies leap into the fray.

> SARAH
> <u>No! Help me! Goddammit, it's gonna kill us all!!!</u>

She is shouting, pleading, trying to get them to understand what is coming. They grab her thrashing arms and legs. They don't even look where the out-of-control woman is pointing... back along the corridor.

They have her pinned to the cold tiles, a ring of faces above her. Silberman leans down to her, holding a syringe with a heavy dose of trank. Sarah cranes her neck and sees the dark silhouette of Terminator coming up behind them. *It is exactly her nightmare.*
She screams in utter hopelessness.

Terminator, holding the shotgun in one hand, reaches down and grabs one of the orderlies with his other hand. He hurls the 200-pound guy against the far wall of the corridor. SMACK! He drops to the floor.

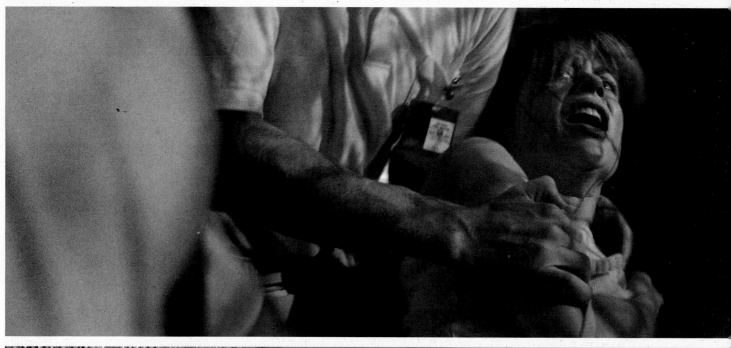

The other two orderlies react instantly, leaping onto the intruder.
Terminator seems to disappear for a moment under the two big guys.
Then there is an explosion of white-clad figures, as the orderlies are flung outward like they stepped on a land mine.
One crashes through a window of safety glass and is caught before a two-story fall by the outer steel bars. The other crashes through an office door, splintering it into kindling.

Silberman has jumped in to hold Sarah. He is grabbed by a roll of skin at the back of his neck and lifted like a cat. The doctor feels his feet pedaling above the ground. He looks into the expressionless face. And it hits him. Sarah was right... this guy *isn't* human.
He feels the fabric of his reality crumbling.
Then he feels himself flying through the air. The wall smacks him, then the floor kicks him in the face. He decides to lie there a second.

Sarah blinks, staring up at the figure looming over her.
John kneels next to her.

> JOHN
> Mom, are you okay?

She looks from Terminator to John. Back to Terminator.
Is this a nightmare? Or has she finally gone truly mad?

Incredibly, Terminator politely reaches his hand down to her, offering to help her up. The last thing she ever expected to see.

> TERMINATOR
> Come with me if you want to live.

The orderlies are stirring.

> JOHN
> It's all right, Mom. He's here to help.

Sarah, in a daze, takes the huge hand in her shaking fingers. Terminator lifts her to her feet.

It was decided during the filming of this scene to have Silberman's role here to be almost completely as a passive observer, basically ignored by all the other characters at this point in the story. This helps creates the sense that Silberman is not even worthy of being Sarah's antagonist, being an ineffectual figure whose authority pales into inaction in the face of the real conflicts and opponents; his main role in the scene is to provide comic relief through the dumbfounded expressions on his face as he watches the morphing and gunplay erupting around him.

73D John sees a GUARD standing thirty feet away, on the other side of the wall of bars. John doesn't know what we know, but he knows something's not right with this guy. Terminator turns to follow John's gaze.
The T-1000 has its pistol in its hand, at its side.
Terminator pushes John behind him. They start backing up.

73E The T-1000 walks forward, reaching the bars. *It doesn't stop.*
Its body divides like jello around the bars. As it squeezes itself through like metal playdough, its surface reforms perfectly on our side. We see it deform and squeeze through like a viscous paste forced past an obstacle.
Silberman has recovered enough to be sitting up and watching this. That faint snapping sound is his mind.

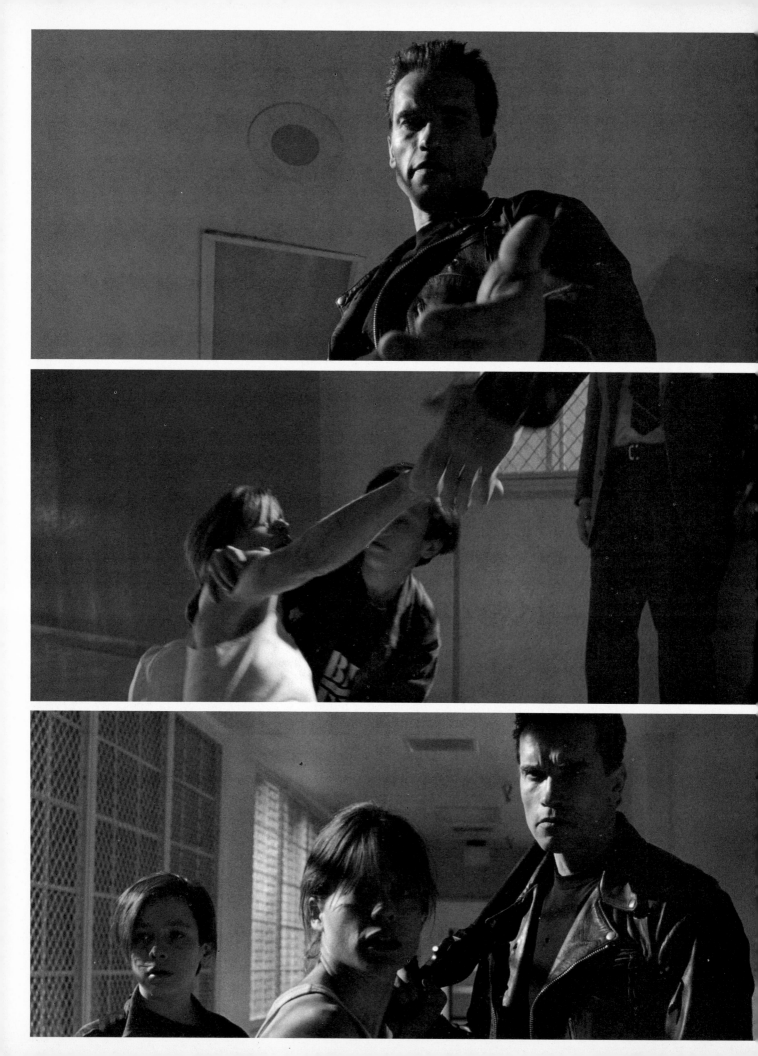

There is a CLINK and we see that the guard's gun has caught against the bars... the only solid object. The T-1000 turns its wrist and tries again, slipping the gun endwise through the gap.

73F   Sarah is agape. Not reacting. It's been a heavy day for her.
Terminator grabs John by the seat of his pants and hooks him up onto his back. John grabs him around the neck. Terminator raises the shotgun and starts backing up.

TERMINATOR
Go! Run!

Sarah doesn't need to be told twice.
T-1000 walks toward them, opening fire with the Browning Hi-Power.
Terminator straight-arms the 12-gauge like a pistol and FIRES.
The stunned orderlies flop face down on the floor as the corridor is filled with high-velocity lead.
One of them, stupidly running for the cross-corridor, gets hit by the T-1000.

Terminator is hammered by several slugs, and the T-1000 is cratered by two buckshot hits. It staggers, but comes on. In the craters we see bright mercury before they close and reseal, disappearing in a second.

73G   Terminator makes it around the corner and breaks into a run. Ahead, Sarah is already at the elevator. Terminator and John pile in and John slaps the button for "Garage Level".

The doors start to close. T-1000 clears the corner.
Terminator slams John and Sarah back against the side walls as the T-1000 charges at them, rapid-firing the Browning.
The rounds hit the steel doors as they close.
T-1000 keeps pumping them at the closing gap.
73H   Inside, they see the backside of the doors denting with the hits that are punching holes in the other side.

73I   The Browning locks open, empty. T-1000 drops it without a glance back. The doors close. K-WHAM! The T-1000 hits them a split second later. The elevator hasn't moved yet. SSWWIKK!

73J   A sword-like blade rams in between the doors, forcing them open. Terminator jams the shotgun through the widening gap. Punches the muzzle right INTO the T-1000's face -- BOOM!!
73K   We get a glimpse of the T-1000's head blown apart by the blast. It is hurled back. The doors close. The car descends.

73L   ON THE T-1000, outside the elevator. Its head, which is blown apart into two doughy masses lying on the shoulders, reforms quickly. There is no trace of the injury.   It sees the closed doors and jams its hands between them, its fingertips becoming pry-bars. It pulls the doors apart with inhuman strength
73M   and LEAPS INTO THE OPEN SHAFT.
It falls two floors and...

74   IN THE ELEVATOR. Our trio hears a loud THUMP on the roof.
Terminator, reloading the shotgun, looks up.
Sarah grabs the .45 from his waistband and aims it at the ceiling.
BEAT...
Then CLANGG!! a swordlike shaft punches through the ceiling and spears down four feet into the elevator car.
It is inches from Sarah's face.
She opens fire, BAM-BAM-BAM-- right through the roof.
Lightning-fast the lance withdraws and thrusts down again, slashing Terminator's jacket, and missing John by inches.
Terminator chambers a round and K-BOOM! the 12-gauge opens a hole in the ceiling.

Terminator rocks out in a fury of firing/cocking/firing as the metal shafts slash down again and again. Sarah yells in pain as one of them slices open her upper arm.

75   The doors open. Sarah pulls John out as soon as the gap is wide enough.
They emerge into the basement. We see the Harley parked nearby.

Terminator, in a rearguard action, fires another blast through the ceiling and runs out. He throws his leg over the Harley, kicks it to life with one powerful stroke and then whips something out of the inner pocket of his jacket. He throws it to John. A road flare!?

76   In the elevator, the T-1000 has bashed a hole in the ceiling big enough to...
Pour itself through.
A massive blob of mercury extrudes from the opening. The mass drops through the hole, down out of frame, then comes back up into frame as Officer X.

It seems to need just a second to get its mental act together after doing this kind of taffy-pull with itself. It opens its eyes and sees--

77   TERMINATOR, *the shotgun held in his teeth*, astride the roaring Harley twenty feet away.
Terminator twists the throttle and pops the clutch.
The back tire screams on the concrete. The front wheel lifts off the ground and the heavy bike launches in a thundering wheelie.

Terminator gets off just before the bike hurtles into the elevator.
The Harley slams the T-1000 square and smashes it right through the back wall of the elevator.
Terminator rolls to his feet.
John strikes the flare on the concrete. Tosses it.
Terminator catches the lit flare with one hand.
Levels the shotgun with the other.
With his last round he blows a big hole in the bike's gas tank.
Gas splashes everywhere, covering the struggling T-1000.
Terminator tosses the flare. KA-VOOOM!

The explosion knocks Terminator backward off his feet, enveloping him in the fireball. He gets up, smoking, and runs after John and Sarah toward the exit ramp.

Terminator's stalling tactic of driving the motorcycle into T-1000 in the elevator and blowing it up was deemed an unnecessary and expensive piece of action and was thus never filmed. This decision not only saved production time and money, but avoided some repetitive gags, such as having a chrome T-1000 come out of another fire, morphing back into the cop as he goes.

---

78   AT THE EXIT RAMP. They are partway up when a blue-and-white hospital security car comes screeching down the other way.
Without breaking stride Sarah runs right at the car. It skids to a shrieking halt. She's in the guy's face with the .45 in both hands.

                    SARAH
          Out of the car!!

The patrol guy is thinking what he can try when BAM! she puts a round through the glass next to his head.

                    SARAH
               RIGHT NOW!

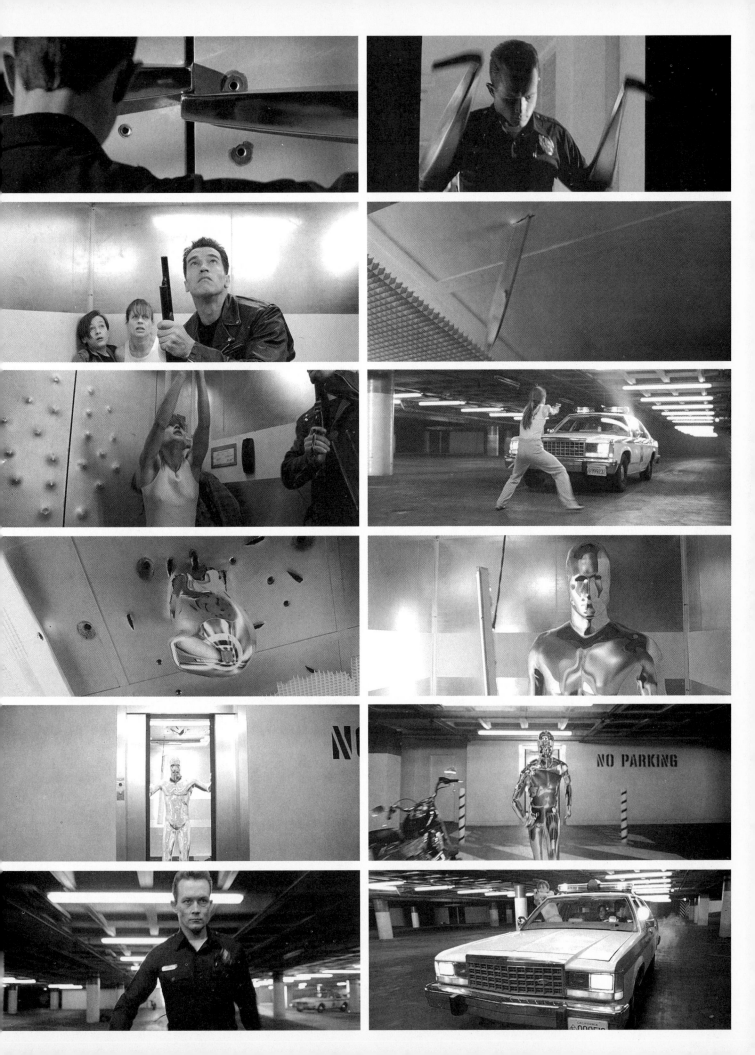

IN THE PARKING GARAGE

①

②

③

④

⑤

HELL'S ANGELS

PACOIMA

The action of Terminator crashing his Harley into the hospital elevator and blowing it up with a road flare --as roughed in by Steve Burg and John Bruno-- was an extra beat of mayhem that was easily omitted; likewise, the companion shot of T-1000 running out of the burning elevator and morphing back to cop from chrome man was too similar to the earlier shot of it walking out of the fire in the canal and was simplified.

The door opens and the guy is coming out with his hands up as Terminator arrives. The cyborg flings the rent-a-cop out of the way and slides behind the wheel. Sarah gets John into the back seat and dives into the front passenger seat as--

78A   Terminator slams the car in reverse and punches it, lighting up the tires on the slick ramp. Terminator hands the shotgun over his shoulder to John and tells him to reload. John pulls some shells from the pocket of his army jacket and starts feeding them in.
Terminator powers backward up the ramp, scraping along one wall, barely in control. Because...

79   *The T-1000 is running at them out of the inferno below.*
This guy won't quit. Shifting from chrome mode to the cop-form as it runs.
It sprints up the ramp after the retreating car. T-1000 is gaining.

80   Terminator hands Sarah another magazine for the .45. She snatches it, drops the other out, and slaps in the new one. Cocks the slide.
The car backs along the service driveway toward the security gate.
John hands the shotgun back to Terminator.
He leans out the window and takes aim at the pursuer.
The T-1000's face is right in the headlights.

80A   Terminator fires, blowing a hole in its shoulder. Shiny liquid metal visible in the hole, which then closes.

80B   Sarah, half out the passenger window, opens fire.
The car crashes backward through the security barricade.

>   TERMINATOR
>   (calmly)
>   Hang on.

He cuts the wheel hard. The car slews into a reverse 180, swapping ends with a screech.
T-1000 is almost on them.
Terminator punches it. The car accelerates forward.

80C   T-1000 leaps. Lands on the trunk.
Its hand is a metal crowbar slammed down through the trunk lid. Feet dragging on the pavement, it slams its other hand down, punching another metal hook into the trunk lid, pulling itself up.
Terminator turns to Sarah.

>   TERMINATOR
>   Drive.

Terminator heaves himself half out of the driver's window. Sarah slaps her foot down on the throttle and steers from the passenger side.

80D   T-1000, fully on the car now, holds on with one hook-hand while it slams the other into the back window, sweeping away the glass and missing John by inches as he ducks.
It draws back for another swing, lunging forward as--

80E   Terminator whips the shotgun down over the roof of the car.
Fires point-blank.
Hits the T-1000's arm just above the "hand" which anchors it to the car. The 12-gauge blows the arm apart, severing the hook-hand.

80F   T-1000 tumbles backward off the accelerating car.
John looks out the back window, his eyes wide.
He sees the T-1000 roll to his feet and continue running.
But he's dropping way behind now. Sarah has the car floored and the liquid-metal killer won't catch them on foot.

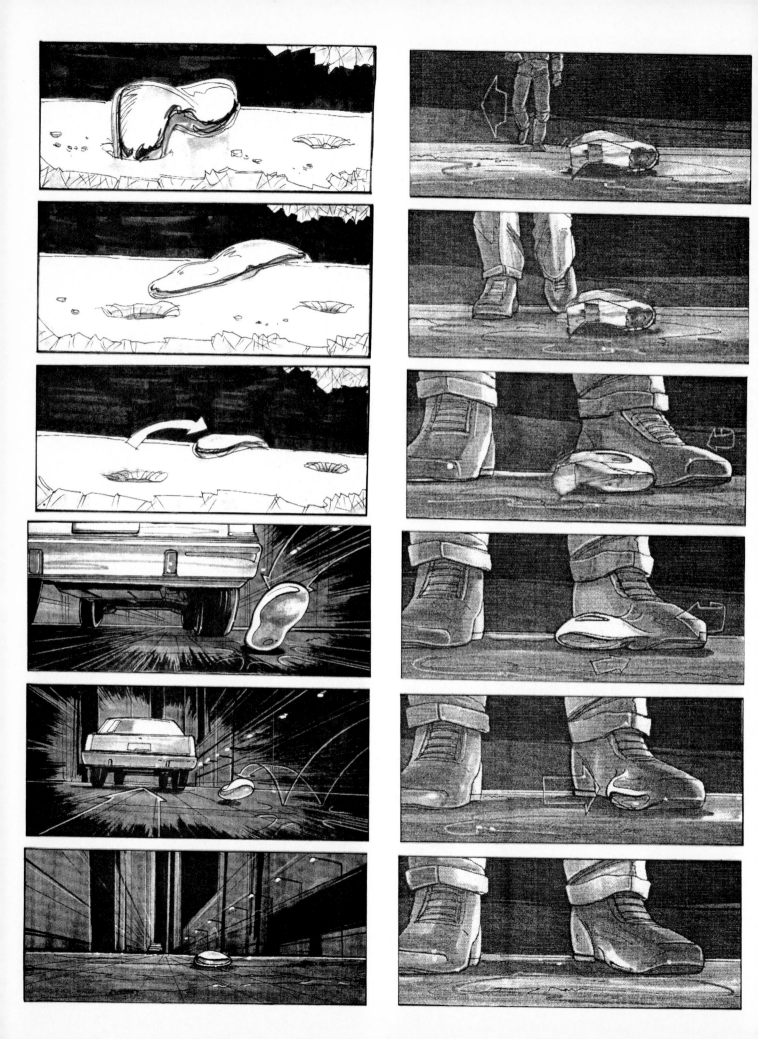

80G   John watches, in awe, as the "crowbar hand", stuck into the trunk right in front of him, reverts to the neutral polyalloy... a kind of thick mercury. The gray metal slides off the trunk of the car and falls onto the road to lie there in a quivering blob.

In an effort to streamline the scene and avoid costly computer graphics shots that did not forward the story, it was decided to have the shot-off crowbar hand remain solid until it rejoins T-1000's shoe. It also gave John Connor something active to do by grabbing the piece and hurling it off the trunk, and is the only time he actually confronts a piece of his nemesis at such close range.

80H   The car speeds off into the night.
REVERSE on the T-1000, walking now, coming right up into closeup, watching the tail lights recede. It looks down.

80I   ANGLE ON BLACKTOP, tight on the liquid metal blob. Next to it is the T-1000's shiny cop shoe. The mercury blob crawls and rejoins the main mass, disappearing into the "shoe".

81   INT./ EXT. SECURITY CAR

A GHOST CAR blasts out of the darkness on a long stretch of moonlit highway. Headlights off, the hospital security car punches a hole in the wind.

81A   INSIDE THE SPEEDING CAR the energy is still high. The air is blasting in the shattered windows as Terminator drives the car easily by electronic night-vision. His eyes glow faintly red.

> JOHN
> Can you even see anything?

81B   TERMINATOR'S POV. A monochrome image of the highway lit bright as day.

81C   Terminator replies in a matter-of-fact tone.

> TERMINATOR
> Everything.

> JOHN
> Cool.

Sarah looks at Terminator, still not quite believing this is happening. But this is a different Sarah than the waitress of 1984.
She spends only a second or two dealing with the unbelievable.
Then she turns to John in the back seat.

> SARAH
> You okay?

He nods. She reaches for John and we think she's going to hug him. She starts to rub her hands over him and we realize she's checking for injuries, very clinically the way a vet checks a dog for broken bones.

He pulls away from her. He hates her always checking him, treating him like he might break, like some piece of rare china.

> JOHN
> I said I was okay.

SCAN LEVELS:
****
234654 453 30
654334 450 16
245261 865 26
453665 766 46
382856 863 09

N
NW   NE
W   E
SW   SE
S

SEARCH CRITERIA
MATCH MODE 5498

ALL LEVELS OPERATIVE

LATERAL SPEED   573 358
TRAJECTORY   600 237
BASE CORRECT   113 355
ACCELERATION   328 589
Z-BUFFER COMP   305 006

IMAGE ENHANCE

Sarah looks at him, exasperated and stern.

                    SARAH
          It was stupid of you to go there.

John stares at her, surprised.

                    SARAH
          Goddammit, John, you have to be smarter than that. You're too
          important!   You can't risk yourself, *not even for me, do you
          understand?*   I can take care of myself. I was doing fine. Jesus,
          John. You almost got yourself killed.

We see his chin quiver. He's a tough kid, but all he really wants is for her to love him. He hasn't
had enough years on the planet yet to be the man of steel she demands.

                    JOHN
          I... had to get you out of that place... I'm sorry, I...

His face crumples. He starts to cry. Sarah gives him a cold stare.

                    SARAH
          Stop it! Right now! *You* can't cry, John. Other kids can afford to
          cry. You can't.

He's trying to be brave, he really is. Terminator turns and sees the water leaking from his eyes.
It doesn't make any sense to him.

                    TERMINATOR
          What is wrong with your eyes?

John turns away, ashamed. Sarah lets her breath out, realizing how keyed up she is. She turns to
Terminator, giving him a wary once-over.

                    SARAH
          So what's *your* story?

Due to the complications of either using a beam-splitter on set or doing an expensive rotoscope job,
Terminator does not have glowing red eyes in this scene. Although filmed, Sarah's berating John for crying
was deemed an unnecessarily harsh extra beat to the scene and was cut from the picture.

                                                        CUT TO:

82 EXT. MENTAL HOSPITAL

The cops have shown up, as they always do. There are black-and-whites everywhere, and
ambulances are arriving. Two cops and an orderly are required to subdue poor Doctor Silberman,
who is raving at the top of his lungs.

                    SILBERMAN
          ...it was all true and we're all going to die and the guy changed,
          I saw him change!!

It's quite pathetic.
A nurse shoots him up with a sedative. They lead him away.

82A   T-1000 walks unperturbed among the milling cops. No one notices it.
        It slips into its cruiser and drives off into the night.

83   INT. CAR

Terminator drives steadily into the black night.

                        SARAH
           This T-1000... what happens when you shoot it?

                        TERMINATOR
           Ballistic penetration shocks it, but only for a few seconds.

Sarah thinks about that. Then:

                        SARAH
           Can it be destroyed?

                        TERMINATOR
           Unknown.

They ride along in silence for a few seconds.
Sarah sees something up ahead, some lonely neon in the blackness.

                        SARAH
           Pull in here. We have to ditch this car.

84   EXT. SERVICE STATION - NIGHT

A rundown gas station with a buzzing neon sign and no one around. They pull into the drive and slowly cruise past the empty office. A sign in the window says CLOSED SUNDAY. They continue around the building to the garage's back door.

AT THE GARAGE DOOR. Terminator breaks the lock on the roll-up door and raises it. Sarah pulls the security car in out of sight. Terminator rolls the door down behind them.

85   INT. GAS STATION

Dark. Sarah switches on the single drop-light. She and Terminator look at each other.
Terminator is shot-up and bleeding, and Sarah has a vicious slash in her upper arm which has
soaked her sleeve with blood.

                    SARAH
          You look like handmade shit.

                    TERMINATOR
          So do you.

                                                            CUT TO:

86   TIGHT ON FIRST-AID KIT from the office, plus some not-so-oily rags, a bottle of rubbing alcohol,
      a few small tools, and other makeshift odds and ends. Terminator's hand comes into shot. Sets
      down a bloody rag. Picks up a clean one.

      WIDER. Sarah sits on an empty crate. Terminator is beside her, suturing her wound with some
      fine wire from the winding of an alternator. Using a pair of needlenose pliers he draws the wire
      through her pale skin with a delicate hand.

                    TERMINATOR
          I have detailed files on human anatomy.

Sarah stares into his face, inches away, fighting the pain. She doesn't like him being this close to
her to begin with, let alone carving on her.

                    SARAH
          I'll bet. Makes you a more efficient killer, right?

                    TERMINATOR
          Correct.
                                                            CUT TO:

87   TIGHT ON TERMINATOR'S BACK. The leather jacket is riddled with bullet holes. Sarah and
      John help pull it off, revealing Terminator's broad, muscled back beneath.

      WIDER. John and Sarah stare in amazement. There are at least twenty bullet holes in him.
      Back. Arms. Legs. Fortunately they're all 9mm. The holes are small and the damage cosmetic.

                    JOHN
          Does it hurt?

                    TERMINATOR
          I sense the injuries. The data could be called pain.

      TIGHT ON SARAH AND TERMINATOR. Sarah starts washing the bullet holes in his broad
      back with alcohol.

                    SARAH
          Will these heal up?

Terminator nods. She reaches into the bloody wounds with pliers and finds the copper-jacketed
bullets, flattened against his armored endoskeleton. Pulls them out. They CLINK one by one into
a glass.

A. COVER PLATE IN PLACE.

B. COVER PLATE REMOVED.

C. INNER PLUG REMOVED

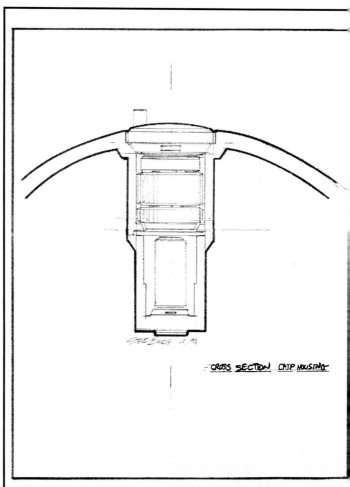

CROSS SECTION CHIP HOUSING

SARAH
That's good. Because if you can't pass for human, you won't be
much good to us.

She concentrates on removing the slugs. CLINK. CLINK.

JOHN
How long do you live? I mean, last?

TERMINATOR
A hundred and twenty years on my existing power cell.

Sarah nods, pulling out another slug. CLINK. The glass is nearly full of flattened bullets. She
begins to sew the holes closed with a few wire sutures. John watches in quiet amazement, the two
warriors calmly fixing each other.

JOHN
Can you learn? So you can be... you know. More human. Not
such a dork all the time.

Terminator turns toward him.

TERMINATOR
My CPU is a neural-net processor... a learning computer. But
Skynet presets the switch to "read only" when we are sent out
alone.

SARAH
(cynical)
Doesn't want you thinking too much, huh?

TERMINATOR
No.

JOHN
Can we reset the switch?

CUT TO:

88   E.C.U. OF AN X-ACTO KNIFE cutting into Terminator's scalp at the base of his skull. His voice
        calmly directs Sarah as she spreads the bloody incision and locates the maintenance port for the
        CPU in the chrome skull beneath.

TERMINATOR
Now open the port cover.

She wipes away the blood and uses the garage-mechanic's air tools to unscrew the port cover.

88A   TERMINATOR POV (DIGITIZED) as he watches her work in a mirror they've taken from the
        washroom. Sarah and John are standing behind him. Her hands are covered with blood, like a
        surgeon's.

TERMINATOR
Hold the CPU by its base tab. Pull.

Following his instructions, she reaches in with a pair of tweezers and PULLS--
There is a BURST OF STATIC and the screen goes BLACK.

CUT TO:

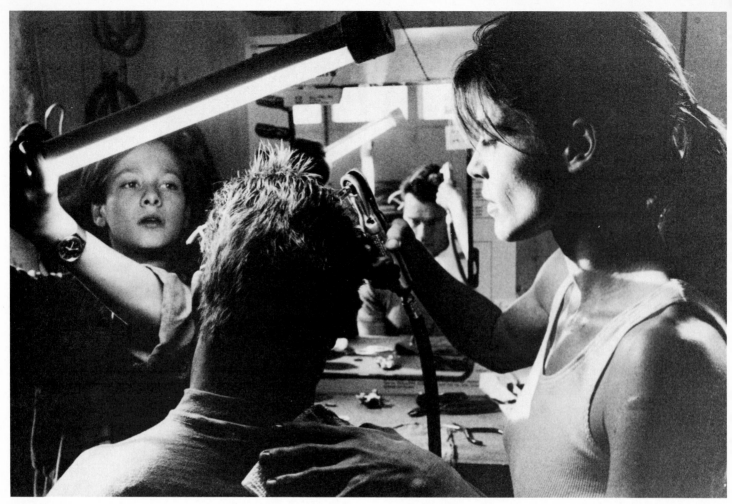

TV-4   Scene 88A

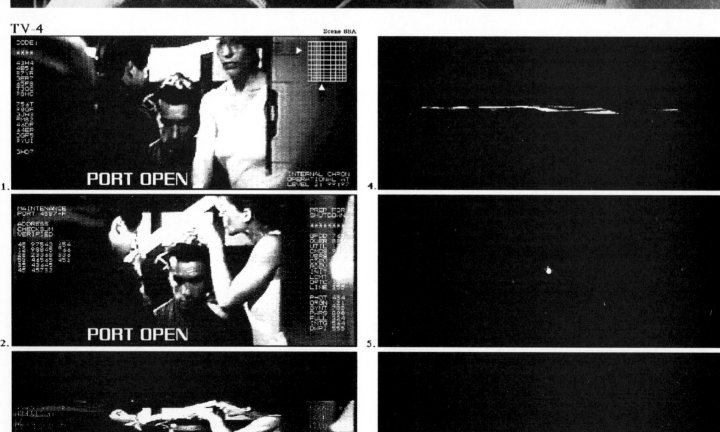

1.

PORT OPEN   INTERNAL CHRON
                             OPERATIONAL AT
                             LEVEL 2: 99.97

2.

MAINTENANCE   PREP FOR
PORT 4597-F   SHUTDOWN
                                     ******
ADDRESS
CHECKSUM
VERIFIED

PORT OPEN

3.   6.

89   TIGHT ON JOHN AND SARAH looking at what she has removed. A reddish-brown ceramic rectangle with a connector on one end. About the size and shape of a domino. On close inspection it appears to be made up of small cubes connected together. It is identical to the shattered one in the vault at Cyberdyne Systems. Now we know what it is that Miles Dyson values so highly. The brain of a terminator.

89A   WIDER. John walks around Terminator and looks at his face.
Eyes open, he is completely inert. Dead.

John lifts his huge hand. The dead servos whine sullenly as he forces them. It's like rigor mortis. He releases the hand and it stays in the lifted position. Sarah examines the CPU chip.

> JOHN
> Can you see the pin switch?

She ignores him. She looks at Terminator.
Then back at the chip.
Then she sets it on the work table and picks up a small sledge hammer. John realizes what she is about to do. Dives at her as the sledge is whistling down.

> JOHN
> No!!!!

He slaps his hand down over the chip.
Sarah barely stops the sledge before smashing his fingers.

> SARAH
> Out of the way, John!

> JOHN
> No! Don't kill him!

> SARAH
> *It,* John. Not *him.* It.

> JOHN
> Alright, *it.* We need *it!*

John keeps his hand right where it is.

> SARAH
> We're better off by ourselves.

> JOHN
> But it's the only proof we have of the future... about the war and
> all that.

> SARAH
> I don't trust it! These things are hard to kill, John, believe me, I
> know. We may never have this opportunity again.

> JOHN
> Look, Mom, if I'm supposed to ever be this great leader, you
> should start listening to my leadership ideas once in a while.
> 'Cause if you won't, nobody else will.

Smart kid. He's got her. She nods, reluctantly. He palms the chip and studies it minutely.

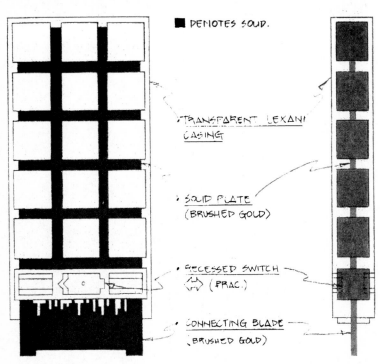

■ DENOTES SOLID.

TRANSPARENT LEXANI CASING

• SOLID PLATE
(BRUSHED GOLD)

• RECESSED SWITCH
(PRAC.)

• CONNECTING BLADE
(BRUSHED GOLD)

• BLADE FIN DETAIL
(BRUSHED GOLD)

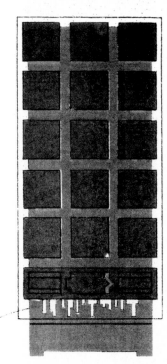

FRONT ELEVATION
3 x F.S.

END ELEVATION
3 x F.S.

REAR ELEVATI
3 x F.S.

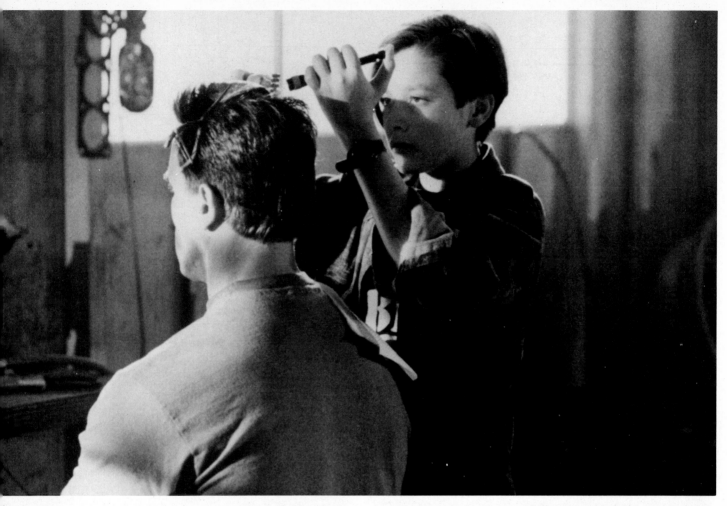

4. SYSTEM INTERRUPT

5. SYSTEM INTERRUPT

6. DIAGNOSTIC

89B   John takes a pin and moves the almost invisible switch to the other position.
It is now in "write" mode. Then he grimaces as he inserts the wafer back into the slot in
Terminator's skull.

89C   TERMINATOR VISION flares back to life in a burst of static. The image forms. Sarah and John
stand behind him in the mirror.

TERMINATOR
Was there a problem?

John glances sheepishly at Sarah. Then smiles at Terminator.

JOHN
No problem. None whatsoever.

One of the major lifts from the film was the entire head operation scene. The scene had been shot in its
entirety and edited in, but was ultimately deemed unnecessary to the plot and was cut for time. To explain
Terminator's ability to use human expressions later in the film, a bridging line of dialogue for Terminator was
added in postproduction: "The more contact I have with humans, the more I learn."

CUT TO:

90   JOHN SLEEPING, lying on a pile of rags next to a stack of tires.
The lights are off.   Sarah sits nearby, cross-legged, her back against the wall.
The .45 is cradled in her lap. She looks weary, but she won't allow herself to sleep with Terminator
present.

By the office windows, in a slash of moonlight, is Terminator. He stands silent and still,
watching the night. Only his eyes move, tracking with the occasional car passing on the road.
His figure silhouetted and still.

DISSOLVE TO:

91   SAME IMAGE. Now DAYLIGHT streams in the dusty windows.
Terminator has not moved. Faithful machine sentinel. He turns at a sound. John stirs, waking
up. He squints at the sunlight. Sarah is still awake. She gets up, wincing at the pain in her arm.

CUT TO:

92   EXT. GAS STATION - DAY (LATER)

John and Terminator walk to an old Chevy pickup parked behind the garage. The day is clear but
windy. Dust devils chase themselves behind the place. The pickup is locked but Terminator
breaks the side window with his fist and opens the door. He and John climb in.

92A   IN THE PICKUP. Terminator has this trick (which you could do too if you had servo-driven steel
fingers) where he smashes the cowl around a steering column with one blow from the palm of his
hand. When it shatters he strips it away with a single move, and then turns the stub of the lock-
mechanism with his fingertips. This starts the vehicle. It takes about three seconds.

In fact, he does it so quickly, the truck is running by the time John flips down the sun visor. A set of
keys drops out and John catches them. Dangles them in front of Terminator's eyes.

JOHN
Are we learning yet?

92B   Sarah comes out. She's found a mechanic's coverall inside, used but fairly clean. It doesn't fit too well but it's better than the stuff from the hospital. She's still barefoot.
The sun, which she hasn't seen in months, hurts her eyes.
Terminator and John pull up in the pickup. She gets in.

92C

TERMINATOR
We need to get as far from the city as possible.

SARAH
Just head south.

CUT TO:

93   INT. / EXT. PICKUP TRUCK / HIGHWAY - DAY

THE OPEN ROAD. The pickup roars through light traffic down a long stretch of highway. They sit three abreast on the bench seat, John in between, like some improbable family on a car trip. Sarah leans over to get a look at the speedometer.

SARAH
Keep it under sixty-five. We can't afford to get pulled over.

Terminator backs off the throttle slightly.

TERMINATOR
Affirmative.

JOHN
No, no, no. You gotta listen to the way people talk. See, you don't say like "Affirmative" or some shit like that. You say... *no problemo*.

Terminator nods, filing away the information. Sarah is ignoring the lesson, lost in thought.

JOHN
If someone comes off to you with an attitude, you say "eat me"... if you wanna shine them on, it's "Hasta la vista, baby".

TERMINATOR
"Hasta la vista, baby"?

JOHN
Yeah, or "later, dickwad." Or if someone gets upset you say "chill out." Like that. Or you can do combinations.

TERMINATOR
Chill out, dickwad.

JOHN
That's great! See, you're getting it.

TERMINATOR
No problemo.

CUT TO:

94-95 OMITTED

96   EXT. ROADSIDE STAND / GAS STATION - DAY

There's a gas pump and a sleazy fast-food stand. Picnic tables are set up at the side of the food stand. A family sits at one, children playing and running about.

96A   The pickup truck pulls into the lot. Stops at the gas pump.
Sarah turns to John.

SARAH
You got any cash?

John pulls what's left of his Ready-Teller money from his pocket.

JOHN
Only a couple of hundred. I'll give you half.

Sarah grabs all of it. Peels off a twenty, hands it to John.

SARAH
Get some food.

She opens the truck door and steps out. John turns to Terminator.

JOHN
No sense of humor.

97   THE ORDERING WINDOW as John and Terminator approach.

JOHN
And that's another thing. You could lighten up a bit, yourself.
This *severe* routine is getting old. Smile once in a while.

TERMINATOR
Smile?

JOHN
Yeah. *Smile.* You know. People smile, right? Watch.

Goes to the order window.

JOHN
(smiling broadly)
Hi. Nice place you got here. How's business?

WINDOW WOMAN
(stone-faced)
Gimme a break.

                    JOHN
                (to Terminator)
            Okay. Bad example. Over there, look.

John points at THREE TEENAGE GUYS standing at a drinking fountain nearby. One of them
has said something funny and the others are laughing, grinning.

                    JOHN
            Like that.

TERMINATOR POV (DIGITIZED) The real-time image continues while a replay of one of the
guys grinning runs in a window. It expands, so that the guy's mouth fills the window. Replays
again in slow motion. A vector-graphic of lips smiling appears, along with an array of symbolic
data.

Terminator tries it. The result is dismal. A rictus-like curling up of the lip. Terminator's next
effort is a marginal improvement.

                    JOHN
            I don't know, maybe you could practice in front of a mirror or
            something.

Another of the major lifts from the film was the "smile" sequence at the roadside stand. Although the sight of
Terminator trying to smile was one of the funniest moments in the film, the lead-up to that payoff was too
long and hard to cut down, so the entire scene was omitted. The film now cuts from their station wagon
pulling up to the roadside stand in Scene 96 to Sarah eating her hamburger in silence in Scene 98.

                                            CUT TO:

98   EXT. REST STOP/PICKUP TRUCK - DAY (LATER)

Sarah and John are eating cheeseburgers and fries, sitting in the truck and on the curb
respectively. They are parked away from the other families, at the end of the gravel parking area.
Terminator is pouring coolant into the radiator. Sarah is deep in thought, turning and turning the
whole thing in her brain. John, unable to deal with her silence, goes around to where Terminator
is working.

98A   John sees two kids playing with machine-gun water pistols nearby, viciously squirting each other.

                    FIRST KID
            You're dead!

                    SECOND KID
            Am not!

                    FIRST KID
            Are so!

John and Terminator watch them rolling on the ground in a fight to the death. Sarah rounds the
front of the truck, and sees the kids. John sighs, solemn. He looks up at the cyborg.

                    JOHN
            We're not gonna make it, are we? People, I mean.

                    TERMINATOR
            It is in your nature to destroy yourselves.

The roadside stand sequence was reduced to its essentials during the editing process. In tightening the film, the need to maintain the forward movement of the story --establishing the characters' destination and motives now that they have escaped (temporarily) from the T-1000-- took priority over the more humorous attempts by John to teach Terminator how to be more "human"; this included the "smile" gag, which paid off in a big laugh but took over two minutes of valuable screen time to set up.

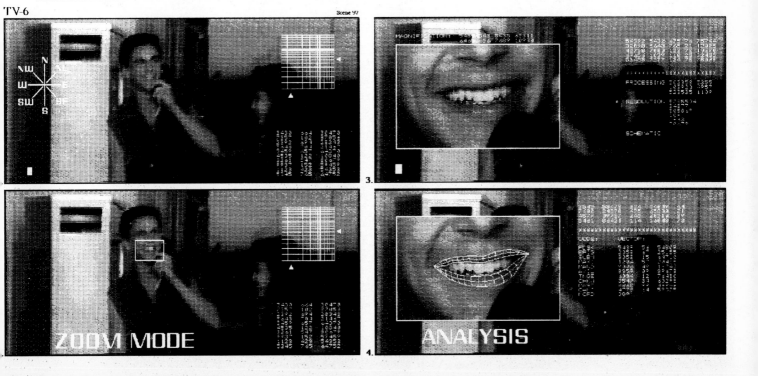

John nods, depressed.

> JOHN
> Yeah. Drag, huh?

The addition of a background throwaway line from the fighting children's mother --"Break it up before I wring both your necks"-- was added in postproduction and serves an ironic counterpoint to Terminator's featured line, "It is in your nature to destroy yourselves." This is a perfect example of taking advantage of every available resource on the soundtrack --even throwaway lines from background extras-- to enrich the depth and meaning of a scene.

> SARAH
> I need to know how Skynet gets built. Who's responsible?

> TERMINATOR
> The man most directly responsible is Miles Bennet Dyson,
> Director of Special Projects at Cyberdyne Systems Corporation.

> SARAH
> Why him?

> TERMINATOR
> In a few months he creates a revolutionary type of
> microprocessor.

> SARAH
> Then what?

98B   Terminator closes the hood and gets into the truck as he speaks.

> TERMINATOR
> In three years Cyberdyne will become the largest supplier of
> military computer systems. All stealth bombers are upgraded
> with Cyberdyne computers, becoming fully unmanned.
> Afterward, they fly with a perfect operational record.

> SARAH
> (getting in behind John)
> Uh huh, great. Then those fat fucks in Washington figure, what
> the hell, let a computer run the whole show, right?

> TERMINATOR
> Basically.
> (starting the engine, backing out)
> The Skynet funding bill is passed. The system goes on-line
> August 4th, 1997. Human decisions are removed from strategic
> defense. Skynet begins to learn, at a geometric rate. It becomes
> self-aware at 2:14 a.m. eastern time, August 29. In a panic, they
> try to pull the plug.

> SARAH
> And Skynet fights back.

They accelerate back onto the highway.

                              TERMINATOR
            Yes. It launches its ICBMs against their targets in Russia.

                                SARAH
            Why attack Russia?

                              TERMINATOR
            Because Skynet knows the Russian counter-strike will remove
            its enemies here.

                                SARAH
            Jesus.
                        (beat, then)
            How much do you know about Dyson?

                              TERMINATOR
            I have detailed files.

                                SARAH
            I want to know everything. What he looks like. Where he lives.
            Everything.

Sarah's line about "those fat fucks in Washington" was omitted to streamline the expository dialogue, and
her line "Why attack Russia?" was given to John to keep him a part of the scene, and the addition of "Aren't
they our friends now?" serves not only to take into account current events but also points out the irony of
"friends" who still have their military systems set to kill each other.

---

99   INT. DYSON HOUSE - DAY

Miles Dyson sits at the huge desk in his study. He is deep in thought, tapping away at the keyboard
of his home computer terminal. Next to his desk are racks of sophisticated gear. On a Sunday
morning, when most men are relaxing, spending time with their families, Dyson is hard at work.

IN A PROFILE CLOSEUP we see him in deep concentration, his mind prowling the labyrinth of
his new microprocessor.

A WOMAN'S FACE ENTERS FRAME soundlessly behind him. He doesn't hear her. His wife,
TARISSA, extends her tongue and traces it down the back of his neck. He smiles and turns to kiss
her good morning. She's still in her bathrobe, holding coffee. He's been up for hours. He turns
and goes back to work, forgetting instantly that she is standing there.

She watches him work, the arcane symbols moving across the screen. We see her frustration, her
inability to truly enter the magic box of his world.

                              TARISSA
            You going to work all day?

                               DYSON
            I'm sorry, baby. This thing is just kicking my ass. I thought we
            had it with this one...

He points to a metal box on his desk, about two feet long. An assembly of small cubes. It looks like
a dinosaur version of Terminator's CPU.

                    DYSON
... but the output went to shit after three seconds. I'm thinking
now it's in the way I'm matrixing the command hierarchies...

                    TARISSA
You need a break. You'll see it clearer when you come back.

                    DYSON
I can't.

                    TARISSA
Miles, it's Sunday. You promised to take the kids to Raging
Waters today.

                    DYSON
Oh. I can't, honey. I'm on a roll here.

He takes her hands. We see a childlike excitement in his face. He wants so badly to share the
almost orgasmic thrill of discovery, the satisfaction of creation.

                    DYSON
Baby, this thing is going to blow 'em all away. It's a neural-net
process--

                    TARISSA
I know. You told me. It's a neural-net processor. It thinks and
learns like we do. It's superconducting at room temperature.
Other computers are pocket calculators by comparison.
                (she pulls away from him)
But why is that so goddamn important, Miles? I really need to
know, 'cause I feel like I'm going crazy here, sometimes.

                    DYSON
I'm sorry, honey, it's just that I'm thiiis close.

He holds up his thumb and index finger... a fraction of an inch apart.
She picks up the prototype. It doesn't look like much.

                    DYSON
Imagine a jetliner with a pilot that never makes a mistake,
never gets tired, never shows up to work with a hangover.
                (he taps the prototype)
Meet the pilot.

                    TARISSA
Why did you marry me, Miles? Why did we have these two
children? You don't need us. Your heart and your mind are in
here.
                (she stares at the metal box in her hands)
But it doesn't love you like we do.

He takes the anodized box from her hands and sets it down. Then he puts his hands on her
shoulders and kisses her gently. She acquiesces to his kiss.

                    DYSON
I'm sorry.

Tarissa glances over his shoulder. She nods her head toward the doorway to the study. Dyson turns and sees their two kids standing there. Danny (6) and Blythe (4) look rumpled and adorable in their PJs. Dyson wilts at their hopeful expressions.

TARISSA
How about spending some time with your *other* babies?

Dyson grins. The forces of darkness have lost this round. He holds out his hands and his kids run to him, cheering.

Another major lift from the film, the Dyson house introduction scene not only developed the family aspect of Dyson's life but also fleshed out his character as an obsessed scientist caught blindly in the obsessive thrill of discovery without acknowledging the dangerous ramifications of his work. The omission of this scene for time simplified the character but actually made more potent the later disruption of the family by Sarah, in that we infer that Dyson's relationship with his family as being close and idyllic rather than somewhat neglectful, as this scene portrays; fortunately, the essence of Dyson's character remains intact in Joe Morton's performance in Scene 137.

CUT TO:

A100 EXT. DESERT / COMPOUND - DAY

The desert northwest of Calexico. Burning under the sun like a hallucination. Heat shimmers the image, mirage-like.
Terminator turns the pickup off the paved road and barrels along a roadbed of sand and gravel, trailing a huge plume of dust.
A sign at the turnoff says: CHARON MESA   2 MI
                              CALEXICO   15 MI

The rack-focus shot from the approaching car to the row of snake heads on the fence in the final film was a holdover spelled out in the original 5/10/90 draft. To build a little suspense, the approach to Salceda's camp in the desert is played mysterious; the expository road sign mentioned in the script was omitted, since its main purpose was to give the audience a cue to how T-1000 locates the place in a scene that was subsequently never shot.

A101 AHEAD is a pathetic oasis of humanity in the vast wasteland, a couple of aging house-trailers, surrounded by assorted junk vehicles and desert-style trash. There is a dirt airstrip behind the trailers, and a stripped Huey helicopter sitting on blocks nearby.

The truck rolls to a stop in a cloud of dust. The place looks deserted. The door to the nearest trailer bangs in the wind.

SARAH
(to Terminator and John)
Stay in the truck.

A102 ANGLE FROM INSIDE ANOTHER TRAILER, NEARBY.
A DARK FIGURE in the F.G. has an AK-47 trained on the pickup as Sarah gets out.

ON SARAH peering through the backlit dust.
The sound of wind. She approaches the trailer.

SARAH
(in Spanish)
Enrique? You here?

She hears KACHACK! behind her and spins, whipping out her .45 in one motion.

ENRIQUE SALCEDA stands behind a rusting jeep, a 12-gauge pump trained on her. He is mid-forties, a tough Guatemalan with a weathered face and heavy moustache. He wears cowboy boots and a flak vest, no shirt.

SALCEDA
You pretty jumpy, Connor.

To which Sarah replies, "Y tú. *Siempre cómo culébra.*" (" And you. Always like the snake...")

His fierce face breaks into a broad grin. The shotgun drops to his side as he walks toward her. When he reaches her he hugs her, then steps back.

SALCEDA
(in Spanish)
Good to see you, Connor. I knew you'd make it back here sooner
or later.

He grins at John as he steps from the truck, and then clocks Terminator getting out.

SALCEDA
Oye, Big John! Que pasa? Who's your very large friend?

JOHN
(perfect Spanish)
He's cool, Enrique. He's... uh... this is my Uncle Bob.
(to Terminator, in English)
Uncle Bob, this is Enrique.

Terminator smiles. *Sort of.* Salceda squints at him.

SALCEDA
Hmmm. Uncle Bob, huh? Okay.
(yelling)
Yolanda. Get out here, we got company. And bring some
fucking tequila!

A thin Guatemalan KID, FRANCO, eighteen or so, comes out of the trailer with the AK-47, followed by Salceda's wife, YOLANDA. She has THREE younger children with her, from a five-year-old GIRL, JUANITA, to a year-and-half-old BOY. She waves at John. They exchange greetings in Spanish. They seem like nice people.
Terminator looks down at John, next to him. He says quietly...

TERMINATOR
Uncle Bob?

SALCEDA
(to Sarah)
So, Sarahlita, you getting famous, you know that? All over the
goddamn TV.

Salceda rips the cap off the tequila bottle. The two-year-old toddles to Terminator and grabs his pants, sliming them with drool.

Terminator looks down at the tiny kid, fascinated. What is it?

He picks the child up with one huge hand. Looks at it. Turns it different ways. Studying it. Then sets it down. The kid waddles off, a little dizzy.

> SALCEDA
> Honey, take Pacolito. Thanks, baby.

She hands him the tequila and takes the child. Salceda takes a long pull from the Cuervo bottle.

> SALCEDA
> (to Terminator)
> Drink?

Terminator gestures "no" at the proffered bottle, but Sarah grabs it and takes a long plug. She lowers it without expression. Her eyes don't even water.

> SARAH
> I just came for my stuff. And I need clothes, food, and one of your trucks.

> SALCEDA
> (grinning)
> Hey, how about the fillings out of my fucking teeth while you're at it?

> SARAH
> Now, Enrique.
> (turns to Terminator and John)
> You two are on weapons detail.

> CUT TO:

A103   EXT. COMPOUND/ BEHIND THE TRAILERS

There is an aging and rusted Caterpillar sitting behind one of the trailers. John expertly backs it toward Terminator who is holding one end of a piece of heavy chain which disappears into the sand.

> JOHN
> Hook it on.

Terminator hooks the chain onto the towhook on the back of the tractor. John hits the throttle and the Cat churns its treads, pulling some massive load. A six-by-eight foot sheet of steel plate moves slowly under six inches of sand.

John drags it far enough to reveal... .a rectangular hole in the ground. Like the mouth of a tomb. The kid drops down from the tractor and walks to the hole.

> JOHN
> One thing about my mom... she always plans ahead.

A104   INT. WEAPONS CACHE

From inside the "tomb". Sunlight slashes down into a cinder-block room, less than six feet wide but over twenty long. Sand spills down the steps. The walls are lined with guns.

John precedes Terminator into Sarah's weapons cache. Rifles, pistols, rocket launchers, mortars, RPGs, radio gear. At the far end, boxes containing ammo, grenades, etc. are stacked to the ceiling. Terminator gets real alert. Scanning, wondering where to begin.
He picks up a MAC-10 machine pistol. Racks the bolt.

                    TERMINATOR
        Excellent.

                    JOHN
        Yeah, I thought you'd like this place.

A105   EXT. COMPOUND / NEARBY

Sarah emerges from a trailer. She has changed. Boots, black fatigue pants, T-shirt. Shades. She looks hard.
Salceda is nearby, packing food and other survival equipment with Yolanda. He looks up as Sarah approaches, and slaps the side of a BIG FOUR-BY BRONCO next to him.

                    SALCEDA
        This is the best truck, but the water pump is blown. You got the
        time to change it out?

                    SARAH
        Yeah. I'm gonna wait till dark to cross the border.
            (she pulls him away from Yolanda)
        Enrique, it's dangerous for you here. You get out tonight, too,
        okay?

                    SALCEDA
        Yeah, Sarahlita. Sure.
            (he grins)
        Just drop by any time and totally fuck up my life.

She claps him on the shoulder.

In the final film, this scene cuts right after Sarah's line about crossing the border; the hint of a stronger relationship between Sarah and Enrique in the performance of the subsequent dialogue was a nice moment, but ultimately did not contribute to the drive of the narrative and was cut.

                                            CUT TO:

A106   INT. WEAPONS CACHE

Terminator returns from carrying out several cases of ammo. John is selecting rifles from a long rack.

                    JOHN
        See, I grew up in places like this, so I just thought it was how
        people lived... riding around in helicopters. Learning how to
        blow shit up.

John grabs an AK-47 and racks the bolt with a practiced action. Inspects the receiver for wear. Doesn't like what he sees. Puts it back. His movements are efficient. Professional. Uninterested.

                    JOHN
        Then, when Mom got busted I got put in a regular school. The
        other kids were, like, into Nintendo.

Terminator has found a Vietnam-era "blooper" M-79 grenade launcher. A very crude but
effective weapon. He opens the breech and inspects the bore.

                    JOHN
        Are you ever afraid?

Terminator pauses a second. The thought never occurred to him. He searches his mind for the
answer...

                  TERMINATOR
        No.

Terminator slings the M-79 and starts looking for the grenades.

                    JOHN
        Not even of dying?

                  TERMINATOR
        No.

                    JOHN
        You don't feel any emotion about it one way or the other?

                  TERMINATOR
        No. I have to stay functional until my mission is complete.
        Then it doesn't matter.

John is idly spinning a Sig Saur 9mm pistol on his finger... backwards and forwards like Bat
Masterson.

                    JOHN
        Yeah. I have to stay functional too.
            (sing-songy)
        "I'm too important".

Terminator pulls back a canvas tarp, revealing a squat, heavy weapon with six barrels clustered
in a blunt cylinder. Chain-ammo is fed from a cannister sitting next to it. A G.E. MINI-GUN.
The most fearsome anti-personnel weapon of the Vietnam era.
Terminator hefts it. Looks at John as if to say "Can I? Please?"

                    JOHN
        It's definitely you.

The majority of the dialogue in this scene, specifically the discussion about being afraid and staying
functional, was omitted as unnecessary to the flow of the plot; John's first line is heard over Terminator's
uncovering and hefting of the minigun. Terminator grins for the first time in this scene as he holds the minigun
and looks at John; even though the "smile" scene at the roadside stand was omitted, this moment plays as
a big laugh and feels appropriate, as if a big weapon is exactly what a terminator would smile about.

                                              CUT TO:

Sarah and John have their weapons and supply selections laid out on two battered picnic tables for cleaning and packing. Maps, radios, documents, explosives, detonators... just the basics. Sarah is field-stripping and cleaning guns, very methodically. There is no wasted motion.

Not far away, John and Terminator are working on the Bronco. They're greasy up to their elbows, lying on their backs under the engine compartment, ratcheting bolts into place on the new water pump.

> JOHN
> There was this one guy that was kinda cool. He taught me engines. Hold this a second. Mom screwed it up, of course. Sooner or later she'd always tell them about Judgment Day and me being this world leader and that'd be all she wrote.

John thinks he's being casual, but his longing for some kind of parental connection is obvious.

> TERMINATOR
> Torque wrench please.

> JOHN
> Here. I wish I coulda met my real dad.

> TERMINATOR
> You will.

> JOHN
> Yeah. I guess so. My mom says when I'm, like, 45, I think, I send him back through time to 1984. But right now he hasn't even been born yet. Man, it messes with your head. Where's that other bolt?
>   (Terminator hands it to him)
> Thanks. Mom and him were only together for one night, but she still loves him, I guess. I see her crying sometimes. She denies it totally, of course. Like she says she got something in her eye.

They crawl out from under the truck into the bright sunlight.

> TERMINATOR
> Why do you cry?

> JOHN
> You mean people? I don't know. We just cry. You know. When it hurts.

> TERMINATOR
> Pain causes it?

> JOHN
> Uh-unh, no, it's different... It's when there's nothing wrong with you but you hurt anyway. You get it?

> TERMINATOR
> No.

Terminator gets into the Bronco and turns the ignition key and the engine catches with a roar.

                    JOHN
          Alriiight!! My man!

                  TERMINATOR
       No problemo.

John grins and does a victorious thumbs up.
Terminator imitates the gesture awkwardly.
John laughs and makes him get out of the truck, to try the move again.

As originally scripted, John talks and does most of the work on the car while Terminator assists him; in the film, it is Terminator who does the majority of the repair work while John talks, which not only seems more appropriate but is a more balanced playing of the scene in terms of character and action.

A108   SARAH, across the compound, pauses in her work to watch John and Terminator.

A109   SARAH'S POV... we don't hear what John and Terminator are saying. It is a soundless pantomime as John is trying to show some other gestures to the cyborg. Trying to get him to walk more casually. John walks, then Terminator tries it, then John gestures wildly, talking very fast... explaining the fundamental principles of cool. They try it again. Continued ad lib as we hear:

                  SARAH (V.O.)
       Watching John with the machine, it was suddenly so clear. The
       Terminator would never stop, it would never leave him... it
       would always be there. And it would never hurt him, never
       shout at him or get drunk and hit him, or say it couldn't spend
       time with him because it was too busy. And it would die to protect
       him. Of all the would-be fathers who came and went over the
       years, this thing, this machine, was the only one who measured
       up. In an insane world, it was the sanest choice.

Sarah clenches her jaw and goes grimly back to work... a strong woman made hard and cold by years of hard choices.

                                        CUT TO:

A110   EXT. ROAD - DAY

A police cruiser is parked off the side of a quiet, empty road on the outskirts of Los Angeles. A ribbon of traffic moves steadily by on a freeway in the distance. Nothing stirs around the cruiser except some pump-jacks sucking the earth on the hill behind it.

A111   IN THE CRUISER. The T-1000 sits inside. John's notes and letters are spread out on the seat beside it. Sarah's voice speaks from a cassette deck. John's tapes. Her voices mixes with the static filled chatter of the radio that T-1000 monitors for any sign of its target.

> SARAH
> ... if we are ever separated, and can't make contact, go to
> Enrique's airstrip. I'll rendezvous with you there.

T-1000 whips around and rewinds the tape, replaying the last section. It then snaps up the envelope of photos we saw earlier.

ECU on envelope. We see the postmark: "Charon Mesa, Calif."

TIGHT ON T-1000 staring at the postmark on the envelope. It glances up at the sound of crunching gravel. In the rear-view it sees a BIKE COP pulling onto the shoulder behind it. The big KAWASAKI 1100 idles up next to the T-1000, still seated in the cruiser.

> BIKE COP
> Howdy. I saw you pulled over here earlier. Everything okay?

> T-1000
> Everything's fine. Thanks for checking.
> (it gets slowly out of the car)
> Since you're here, though, can I talk to you a second...

CUT TO:

A112   EXT. HIGHWAY - DAY / MINUTES LATER

The T-1000 thunders along on the Kawasaki 1100, doing about a hundred and twenty. PAN WITH IT until it recedes toward the horizon.

These scenes were scheduled but never shot, for several reasons: first, they beg the already-omitted scene of T-1000 going to Salceda's camp (see annotation below); and second, the other reason for the existence of the scene --T-1000's acquisition of the motorcycle-- was taken care of earlier in Scene 82A. As before, it was found that there was no need to repeat the same idea at every location to show that the T-1000 is always one step behind our heroes.

CUT TO:

A113   EXT. COMPOUND - DAY (LATE AFTERNOON)

Sarah sits at the picnic table. The weapons are cleaned and her work is done. She hasn't slept in twenty-four hours and she seems to have the weight of the whole world on her shoulders.
She draws her knife from its belt sheath.
Idly starts to carve something on the table top... the letter "N".

A114   NOT FAR AWAY, John and Terminator are packing the Bronco for the trip.

A115   ON SARAH, AT THE TABLE as she looks up from her carving, thinking. She watches Salceda's kids playing nearby... wrestling with a mutty dog and loving it. Sarah watches Yolanda walking her toddler by the hands. Backlit, stylized. She looks over at John. Loading guns and supplies.

A116   ANGLE ON kids playing.

A117   SARAH'S HEAD droops. She closes her eyes.

118   *TIGHT ON small children playing. Different ones.*
       Wider now, to reveal a playground in a park. Very idyllic. A dream playground, crowded with
       laughing kids playing on swings, slides, and a jungle gym. It could be the playground we saw
       melted and frozen in the post-nuclear desolation of 2029. But here the grass is vibrant green and
       the sun is shining.

118A   *Sarah, short-haired, looking drab and paramilitary, stands outside the playground. An outsider.*
       Her fingers are hooked in a chain-link fence and she is staring through the fence at the young
       mothers playing with their kids.   A grim-faced harbinger.

118B   *Some girls play skip-rope. Their sing-song chant weaves through the random burbling laughter*
       of the kids. One of the young mothers walks her two-year-old son by the hands. She is wearing a
       pink waitress uniform. She turns to us, laughing.
       It is Sarah. Beautiful. Radiant. Sarah from another life, uncontaminated by the dark future. She
       glances at the strange woman beyond the fence.

118C   *Grim-faced Sarah presses against the fence. She starts shouting at them in SLOW MOTION. No*
       sound comes from her mouth.   She grabs the fence in frustration, shaking it. Screaming
       soundlessly.
       Waitress Sarah's smile falls. Then returns as her little boy throws some sand at her. She laughs,
       turning away, as if the woman at the fence were a shadow, a trick of the light.

118D - 118F OMITTED

Scenes 118D through 118F constituted the "missile dream" (see the appendix of omitted sequences), a part
of Sarah's recurring nuclear nightmare which was deleted from the script due to the production
complexities and cost of doing the sequence. In the final film, this sequence reflects the consolidation of
both dream sequences into one powerful tour-de-force nightmare, and provides the visceral reaction that
galvanizes Sarah into pursuing her deadly course of action.

118G   <u>*THE SKY EXPLODES.*</u> *The children ignite like match heads. Sarah is burning, screaming*
       silently, everything silent and overexposed.

118H   *THE BLAST WAVE HITS... devouring the cowering mothers and children. Sarah's scream*
       merges with the howl of the wind as the shockwave rips into her, blasting her apart and she...

119   Wakes up.
       All is quiet and normal. The children are still playing nearby.   Less than fifteen minutes have
       gone by.

       Bathed in sweat, Sarah sits hunched over the table.
       Every muscle is shaking. She is gasping.
       Sarah struggles to breathe, running her hand through her hair which is soaked with sweat. She
       can escape from the hospital, but she can't escape from the madness which haunts her.

       She looks down at the words she has carved on the table, amid the scrawled hearts and bird-
       droppings. They are: "NO FATE."
       Something changes in her eyes. She slams her knife down in the table top, embedding it deeply in
       the words. Then gets up suddenly and we--

                                                                              CUT TO:

A120   LONG LENS on Sarah walking toward us, striding across the compound with grim purpose. She
       carries a small nylon pack and a CAR-15 assault rifle. Her face is an impassive mask. She has
       become a terminator.

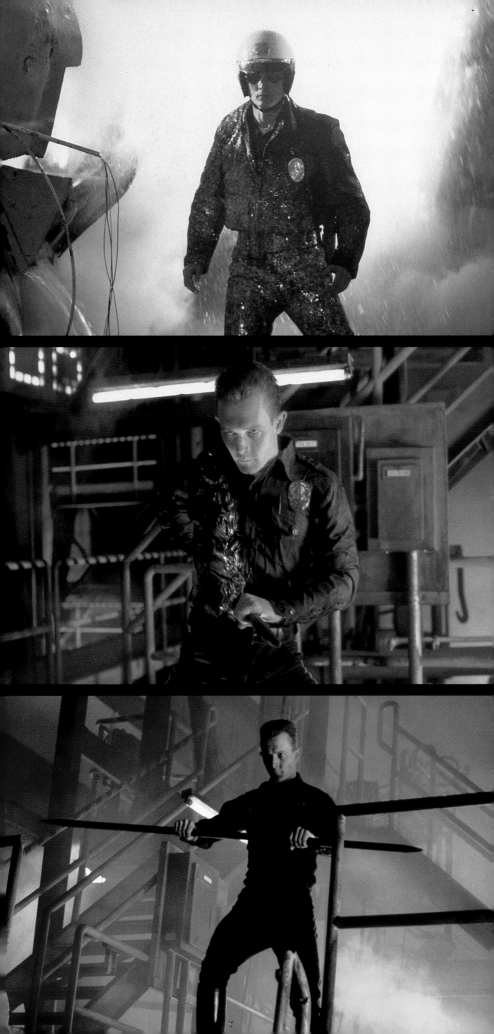

A120A JOHN LOOKS UP from his work in time to see Sarah throw the rifle behind the seat of their stolen pickup, jump in and start it. She slams it in gear. Salceda walks up to John.

> SALCEDA
> She said you go south with him...
>> (he points at Terminator)
> ...tonight, like you planned. She will meet you tomorrow in...

But John is moving, running after her.

> JOHN
> Mommm!! Wait!!

A120B MOVING WITH SARAH as she leaves the compound. We see John running after her... yelling. Can't hear his words. She looks in the rear-view mirror but doesn't slow down.

CUT TO:

A121   EXT. COMPOUND - DUSK / MINUTES LATER

John and Terminator ponder the message carved into the top of the picnic table. Sarah's knife is still embedded there.

> JOHN
> "No fate." No fate but what we make. My father told her this... I mean I made him memorize it, up in the future, as a message to her--
> Never mind. Okay, the whole thing goes "The future is not set. There is no fate but what we make for ourselves."

> TERMINATOR
> She intends to change the future somehow.

> JOHN
> I guess, yeah--
>> (snaps his fingers as it hits him)
> Oh shit!!

> TERMINATOR
> Dyson.

> JOHN
> Yeah, gotta be! Miles Dyson! She's gonna blow him away!

John motions to Terminator and breaks into a run.

> JOHN
> Come on. Let's go. LET'S GO!!

CUT TO:

A122   INT. / EXT. SARAH'S JEEP - DUSK

Sarah speeds through the darkening desert. Expressionless. In her dark glasses, she looks as pitiless as an insect.

DISSOLVE TO:

A123   EXT. HIGHWAY - NIGHT

TRACKING WITH THE BRONCO, Terminator and John heading toward L.A.

                    TERMINATOR
          This is tactically dangerous.

                    JOHN
          Drive faster.

                    TERMINATOR
          The T-1000 has the same files that I do. It could anticipate this
          move and reacquire you at Dyson's house.

                    JOHN
          I don't care. We've gotta stop her.

                    TERMINATOR
          Killing Dyson might actually prevent the war.

                    JOHN
          I don't care!! There's gotta be another way. Haven't you
          learned anything?! Haven't you figured out why you can't kill
          people?

Terminator is still stumped.

                    JOHN
          Look, maybe you don't care if you live or die. But everybody's
          not like that! Okay?! We have feelings. We hurt. We're
          afraid. You gotta learn this stuff, man, I'm not kidding. It's
          important.

PANNING as they pass, revealing the lights of the city ahead.

In the final film, the scene ends on Terminator's blank reaction to John's question "Haven't you figured out why you can't kill people?" John's last speech in the car on the way to Cyberdyne --about man's fear of death-- was deemed somewhat preachy and unnecessary and was cut.

                                                            CUT TO:

A124   EXT. DYSON'S HOUSE - NIGHT

The house is high-tech and luxurious. Lots of glass. Dyson's study is lit bluish with the glow from his computer monitors. He is at the terminal, working. Where else? We see him clearly in a long shot from an embankment behind the house.

A DARK FIGURE moves into the foreground. Rack focus to Sarah as she turns into profile. She raises the CAR-15 rifle and begins screwing the long heavy cylinder of a sound-suppressor onto the end of the barrel.

                                                            CUT TO:

In the 9/10/90 revision, there was a suspenseful scene of T-1000 wreaking havoc at Salceda's camp (see the appendix of omitted sequences), which was deleted from the script just prior to the start of principal photography, due to a number of production and technical considerations as well as unnecessary repetition of both narrative elements and certain T-1000 interrogation gags.

129   OMITTED

129A   INT. DYSON HOUSE

Dyson's kids, Danny and Blythe, are playing in the halls with a radio-controlled off-road truck. Danny drives and Blythe scampers after it, trying to catch it. They stop in the hall outside Dyson's study and see him working at his terminal. Danny puts a finger to his lips, shushing Blythe. His expression is mischievous.

129B   EXT. DYSON'S HOUSE

With the silencer in place, Sarah eases back the bolt and then slips it forward, chambering a .223 round. Then she lies down on the embankment.
Her cheek pressed against the cool rifle-stock, she slides one hand slowly forward to brace the weapon, taking the weight on her elbow. Her other hand slips knowingly to the trigger.

Her expression is cold, impassive. She looks through the scope at the man in the house. She feels nothing as she raises the rifle.

In the final film, all of Sarah's preparations outside the Dyson house (Scenes 129, 130, etc.) have been cut; it is much more ominous to concentrate on the Dyson family happy at home and then introduce the red dot of Sarah's laser designator appear out of nowhere on Dyson's back. The shock of seeing the dot appear plays better than the crosscutting suspense build as written in the script, and has the added value of driving home the coldness of Sarah as a terminator --the first time we see her here, she's already set up as an assassin. The final cut of this Dyson house sequence also makes up for the omission of the earlier Dyson scenes by not only retaining the essence of his character --a man obsessed with his work even at home-- but establishing just enough of the normal everyday family routine for the audience to relate to and sympathize with just prior to shattering it. Dyson's son Danny has become an only child in the translation from script to screen, however; his sister Blythe, present briefly in the omitted Scene 99, did not appear in the night scenes due to some scheduling conflicts.

130   OMITTED

130A   INT. DYSON'S HOUSE

DYSON, in deep thought. The rhythmic sounds of keys as he works. Symbols on the screen shift.

ON HIS BACK we see a glowing red dot appear. It is the target dot of Sarah's laser designator. It moves silently up his back toward his head.

131   EXT. DYSON HOUSE/ EMBANKMENT

IN EXTREME CLOSEUP we see Sarah's eye at the night-scope.
TIGHT INSERT on her finger as it tightens on the trigger, taking out the slack. She takes a deep breath and holds it. Adjusts her position minutely.

132   INT. DYSON HOUSE

The laser dot jiggles on the back of Dyson's neck and then rises, centering on the back of his skull.

132A   LOW ANGLE as Danny's Bigfoot truck roars toward us-- FILLING FRAME.
Thump. It hits Dyson's foot. He jerks, startled, and looks down as--
POP!!

132B   His monitor screen is BLOWN OUT spraying him with glass. He jerks back, utterly shocked... and spins to see the huge hole blown through the window behind him. This saves him as K-THUMP! -- the second shot blows the top of his high-backed chair into an explosion of stuffing an inch from his head.
Instinctively he dives to the carpet as --

BLAM BLAM BLAM -- rounds blast through the window, tearing into his desk and computer, blowing his keyboard into shrapnel.

132C   With the monitor screen blown out, the room is in darkness. Sarah can't see Dyson now, down behind the desk. She puts round after round into the heavy desk, blasting one side of it into kindling.

132D   Dyson, scared out of his mind, has his face jammed against the carpet, terrified to move. He sees his kids in the hall.
                    DYSON
          Run, kids! Go! Run!

132E   IN THE HALL, TARISSA rounds the corner at a dead run. She sees the kids running toward her and grabs them in her arms. Down the hall, in the dark study, she sees Dyson on the floor amid the splinters and shrapnel of the continuing fusillade.

                    TARISSA
          Miles! Oh my God!!

                    DYSON
          Stay back!!

132F   ON THE FLOOR, Dyson flinches as chunks of wood and shattered computer components shower down on him. He looks desperately toward the door, but knows he'd be totally exposed. He'd never make it.

133   SARAH's rifle empties with a final CLACK!
She throws it down and draws her .45 smoothly from a shoulder holster. She starts toward the house, snapping back the slide on the pistol, chambering a round. She is in a fast, purposeful walk, keeping her eyes fixed on the target. She is utterly determined to kill this man.

134   FROM UNDER THE DESK Dyson can see a sliver of the backyard. He sees Sarah's feet as she strides toward him. He tenses to make a break for the door.

Sarah raises the pistol, eyes riveted ahead, controlling her breathing. Dyson springs up in a full-tilt sprint. She tracks him.
He hooks a foot on the cord of a toppled disk drive.
BOOM! Her shot blows apart a lamp where his head was.
He hits the floor hard, but keeps moving, scrambling forward.

Crunch of glass behind him as Sarah's dark form is framed in the blown-out floor-to-ceiling window. Dyson leaps toward the hall.
BOOM! Her second shot spins him. He hits the floor in the hallway. Tarissa is screaming.
Dyson struggles forward, stunned. There is a .45-caliber hole clean through his left shoulder. He smears the wall with blood as he staggers up. Looking back, he sees the implacable figure behind him, coming on.

He topples through a doorway as ---
BOOM! BOOM! Shots blowing away the molding where he just was.

135   EXT. DYSON HOUSE/ STREET

Terminator and John leap from their jeep, sprinting toward the house. The shots sound muffled from outside.

                    JOHN
          Shit, we're too late!

136   INT. HOUSE

Advancing with Sarah we enter the living room. Tarissa has Blythe and she's screaming at Danny, who has run back to his collapsed father.

                    TARISSA
          Danny! DANNY!

                    DANNY
          Daaaaddddeeee!

Danny is pulling at Dyson, crying and screaming, as his father tries to stagger forward. Tarissa drops Blythe and runs back for Dyson, grabbing him. Sarah looms behind them with the pistol aimed.

                    SARAH
          Don't fucking move! Don't FUCKING MOVE!!
               (she swings the gun on Tarissa)
          Get on the floor, bitch! Now!! Fucking down! NOW!!

Sarah is crazy-eyed now, shaking with the intensity of the moment. The kill has gone bad, with screaming kids and the wife involved... things she never figured on. Tarissa drops to her knees, terrified as she looks into the muzzle of the gun. Blythe runs to Dyson and hugs him, wailing.

                    BLYTHE
          Don't you hurt my father!

                    SARAH
               (screaming)
          Shut up, kid! Get out of the way!!

Dyson looks up, through his pain and incomprehension. Why is this nightmare happening? The black gun muzzle is a foot from his face.

                    DYSON
               (gasping)
          Please... let... the kids... go...

                    SARAH
          Shut up! SHUT UP!! Motherfucker! It's all your fault! IT'S
          YOUR FAULT!!

We see her psyching herself to pull the trigger... needing now to hate this man she doesn't know. It's a lot harder face-to-face. She is bathed in sweat, and it runs into her eyes. Blinking, she wipes it fast with one hand, then gets it back on the gun. The .45 is trembling.

TIGHT ON SARAH as we see the forces at war behind her eyes.
She looks into the faces of Dyson, Tarissa, Blythe, Danny.
Sarah takes a sharp breath and all the muscles in her arms contract as she tenses to fire.
But her finger won't do it.
She lowers the gun very slowly. It drops to her side in one hand.

All the breath and energy seems to go out of her.
She weakly raises her other hand in a strange gesture, like "Stay where you are, don't move". As if, should they move, the fragile balance might tip back the other way.
She backs away from them slowly, panting. It's as if she's backing away in terror from what she almost did. She reaches a wall and slumps against it. Slides down to her knees. The gun falls limply from her fingers.
She rests her cheek against the wall.

136A   The front door is kicked in.
Terminator steps inside. John grabs his sleeve and pushes past him.
He scopes out the situation in two seconds... Sarah, the gun, the sobbing family. John moves to Sarah while Terminator checks Dyson.

John kneels in front of his mother. She raises her head to look at him. He sees the tears spilling down her cheeks.

> JOHN
> Mom? You okay?

> SARAH
> I couldn't... oh, God.
> (she seems to see him for the first time)
> You... came here... to stop me?

> JOHN
> Uh huh.

She reaches out and takes his shoulders suddenly, surprising him... drawing him to her. She hugs him and a great sob wells up from deep inside her, from a spring she had thought long dry. She hugs him fiercely as the sobs wrack her.

John clutches her shoulders. It is all he ever wanted.

> JOHN
> It's okay. It'll be okay. We'll figure it out.

> SARAH
> I love you, John. I always have.

> JOHN
> I know, Mom. I know.

TARISSA looks around at the bizarre tableau. Terminator has wordlessly ripped open Dyson's shirt and examined the wound.

> TERMINATOR
> Clean penetration. No shattered bone.
> Compression should control the loss of blood.

He takes Tarissa's hands and presses them firmly over the entrance and exit wounds.

> TERMINATOR
> Do you have bandages?

173

DYSON
In the bathroom. Danny, can you get them for us?

Danny nods and runs down the hall.
John disengages from Sarah. She wipes at her tears, the instinct to toughen up taking over again.
But the healing moment has had its effect, nevertheless.

John walks toward Dyson and Terminator.

DYSON
Who are you people?

John draws the Biker's knife from Terminator's boot. Hands it to him.

JOHN
Show him.

Terminator takes off his jacket to reveal bare arms.
John takes Blythe by the hand and leads her down the hall, away from what is about to happen.

136B   TIGHT ON TERMINATOR'S left forearm as the knife makes a deep cut just below the elbow. In one smooth motion, Terminator cuts all the way around his arm. With a second cut, he splits the skin of the forearm from elbow to wrist.

TERMINATOR grasps the skin and strips it off his forearm like a surgeon rips off a rubber glove. It comes off with a sucking rip, leaving a bloody skeleton.

But the skeleton is made of bright metal, and is laced with hydraulic actuators. The fingers are as finely crafted as watch parts... they flex into a fist and extend. Terminator holds it up, palm out, in almost the exact position of the one in the vault at Cyberdyne.

HOLD ON DYSON reacting to the servo-hand in front of him.
He's seen one of these before.
Tarissa is screaming now, but he doesn't hear her.

DYSON
My God.

TERMINATOR
Now listen very carefully.

137   INT. HOUSE/ KITCHEN - LATER

Sarah puts out her fifth cigarette. She's sitting on the counter. John, Terminator, Dyson, and Tarissa are at the kitchen table, under a single overhead light.

Dyson looks like that guy on the Sistine Chapel wall, the damned soul... eyes fixed and staring with terrifying knowledge. His shoulder is bandaged. Terminator's arm is wrapped with a blood-soaked bandage below the elbow. The steel forearm and hand gleam in the harsh kitchen light. TRACKING AROUND THE TABLE as Terminator speaks... we don't hear the words.

SARAH (V.O.)
Dyson listened while the Terminator laid it all down. Skynet.
Judgment Day... the history of things to come.   It's not every
day you find out you're responsible for 3 billion deaths.
He took it pretty well, considering...

Terminator finishes speaking.

                              DYSON
                    I feel like I'm gonna throw up.

He looks around at them, clutching the table like he's about to blow away. His face, his posture, his
ragged voice express soul-wrenching terror. This is a man ripped out of normal life into their
grim world. His voice is pleading.

                              DYSON
                    You're judging me on thing's I haven't even done yet. Jesus.
                    <u>How were we supposed to know</u>?

Sarah speaks from the shadows behind them. Dyson turns to find her looking right at him.

                              SARAH
                    Yeah. Right. How were you supposed to know? Fucking men...
                    all you know how to do is thrust into the world with your...
                    fucking ideas and your weapons.   Did you know that every gun
                    in the world is named after a man? Colt, Browning, Smith,
                    Thompson, Kalashnikov... all men. Men built the hydrogen
                    bomb, not women... men like you thought it up. You're so
                    creative.   You don't know what it's like to *really create*
                    something... to create a life. To feel it growing inside you. All
                    you know how to create is death... you fucking bastards.

                              JOHN
                    Mom, Mom, we need to be more constructive here. I don't see
                    this as a gender-related issue.
                              (to the Dysons)
                    She's still tense.
                              (to Sarah)
                    We still have to figure out how to stop it all from happening.
                    Right?

                              TARISSA
                    But I thought... aren't we changing things? I mean... right
                    now? Changing the way it goes?

                              DYSON
                              (seizing on that)
                    That's right! There's no way I'm going to finish the new
                    processor now. Forget it. I'm out of it. I'm quitting Cyberdyne
                    tomorrow... I'll sell real estate, I don't care--

                              SARAH
                              (coldly)
                    That's not good enough.

Dyson's voice is pitiful.

                              DYSON
                    Look, whatever you want me to do, I'll do. I just want my kids to
                    have a chance to grow up, okay?

                              TERMINATOR
                    No one must follow your work.

                              DYSON
                        (thoughts racing)
              Alright, yeah. You're right. We have to destroy the stuff at the
              lab, the files, disk drives... and everything I have here.
              Everything! I don't care.

In the final film, Sarah's diatribe about "fucking men..." has shifted from a gender-related speech to a more
general reaction against those who will not take responsibility for their research. While an interesting
consideration, the gender-blaming was not relevant to the narrative and also gave the perception of
Sarah as man-hating, which at this point in the story seemed to come out of nowhere. Sarah should be also
softening at this point after her catharsis at not being cold enough to kill Dyson, although her bitterness still
tries to rise to the surface before John brings her back down. The narrative trick applied here is the
anticipation of the audience's awareness of Sarah's pontification and playing off of it; thus, John's reaction
to her speech and cutting her off before she gets too carried away does exactly what the audience wants
it to do: stop her heavy-handed moralizing. Terminator is wearing a black glove on his left hand to
conveniently bypass the puppet rig (and precious production time) needed to set up the articulated
mechanical endo hand depicted in the script.

                                                                    CUT TO:

138   FIRE ROARING IN A METAL TRASH BARREL.
        Stacks of files are dumped onto it.
        WIDER reveals we are in--

138A   EXT. DYSON'S BACKYARD - NIGHT

        Terminator dumps lighter fluid liberally over the fire, which flares up, lighting his face
        demonically. Sarah, Dyson, Tarissa, and John return from his office with more stuff-- files,
        notes, optical disks. Even his kids are carrying stuff. It all goes into the fire. Dyson drops the
        prototype processor onto the fire... his eyes hollow and distant.

        He stares into the fire, watching his world burning. Then has a sudden thought.

                              DYSON
              Do you know about the chip?

                              SARAH
              What chip?

                              DYSON
              They have it in a vault at Cyberdyne...
                        (to Terminator)
              It's gotta be from the other one like you.

                              TERMINATOR
                        (to Sarah)
              The CPU from the first terminator.

                              SARAH
              Son of a bitch, I knew it!

                              DYSON
              They told us not to ask where they got it. I thought... Japan...
              hell, I don't know. I didn't want to know.

                              SARAH
              Those lying motherfuckers!

DYSON

It was scary stuff, radically advanced.   It was shattered...
didn't work. But it gave us ideas. It took us in new directions...
things we would never have thought of. All this work is based on
it.

In the final film, the dialogue in this exterior scene is absorbed into the previous interior scene in an effort to simplify the location shooting. The burning of Dyson's papers and equipment is mentioned but not shown in this scene, but is later corroborated by T-1000's discovery of the burning trash can upon his arrival at the Dyson house in Scene 146. Dyson's obvious fascination and excitement in talking about the chip's technology before he realizes what he's saying is a pivotal glimpse into the man's character that compensates for the loss of Scene 99. The tail of scene is cut short, going directly from Dyson's line, "Now?" to the approach to Cyberdyne, which streamlines the narrative by sending the characters immediately toward their next goal.

TERMINATOR

It must be destroyed.

SARAH

(to Dyson)
Can you get us in there, past security?

DYSON

I think so, yeah. When?

Dyson looks at her, Terminator, then John. Sees his answer.

DYSON

Now?
            (he takes a breath)
Yeah, right.

He turns to his wife. Her face is streaked with tears, but her eyes are strong and clear. Tarissa puts her hands on his arm. She is stunned by what she's heard, but dealing with it. She believes them.

TARISSA

Miles, I'm scared. Okay. But the only thing that scares me
more than you going... is you *not going*.

He nods. She's right.

SARAH

(to Terminator)
Is it safe for them here?

TERMINATOR

(to Tarissa)
Take your kids. Go to a hotel. Right now.
Don't pack.
            (to the others)
Let's go.

CUT TO:

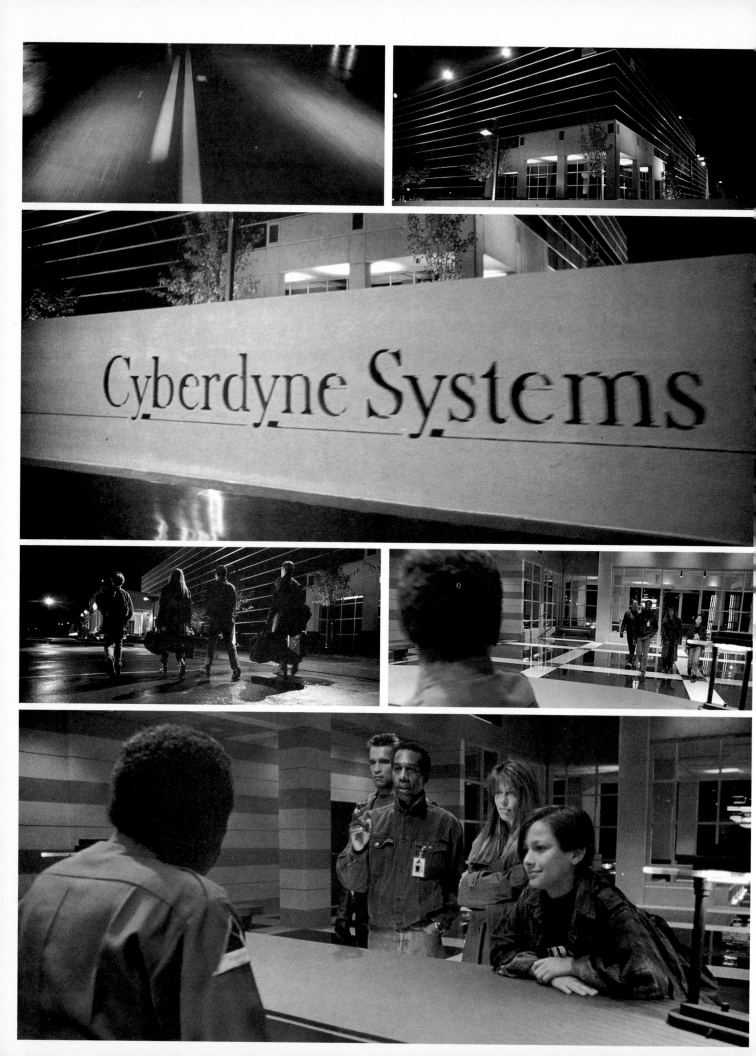

138B   EXT. HIGHWAY - NIGHT

Pavement rushing at us, lit by headlights. Beyond, darkness.

> SARAH (V.O.)
> The future, always so clear to me, had become like a black
> highway at night.   We were in uncharted territory now...
> making up history as we went along.

TILT UP to reveal a rectangle of light ahead. The Cyberdyne Building...

139   INT. CYBERDYNE SYSTEMS BUILDING/ LOBBY - NIGHT

TIGHT ON A CARD-KEY SCANNER as Dyson's hand zips his security card through the slot in one motion. There is the sound of a servo-lock, and--

139A   DYSON enters the spacious lobby, followed by Sarah, John, and Terminator last of all. In a frontal angle, the others block Terminator from view.

THE GUARD at the front desk, GIBBONS, looks up as Dyson moves toward him. Dyson is pale and sweaty, but smiles warmly at the guard, speaking well before he reaches the desk.

> DYSON
> Evening, Paul. These are friends of mine from out of town, I
> just thought I'd take them up and show them around.

> GIBBONS
> I'm sorry, Mr. Dyson. You know the rules about visitors in the
> lab. I need written authoriz--

K-CHAK! Gibbons is staring down the barrels of Sarah's .45 and Terminator's MAC-10.

> TERMINATOR
> I insist.

The guard is too stunned to move. We see that Terminator is wearing his jacket and one black glove.
Gibbons' eyes go to the silent alarm button on the console.

> SARAH
> Don't even think about it.

Gibbons nods. He stays frozen. Terminator circles quickly and gets the guard out of the chair. John pulls a roll of duct-tape from his knapsack and tears off a piece.

140   INT. SECOND FLOOR CORRIDOR

ELEVATOR DOORS OPEN and Terminator leads the group warily into the corridor. They have a cart piled high with gear in nylon bags. Dyson motions down the corridor to the right. As they walk, he continues to fill them in--

> DYSON
> The vault needs two keys to open. Mine...
> (holds up key)
> ...and one from the security station. It's in a locker but my card
> should access it. Here we go.

They stand in front of a wide security door. A sign above reads SPECIAL PROJECTS DIVISION: AUTHORIZED PERSONNEL ONLY. Dyson zips his key-card through the scanner and the door unlatches.

141   OMITTED

142   INT. FIRST FLOOR CORRIDOR/ LOBBY

A ROVING GUARD, MOSHIER, strolls down the long corridor from the first-floor office block. A punch clock swings at his hip, and he's just completed his circuit of the building. He passes the bank of elevators and rounds the corner to the front desk, calling out--

                    MOSHIER
          Honey, I'm home...

He sees the desk is deserted and frowns. Figures Gibbons must be in the can, so check that first before getting alarmed.
TRACKING WITH HIM to the restroom around the corner.

                    MOSHIER
          Hey, man, you shouldn't leave the --

142A   OVER HIS SHOULDER we see past the door as he pushes it open, revealing Gibbons handcuffed to the urinal. Moshier spins on a dime and sprints to the desk where he slaps his hand down on the silent alarm button.

143   INT. SECURITY STATION

The security station is a pass-through area with a counter, behind which are desks and a bank of monitors, showing boring movies about empty corridors. Dyson crosses quickly to a locker behind the monitor area. He swishes his card repeatedly through the scanner slot on the locker. Nothing happens. The light on the locker is blinking red. Sarah notices Dyson's alarmed expression.

                    SARAH
          What? WHAT IS IT?

Dyson whips around, staring at a light flashing on the console behind him.

                    DYSON
          Silent alarm's been tripped. It neutralizes the codes throughout
          the building. Nothing'll open now.

We see his nerve snapping.

                    DYSON
          We should abort.

                    SARAH
          NO!! We're going all the way! You got that, Dyson?

She's right in his face. Somehow, it works for him. He nods, getting some resolve from somewhere.

144   INT. LOBBY

Moshier's gotten Gibbons loose. He's on the phone to the cops.

GIBBONS
... multiple armed suspects. Look, I think it's the guy from that
mall shootout, and the woman... yeah, her. Pretty sure. Just
send everything you've got in the area--

In all but the final revision, the second-floor security station is manned by three guards, one of whom has the second vault key on a chain around his neck. Dyson, Sarah, John, and Terminator enter the lab and strong-arm the guards into surrendering the key by having Terminator pick up one of the guards by the throat, with John pretending to try to pull him off while telling the guard "I can't reason with this guy when he gets like this. I've seen him do things made the coroner puke." They then tie up and gag the guards, and in the omitted Scene 152 they chase them down the stairwell, Terminator firing a machine gun over their heads and saying "Later, dickwads," to get them out before our heroes set off the explosive charges to blow the lab. During production, the security guards were omitted from the security station to simplify both the narrative and the shooting schedule.

---

145   INT. SECURITY STATION./ LAB

John jumps up on a desk next to the wall-mounted locker. Dyson stares in amazement as John starts pulling his counter-electronics gear out of his knapsack. It's just another Ready-Teller to him.

JOHN
You guys get started on the lab... I can open this.

145A   Dyson leads Terminator and Sarah to the main lab doors. Another servo-lock.
He tries his card. Nothing.

DYSON
No good.

TERMINATOR
Let me try mine.

He unslings the M-79, pulling it over his shoulder in one motion.
Sarah grabs Dyson and drags him back down the hall.
Terminator opens the breech and slides in one of the fat 40mm H.E. grenades. He flips the thing closed with a snap of the wrist.

SARAH
(yelling as she runs)
John! Fire-in-the-hole!

John drops what he's doing, and covers his ears.
Terminator fires at inhumanly close range.
145B   The door EXPLODES into kindling. The concussion blows his jacket open, and flying shrapnel whizzes all around him. Before the thunderclap has faded Terminator walks into the fire and smoke.
John goes back to work without missing a beat.
Sarah and a stunned Dyson walk through the burning doorframe into the Artificial Intelligence Lab.

A SIREN is sounding. The HALON FIRE-CONTROL SYSTEM has been triggered. The invisible gas roars in, putting out the flames.

DYSON
Fire's set off the halon system! Here... hurry!

Dyson runs to a wall cabinet and pulls out some BREATHING MASKS. He hands one to Sarah and dons the other. Then he reaches out to hand one to Terminator.

> DYSON
> Here!

Terminator doesn't need a mask, since his oxygen requirements are so low. He ignores Dyson as he removes his massive backpack and opens it. Dyson shrugs and tosses the mask on a desk. He turns to Sarah.

> DYSON
> (yelling through the mask)
> We'll have to keep these on a couple minutes, till the gas clears.

Terminator pulls two five-gallon jerry-cans of gasoline from his pack.
Sarah starts pulling out book-sized, olive-drab CLAYMORE MINES, stacking them next to the gasoline. Dyson stares. Part of him can't believe they're really doing this.

In the final film, Terminator strides into the lab, ignoring the halon gas pouring into the room, and retrieves some emergency breathing gear to give to Sarah and Dyson. This action not only makes Terminator more heroic, but also actively drives home the point that Terminator doesn't need a gas mask --a point which is only passively made in the script by Terminator's ignoring of the mask Dyson hands him. Although the scenes of the characters ransacking the lab, gathering materials, and destroying equipment --in particular the shots of Terminator "reprogramming" many of Cyberdyne's computers with a fire axe-- were filmed, they were deemed unnecessary to the narrative (since they will be blowing up the entire lab anyway), and were cut from the picture.

CUT TO:

146   INT. DYSON HOUSE - NIGHT

The T-1000 moves slowly through the ravaged office, analyzing what has happened here. It walks down the dark hallway. The place is deserted. The police-walkie clipped on its belt (real, not simulated) blares to life.

> DISPATCHER (V.O.)
> All units, all units. 211 in progress at 2144 Kramer Street, the
> Cyberdyne building. Multiple suspects, armed with automatic
> weapons and explosives. SWAT unit is en route...

In the final film, T-1000 arrives at the Dyson house in an abstract and stylized closeup, where it sees the burning trash can of Dyson's notes and materials. The arrival of the police, SWAT teams, and the helicopter immediately follow T-1000's walkthrough of Dyson's ruined office, and the two scenes are bridged by the police chatter over the walkie-talkies. The walkie chatter not only identifies Sarah by name, giving T-1000 confirmation of their whereabouts, but also notes that the other individual involved is a "white male fitting the description of the individual wanted for the murder of police officers in 1984." This use of sound and voiceover brings all of the elements together both editorially and narratively, not only easing the transition between scenes, but also explaining why there are so many cops at the scene.

147   EXT. HOUSE/ STREET

The T-1000 sprints up and throws its leg over the big C.H.P. Kawasaki. Fires it up. It smokes an arcing scorch-mark on the pavement as it spins around and roars away.

                                                              CUT TO:

148   INT. CYBERDYNE BUILDING/ LAB

TIGHT ON A LARGE DISK DRIVE. State-of-the-art. Very expensive. A FIRE AXE smashes down through the housing, shattering the disk.

148A   WIDER, revealing a scene of high-tech pillage. Terminator beats the disk drive into junk and steps to another. WHAM. Same routine. He's already demolished half a dozen.
Sarah topples a file cabinet, scattering the files.
Dyson staggers up with an armload of heavy M-O (magnetic-optical) disks and drops them on a growing stack in the middle of the floor. He and Sarah have their breathing masks hanging down around their necks, since the halon gas has dissipated.

                        DYSON
                  (to Sarah, panting)
            Yeah, all that stuff! And all the disks in those offices.
            Especially my office... everything in my office!
                  (to Terminator)
            These, too! This is important.
                  (SMASH!)
            And all this here... that's it.

148B   Sarah goes into Dysons office and starts hurling everything out the door onto the central junkpile... books, files, everything on the desk.
A FRAMED PHOTO of Dyson's wife and kids lands on top of the heap. Tarissa, hugging Danny and Blythe, all grinning. The glass is shattered.

148C   Terminator cuts a swath, under Dyson's direction, exploding equipment into fragments with his inhuman swings.
SMASH! It's carnage. Millions in hardware, and all the irreplaceable fruits of their years of research... shattered, broken, dumped in a heap for the big bonfire of destiny.
Dyson stops a second, panting.

                        DYSON
            Give me that thing a second.

Terminator hands him the axe. Dyson hefts it one-handed. He turns to a lab table... on it is another prototype processor.

                        DYSON
            I've worked for years on this thing.

Swinging awkwardly but with great force he smashes the axe down onto the processor prototype, exploding it into fragments. His shoulder is agony, but he looks satisfied.

_____

Although filmed, the scene of Dyson destroying the prototype neural-net processor was omitted to streamline the narrative; with the omission of both the scenes showing the smashing of the other computer hardware and the previous scenes establishing the look of the processor, this scene became unnecessary; as it is, no one recognizes the processor since it is not featured prominently in other remaining scenes. Dyson thus comes off as more appropriately numbed and pensively resigned to their course of action, rather than gung-ho about destroying his life's work.
_____

149 **INT. SECOND FLOOR SECURITY STATION**

John taps away at his little lap-top, which is running code combinations into the card-key lock. Suddenly, the green light on the locker goes on and it unlocks with a clunk.

> JOHN
>
> Easy money.

He whips it open, revealing a rack of keys. But the VAULT-KEY is distinctive, a long steel rectangle on a neck-chain. John grabs it and runs toward the lab.

In the final film, John is caught in the sweep of the searchlight of the helicopter hovering outside the second-story window; he looks at the bank of exterior surveillance monitors and sees the building surrounded by the police and SWAT teams. Muttering "Not good, not good," he heads for the lab. This piece of business explains visually how they know the police and SWATs have surrounded the building, whereas in the script, they just hear the sound of sirens outside. When John runs into the lab, the actors improvised some lines on set: Sarah asks, "How many?" and John replies,"All of them, I think."

---

150 **INT. LAB**

Sarah and Terminator are working like a crack team, rigging the explosives. She is taping the claymores to the gas cans with duct tape to create powerful incendiary bombs. Terminator is attaching claymores and blocks of C-4 plastic explosive to the large MAINFRAME COMPUTER cabinets nearby. All the claymores are wired back to one detonator which has a RADIO-CONTROL RELAY switch.

> DYSON
>
> How do you set them off?

Terminator shows him a REMOTE DETONATOR, a small transmitter with a red plunger.

> TERMINATOR
>
> Radio remote.

He makes a plunger-pushing motion with his thumb and an accompanying "click" sound. Dyson nods.
Just then John comes running in, holding up the key.

> JOHN
>
> I got it. Piece of cake.

> SARAH
> (to Dyson and Terminator)
> Go! I'll finish here.

They run out as the SOUND OF SIRENS grows louder outside.

> TERMINATOR
>
> I'll deal with the police.

> JOHN
>
> Remember what I said, you can't...

> TERMINATOR
>
> Trust me.

151   EXT. CYBERDYNE BUILDING

The security duo of Moshier and Gibbons cowers behind cars in the parking lot in front of the
building. They turn as L.A.P.D. BLACK-AND-WHITES pour into the lot, turning the area into a
disco of whirling blue and red lights.

152   OMITTED

153   EXT. CYBERDYNE BUILDING

The cops are jumping from their cars and ducking behind them. Emphasis on small arms here.
Behind them an ugly BLACK SWAT VAN screeches into the
lot.

153A   We hear the THUMP OF ROTORS as a POLICE CHOPPER arrives and swings in close to the
building. It rakes its XENON SPOTLIGHT through the second floor offices.

154   INT./EXT. SECOND FLOOR OFFICE
Terminator crosses the office toward the floor-to-ceiling windows. He is outlined starkly by the
spotlight as it rakes through the dark offices. Without breaking stride he kicks an executive desk
toward the window.
154A   Glass explodes outward and the desk topples, falling to the sidewalk below.

154B   Terminator, standing at the edge, FIRES A LONG BURST which strafes the police cars lined up
below. Cops duck as glass flies. Terminator, with his superb aim, hits no one. But notice is
served.

In the final film, a TermoVision POV shot --scanning the parking lot for human casualties and finding none--
was added to visually drive home the point that Terminator does not kill anyone in his assault from the
second-story window on the police forces in the parking lot below.

154C   The cops (surprise) FIRE BACK. Terminator turns and is walking calmly from the windows as
glass, office furniture, drapes etc. are riddled by return fire.   A few rounds hit his back, but he
doesn't notice. He reloads as he walks.

155   INT. VAULT ANTECHAMBER

TIGHT ON A KEY inserted into one of the vault locks.

WIDER as John and Dyson stand poised, hands on keys.

                          JOHN
          And let's see what's behind door number one.

Dyson nods and they turn the keys together. The vault grumbles to itself, withdrawing its locking
bolts with a final KLONK!
Together Dyson and John swing the door open.

156   EXT./ INT. LOBBY

The varsity takes the field as the SWAT TROOPERS sprint forward by squads. They flank the
lobby and work their way inside, deploying rapidly. They move and freeze, behind cover,
quivering with adrenalin. They have all that great SWAT equipment: body armor, gas-masks,
M-16s, tear-gas launchers, ropes. The works. They make a lot of hand signals and keep their
mouths shut. They're well-trained and deadly.

SCAN
AXIL
CAMI
CHKW
EPIG
FDSK
MAND
MAST
MAXI
MORD
SUBM
TNGE

HUMAN
CASUALTIES: 0.0

157   OUTSIDE we see cops firing TEAR GAS grenades through the broken windows into second-floor offices.

158   INT. VAULT

John and Dyson are isolated from the world in this silent steel womb. Dyson opens the cabinet containing the terminator relics.   It's John's turn to stare with uneasy déjà-vu as he sees the terminator hand and CPU.

Then in one vicious move he sweeps his arm behind the inert-gas flasks and hurls them to the floor. They SHATTER. John snatches the CPU and the metal hand out of the broken glass.

                    JOHN
          Got ol' Skynet by the balls now, Miles. Come on, let's book!

Clutching the steel hand and pocketing the chip like it's a Mars bar he just bought, John runs out. Dyson follows.

159   INT. FIRST FLOOR CORRIDOR/ STAIRWELL

We see the advance squad of SWATs make it to one of the stairwells. They start up, two at a time, covering each other ritualistically by the numbers.

160   INT. LAB/ HALL

John pelts into the lab with Dyson stumbling along behind him.
Sarah has just finished wiring all the charges to the central detonator.

                    JOHN
          Ready to rock?

                    SARAH
          Ready.

John tosses her the metal hand. She catches it and bends to put the hand in her empty back-pack. Sarah zips the pack and starts to shuck into it.

Dyson's running out of steam. The bandages at his shoulder are soaked with seeping blood. He stands in the middle of the lab, saying goodbye in his mind, looking weak and empty. Terminator strides into the lab.

                    TERMINATOR
          Time to go. *Right now.*

He and John head back the way they came, through security.
Sarah sees that in her work, she has set the detonator down twenty feet away, near where Dyson is standing.

                    SARAH
          Dyson, hand me the detonator. Let's go--

He gingerly picks up the detonator. Starts toward her. Then--
160A   CRASH!! THE DOORS AT THE BACK OF THE LAB ARE KICKED OPEN.
SWAT LEADER and two others OPEN FIRE.
Their M-16s rake the room. Sarah dives behind a computer cabinet.
Dyson is HIT. He is slammed to the floor by the impacts.

161   IN THE HALL, John hears the firing and spins to run back.

JOHN

Mommm!!!

Terminator grabs him as bullets slam into his broad back. He makes it around the corner with John, out of the line of fire.

162   IN THE LAB, bullets rake over Sarah's head, smacking all around her, clanging into the machine protecting her. She can see Dyson, slumped on the floor. Debris and flying glass rain on her as the SWATs pour on the fire. The detonator is clutched in his hand. He rolls to face her, his eyes bulging from the pain of his torn-up guts.

DYSON

Go.

162A   Sarah hesitates a split second. Then she snap-rolls and fast-crawls through broken glass and debris into the hall where--

TERMINATOR grabs her by the jacket and hauls her roughly to her feet.
Bullets rake the walls behind them as they sprint forward. They round the corner. John does a fast take that she's not hit and they run together through the security checkpoint.

In the final film, Sarah is pinned down and trapped in the clean room by the SWATs' fusillade; John sees her on one of the surveillance monitors, and Terminator breaks through the wall between the clean room and the security station to get her out. The set was designed and constructed with a breakaway wall with this in mind, not only to add suspense to the scene, but also to give Terminator another heroic action, made more heroic by the fact that John does not even order him to do it, but says "Shit, she's in the clean room! There's no way out of there!"

163   INT. SECURITY STATION/ CORRIDOR

John reaches the door first, and tries it. Locked.
Terminator unslings the M-79 blooper smoothly, opening the breech.

TERMINATOR

Get back.

He pulls a grenade from the bandolier over his shoulder, and slides it into the bore. Flicks his wrist. The breech snaps shut. Sarah and John have a split second to duck and cover.

TERMINATOR

Cover your ears and open your mouth.

163A   They do. KABOOM!!! Twenty feet away the door, and half the wall around it, EXPLODES outward. The backblast hits Terminator full force, but he strides through the smoking hole before the debris has even hit the floor.

164   OMITTED

Scene 164 was another scene showing Terminator blowing open a door and was easily omitted.

165   INT. LAB

SWAT LEADER moves cautiously through the lab. Cat-stepping, he circles around a desk which blocks Dyson's body from his view. His M-16 is leveled crisply. We look over his shoulder as he rounds the desk, revealing--

MILES DYSON is not dead. He will be very soon, but at this moment he is conscious. He has propped himself up against the desk, and holds a BOOK in one hand. A heavy technical manual.

Below the book is the detonator, upright on the tile floor.
The message is clear. "Shoot me, the book drops on the plunger. Adios." Dyson wheezes, trying to draw enough breath to talk.

> DYSON
> I don't know... how much longer... I can... hold this thing...

SWAT Leader seems to see the wires, the claymores, the gas cans all around him for the first time.
His eyes, visible through his gas-mask, go very wide.
He spins and motions his squad back.

> LEADER
> <u>Fall back</u>!! Everybody out! <u>Move</u> <u>it</u>! <u>OUT NOW</u>!

They retreat so fast they crash into the next group coming up the stairs.

166   INT. CORRIDOR

Terminator reaches the main elevators. Hits the button. Sarah and John are coughing and stumbling in the choking darkness, buddy-breathing with the single mask. The doors open. They get in the elevator and head down.

167   INT. LAB

Dyson is lying amid the ruins of his dream. Sprawled on the floor, he has his back propped up against the desk. He is bathed in his own blood, which runs out in long fingers across the tiles. His breathing is shallow and raspy. He still holds the book, trembling, above the switch.

In his lap is the picture from his desk. He has pulled it from the debris next to him. A tear trickles from his eye. His wife and children smile up at him through broken glass.

168   OMITTED

169   CUT TO THE PUPIL OF HIS EYE, at the moment of death, the instant the light fades from his eyes and he is gone--
His arm drops and the book hits the switch--

In all but the final revision of the script, Dyson's death consists of a more lyrical, stylized vision (refer to the appendix of omitted sequences) that reconciles him with his family and his conviction that his sacrifice is worthwhile. In shooting the scene, it was decided to play the cold reality of his death, his hyperventilating slowing to a gasp and then stopping completely as the camera pushes in on his face to his wide, unseeing eyes. The family picture motif was thus omitted as well in order not to bring up the issue of his family's future without resolving his feelings toward it. Although it is hard to recognize it, Dyson is holding a shattered piece of the prototype processor over the detonator switch in the film, not a heavy technical manual as scripted; the irony is intentional, that the technology that would destroy mankind is now playing a heavy role in saving it, and with the death of the man brings the destruction of his life's work.

---

170   EXT. BUILDING

As the face of the building EXPLODES in an eruption of glass and fire. Remains of the second-floor windows shower the parking lot and a huge fireball rolls out, leaping into the sky.
The cops look up, stunned. The helicopter banks away from the heat. Burning debris falls among the cop cars and a number of officers break ranks, pulling back.

171   ONLY ONE OF THEM seems to be moving with purpose. A BIKE COP who has just arrived drives through the disorganized crowd, directly toward the building.

171A   T-1000 guns the bike up a ramp to a pedestrian bridge which crosses from a parking structure to the Cyberdyne building. It enters on the second floor, which is now a burning maze.

172   INT. SECOND FLOOR/ OFFICE/ CORRIDOR

T-1000 drives into the smoky wreckage. It draws a Hoechler and Koch MPK machine pistol and cruises slowly into the firelit offices, scanning.

172A   IN THE CORRIDOR the bike skirts flaming wreckage as it idles forward.
T-1000 scans the leaping shadows for its prey.

Since there was no adjacent parking structure to the empty office building in the Fremont, California location where the Cyberdyne exteriors and lobby interior were filmed, T-1000 was shot riding through a back entrance and up a flight of stairs to the second floor, taking the same route as the deploying SWAT troopers who entered earlier. The stairwell was actually shot later at the Lakeview Terrace location where the Pescadero State Hospital scenes were filmed, since the empty Cyberdyne building location had no finished stairwells.

173   INT. GROUND FLOOR/ ELEVATOR/ LOBBY

The elevator doors part and Terminator eases a look out into the corridor. The walls on either side of him ERUPT WITH BULLET HITS. The SWATs have the lobby end of the corridor blocked off. They're totally trapped, cut off and screwed.

> JOHN
> (to Sarah)
> Don't forget. It's always darkest right before... you're totally
> fucked.

John's line in the elevator was omitted as an unnecessary quip. Another TermoVision shot --Terminator's POV looking out of the elevator and doing a threat assessment analysis on the SWAT team amassed at the end of the corridor-- was added in the film to show how Terminator is learning to analyze first before shooting; in the text display of the shot, the command "Termination override: disable only" appears.

173A   The SWATs fire a tear-gas grenade toward the elevators. It spews the vicious CS gas out in a swirling cloud which envelopes Sarah and John, who are pressed against the back wall of the elevator.

> TERMINATOR
> Keep your eyes closed. Don't move.
> (they nod, eyes squeezed shut)
> I'll be back.

He slings the grenade launcher over his shoulder and walks out into the corridor.

173B   BLAM. A tear-gas grenade ricochets from wall to wall as it flies down the corridor. It skids to rest in front of Terminator, throwing out a white cloud which quickly fills the corridor.

173C   In the elevator, Sarah and John are choking, handing the breathing mask back and forth desperately. They're scared. This looks like it.

TRAJECTORY LOGGING:
5439 543 5435 65311
6465 656 7689 10930
5439:

THREAT ASSESSMENT ■

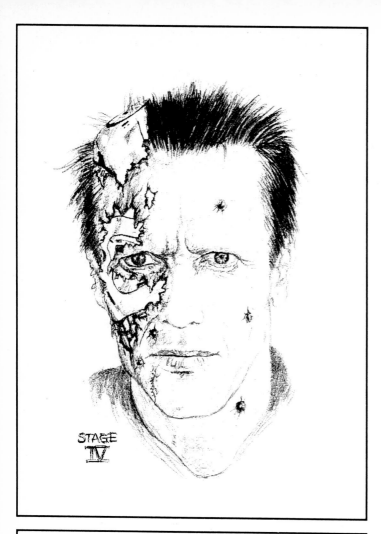

STAGE
IV

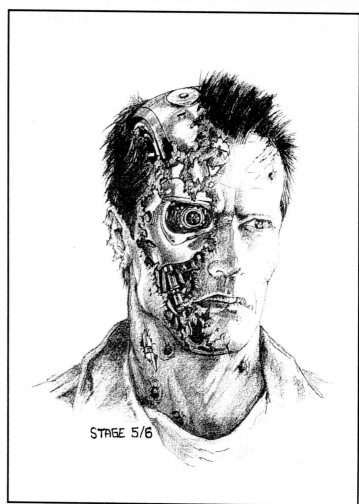

STAGE 5/6

TERMINATOR
STAGE 4
POST-SWAT SHOOTOUT LOOK

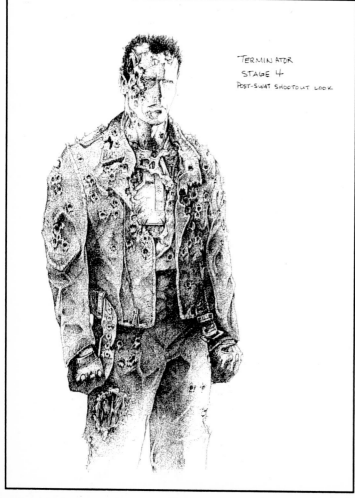

173D   ANGLE ON THE SWAT TEAM, gripping their weapons at the mouth of the corridor. They watch the boiling cloud, waiting.

173E   THEIR POV-- on the wall of boiling smoke. A FIGURE APPEARS. Walking calmly. Totally unaffected. Terminator emerges from the smoke. Not even misty-eyed. Not what they expected.

> LEADER
> (through megaphone)
> <u>Stop where you are. Lie down on the floor, face down. Down on the floor, now!</u>

He continues to stride toward them.
The SWATs tense up. They've never seen anything like this. They're not sure what to do. Closer and closer.

> LEADER
> Drop him.

They OPEN FIRE. The corridor is filled with CRACKING THUNDER. The rounds tear into Terminator's chest. Stomach. Face. Thighs. His leather jacket leaps and jerks as the rounds hit him. The SWATs think the guy's wearing body armor or something. They keep firing. The rounds tear into him, staggering him slightly, but he keeps coming.

> LEADER
> You're not hitting him!

> SWAT #1
> (getting scared)
> Yes I am!

Terminator draws his .45 smoothly. Unhurried. He shoots the nearest man in the left thigh. As he screams and drops, Terminator shoots him in the right thigh. Terminator bends down and picks up the shrieking man's weapon... the TEAR-GAS LAUNCHER.

It is one of those new rotary jobs that holds 12 rounds in a big drum.
Terminator shoots the next SWAT square in the chest with the tear-gas launcher. The gas cannister hits the guy's body armor and doesn't penetrate. But it's like getting slugged in the stomach with a full-swing from a baseball bat. The SWAT folds double and hits the tiles, gasping.

Terminator is an image from Hell, a tall figure in shredded black leather, streaked with blood. One eye is a bloody socket, the metal eye-servos glinting. The flesh of one cheek hangs down in tatters, revealing the chrome cheekbone beneath. The whole front of his jacket is blown open, revealing his metal chest armor.

In the final film, Terminator does not have his right eye servo exposed until later in the steel mill sequence, and only receives "Stage 4" makeup in the Cyberdyne shootout. This decision was made not only to lessen the makeup time required to apply the facial appliances to Arnold Schwarzenegger, but more importantly to preserve for as long as possible Terminator's human expressiveness and the actor's performance --not to mention the fact that with the later makeup stages, Arnold would only be able to see out of one eye and thus would have no stereo vision during the complicated chase and fight sequences in the steel mill.

The remaining SWATs start to fall back. One turns to run and--
KPOW! A gas cannister nails him in the back, sending him sprawling.

173F   Terminator fires three gas grenades into the lobby. It fills rapidly with the white gas, cutting the visibility to a few feet. It is total pandemonium. SWAT LEADER crouches in the fog, white-knuckling his rifle. Terminator looms suddenly out of the mist right in front of him.
POOM! Terminator drills him in the leg with the .45. As the guy screams and drops rifle to clutch his leg, Terminator rips his gas mask off. The SWAT leader drops writhing to the floor, choking and gagging, clutching his bleeding thigh.

Terminator walks up to two SWATs at the front doors. POW-POW. Leg and leg. He snatches off their masks as they fall. The gunfire has stopped. Nobody can see anything. Screams and whimpers echo in the smoke.

174   EXT. BUILDING

Smoke boils out the front door as a figure emerges. Firing the tear-gas launcher with one hand, Terminator launches all remaining rounds among the cop vehicles. Unprotected officers run, choking and half-blind, slamming into cars and tripping over each other. It is a total rout.

175   AT THE SWAT VAN one of the SWATs is rapidly handing out the remaining masks to unprotected cops. A FIGURE appears out of the smoke beside him. He looks up. His mask is ripped off and he is handed the empty launcher. Instinctively he catches it. Terminator grabs his flak vest with one hand and sails him out into the mist.

175A   INT. SWAT VAN

Terminator strides the length of the van and climbs into the driver's seat. No keys in the ignition. He flips down the sun visor. The keys fall into his hand. He starts the van and slams it into gear.

176   INT. / EXT. LOBBY

The tear gas has cleared to a thin haze. The uninjured SWATs are tending their wounded. They look up at the sound of shouts and a roaring engine.

176A   THE SWAT VAN CRASHES INTO THE LOBBY in an explosion of glass and debris. Cops scatter as the van screeches across the lobby in a smoking one-eighty, sliding to a stop across the corridor which leads to the bank of elevators. Terminator backs up until-- crunch-- he seals the corridor with the back of the van.

176B   Sarah and John stumble along the corridor, coughing.
They leap into the back of the van and Terminator hits the throttle.
The van roars across the lobby and exits through blown-out windows.

CUT TO:

177   INT. / EXT. SECOND FLOOR

T-1000, astride the Kawasaki, looks down from a second-floor office and sees the van tearing away across the parking lot with the remaining cops firing at it. It knows. It looks around. Analyzing options. It sees the helicopter hovering outside the building at the end of this corner office block...
It twists full throttle on the powerful bike.
Roars through the office, accelerating fast, straight at the windows--

178   T-1000 BLASTS OUT THROUGH THE GLASS, airborne on the motorcycle. It rockets across the gap to the hovering chopper and--

178A   SLAMS into the canopy. The impact of bike and rider pitches the chopper radically. The startled PILOT fights to regain control as the bike tumbles to the pavement below.

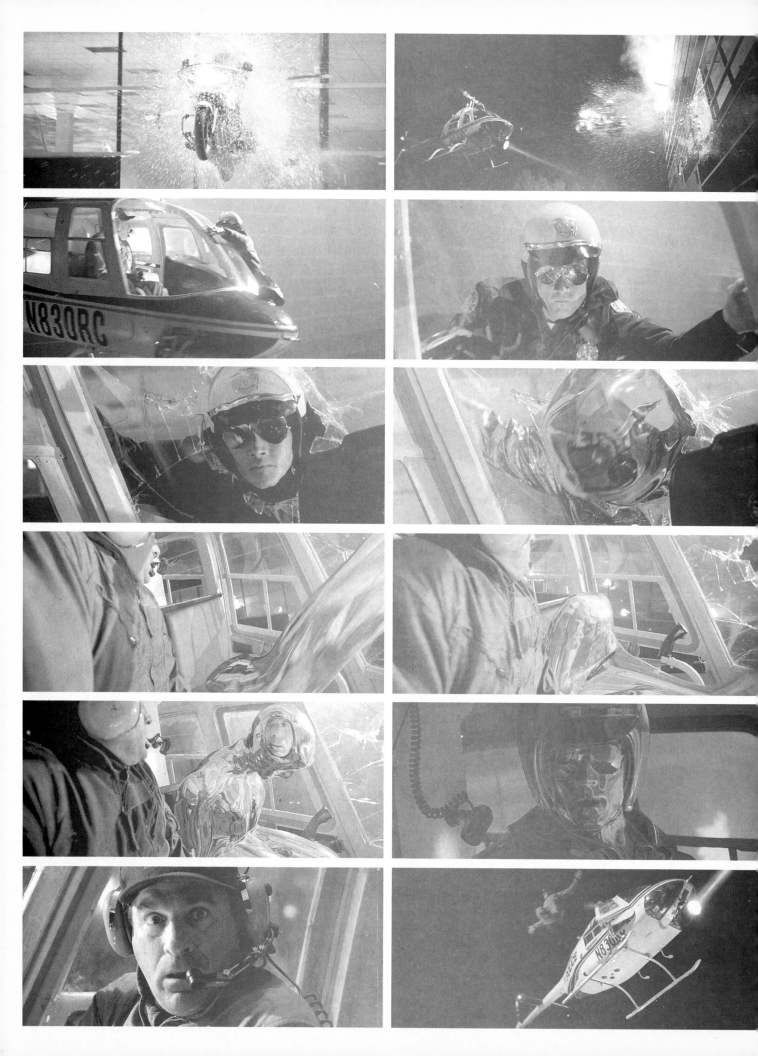

178B   The T-1000 doesn't. It clings to the shattered canopy. Nightmarishly, the pilot watches as the T-1000 smashes its head through the plexiglas canopy and rapidly POURS ITSELF through the jagged hole.   It reforms instantly into its previous self on the passenger seat.

178C   It hurls the pilot out of the chopper and slides into the driver's seat.
The chopper is auto-rotating, spinning out of control. It drops toward the parking lot. T-1000 recovers control ten feet above the ground.

In the final film, T-1000 reforms in the helicopter seat and --still chrome-- turns to the pilot and says calmly, "Get out," whereupon the wide-eyed pilot nods, opens the door, and leaps. The gag not only is a funnier bit of action than scripted, but it echoes a scene from the first film in which Terminator says the exact same thing to commandeer a tanker truck.

178D   Cops hit the deck as the tail-boom swings around, going over them by inches.
The chopper lifts out in a power climb, roaring away across the parking lot toward the fleeing SWAT van.

OKAY, BUCKLE YOUR SEATBELTS, HERE IT COMES...

179   INT. / EXT. SWAT VAN / HIGHWAY - NIGHT

Terminator looks back at his two passengers as he turns the boxy van onto a divided highway. Sarah and John are catching their breath, still coughing from the CS gas. Terminator looks to the rear-view mirror.   He sees the xenon searchlight of the chopper behind them, gaining.

Sarah looks around the inside of the SWAT van. It is a rolling armory. There are rifles, ballistic vests, all manner of equipment.

                    SARAH
         John, get under these. Hurry!

He sits against the front bulkhead of the van and she piles bullet-proof vests on top of him, completely covering him. Then she grabs two M-16s from the wall-rack and loads them.   She starts on a shotgun as--

180   The SWAT van weaves through sparse traffic at high speed.
Terminator slews the unstable van around cars and trucks which seem to be crawling. The van hits its top speed of 80. They swerve to miss the back end of A WHITE 18-WHEEL TANKER .
180A   The chopper swings in behind them, closing fast.
180B   T-1000 reaches through the shattered canopy with the MPK machine pistol and FIRES. The back of the van CLANGS WITH HITS. The door windows are BLOWN IN.

Terminator weaves the van, trying to throw off the T-1000's aim.
The unstable vehicle screeches and wobbles on the edge of control.
One of the doors is kicked open. Sarah, wearing a ballistic vest, crouches in the doorway, whipping up the M-16. SHE OPENS FIRE.

180C   Bullets riddle what's left of the chopper's canopy as the T-1000 returns fire.
The van is stitched with hits.

180D   INSIDE THE VAN holes are punched through the thin sheet-metal walls, ripping up the interior. The vests covering John are hit repeatedly. We see that Sarah has hung two Kevlar vests on the inside of the back door and she ducks behind these as bullets hit around her. She pops back out and fires in controlled bursts. The M-16 empties and she grabs another.

180E   Terminator serves around a car which is changing lanes, hitting it and knocking it skidding.

181   OMITTED

In the 7/18/90 draft, the helicopter chases the SWAT van into a tunnel, where all of the subsequent crash and vehicle changeovers was to occur. Tunnel locations were scouted and effects houses put in bids to do the sequence in miniature; however, the financial, logistical, and safety considerations of this sequence were enormous, and even to do much of the sequence in miniature would have required a large-scale helicopter model --and thus a very large tunnel miniature-- to make it look realistic as the rotors smash the light fixtures and the skids scrape the pavement. The tunnel idea proved unfeasible to shoot and the location was moved to an open stretch of freeway in Long Beach; the one element that was retained was the action of the helicopter flying at high speed under an overpass. An interesting note: to address the logical question of how T-1000 can fly a helicopter (which requires two hands) and shoot/reload its weapon (another two hands) at the same time, there are several cuts in the film showing that T-1000 has sprouted *four* arms during the chase!

181A   Sarah reloads and keeps firing. The van swerves around a Toyota. A moment later the helicopter passes it, the rotor just clearing the top of the car.

181B   T-1000 FIRES the machine pistol.

181C   Sarah has popped out to fire. She takes a HIT in the thigh, and several rounds hammer into her Kevlar vest. She is thrown back onto the floor of the van. She lies there, an exposed target...

181D   Terminator sees the T-1000 preparing to fire again.
        He locks up the van's brakes. Tires scream as the vehicle shimmies. Sarah is thrown forward, sliding up to the bulkhead next to John.

182   And the helicopter SLAMS RIGHT INTO THE BACK OF THE VAN.
        The rotor disintegrates. The back doors of the van are crushed in as the canopy, the whole front of the fuselage is HAMMERED INTO JUNK, trapping the T-1000 inside twisted metal. The chopper hits the pavement, flips sideways, and cartwheels... smashing itself into a shapeless mass of twisted metal.
        It falls away behind the van, tumbling end over end.

182A   Terminator fights to control the van, which is fishtailing violently from the impact. It smashes up against the center divider, screeching along the concrete, and then pulls away. Terminator puts the hammer down and the van accelerates. He swerves to avoid an UGLY PICKUP crawling like a snail ahead.

        THE RIGHT FRONT FENDER of the van, crumpled by slamming the wall, is sawing into the tire. The tire blows and peels clean off the rim. The steel wheel grinds across the pavement, striking trails of sparks, and the van slides sideways and topples--
        STEEL SCREAMS on pavement as the van grinds to a stop on its side.

182B   INSIDE THE VAN, John crawls to Sarah, who is groaning and holding her bleeding leg. She is white and shocky. Terminator starts to extricate himself from the crumpled driver's seat.

183   BACK DOWN THE ROAD, THE HELICOPTER wreckage is a crumpled ball of junk metal, unrecognizable. Behind it, the TANKER TRUCK brakes hard, shuddering and groaning, trying to stop. The big tires lock up in clouds of tire-smoke. The rig comes to a shuddering stop just short of the wrecked chopper.

183A   The shaken DRIVER jumps down.
        From behind the wreckage a cop emerges, walking toward him.

                              DRIVER
                    Goddamn, are you alri---

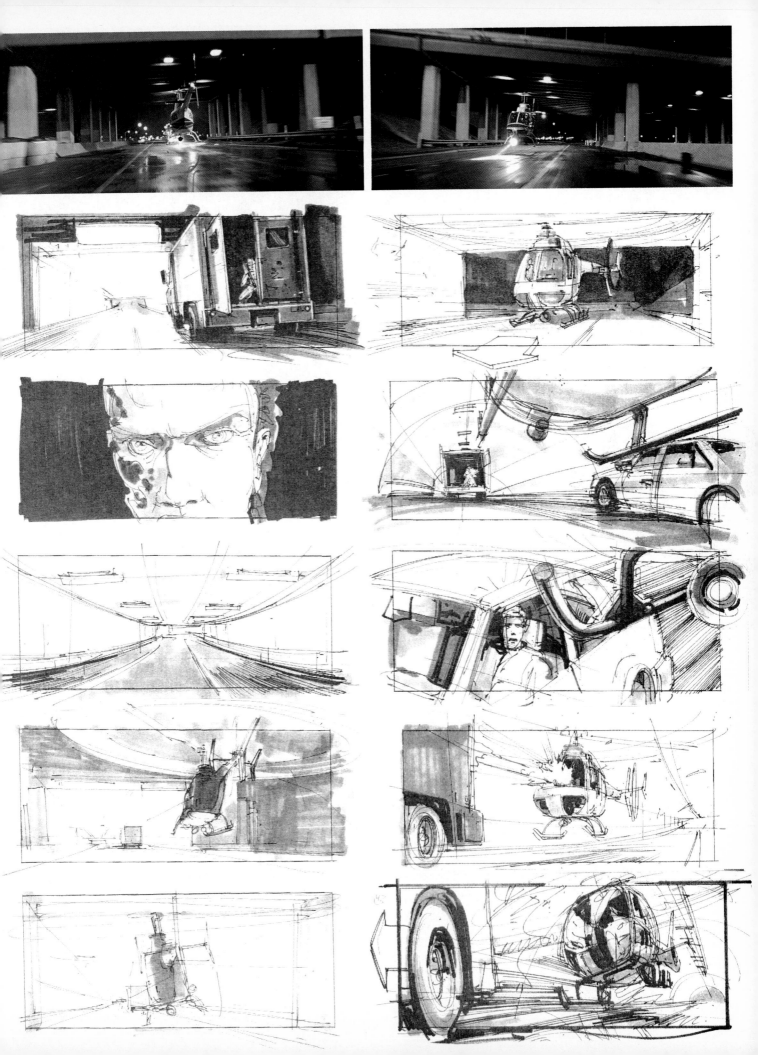

183B   SSSSHHCK! T-1000 drives a blade through the man's abdomen and walks on past without slowing, or even looking at him.

183C   It climbs into the open cab of the tanker. Releases the brake.
As the truck bellows and rolls forward we see the large blue letters on the side which say "CRYOCO INC. LIQUID NITROGEN SUPPLY".

184   AT THE SWAT VAN John and Terminator are carrying Sarah out of the wreck. Terminator has the M-79 slung over his shoulder, the bandolier of grenades, and his .45 stuck in his waistband. John has borrowed a 12-GAUGE RIOT GUN from the SWATs.

184A   The pickup they passed seconds earlier pulls up to them. The DRIVER, a Hispanic guy in his 50's, is getting out to help them. Terminator and John hear a CRASH and look back as the
185   helicopter wreckage is knocked aside by the accelerating tanker truck.

186   JOHN
                Holy shit. Come on, Mom... we gotta keep moving... come on--

                                  TERMINATOR
                              (to the pickup owner)
                          We need your truck.

The guy seems to know better than to try and stop him as Terminator slides Sarah into the front seat and climbs behind the wheel. John runs to the passenger side.

187   THE TANKER ROARS, spewing smoke from its chrome stacks as it shifts up through the gears.

188   Terminator slams the pickup in gear, checking the rear-view. The tanker is a hundred feet behind them now, and really moving. Terminator puts the throttle down, but the pickup is an old slug loaded down by a heavy home-made wooden camper-shell. It accelerates slowly.

189   THE TANKER slams into one end of the SWAT van, spinning it out of the way with a roar and screech of twisting metal. The 18-wheeler shifts to a higher gear, still accelerating.

190   INT. / EXT. PICKUP TRUCK

With the tanker right behind them, Terminator cuts the wheel, swerving the pickup back and forth across the lanes.
The big rig stays right on them, its tanker whiplashing violently.

                                    JOHN
                          Faster! He's right on us!

Terminator doesn't reply. He rapidly unslings the blooper, still around his neck, and reaches for a grenade.

As the tanker gains on the pickup, John says,"Step on it!" Terminator replies, "This is the vehicle's top speed," to which John retorts, "I could get out and run faster than this!"

---

191   LOW ANGLE ON THE TRACTOR-TRAILER as it roars right up to the lens, filling frame with chrome and lights.

191A   K-WHAM!! It rams the back of the pickup, sending it skidding.

191B   Then the T-1000 pulls the tractor trailer up alongside the pickup and crabs over, sandwiching it against the center divider. The spinning chrome hubs tear into the passenger side door and the guard rail screeches along the other side.

The pickup bucks and shakes insanely. It ricochets violently between the big-rig and the divider.
Horrible SCREECH of tortured steel.
Sparks pour in sheets of fire from both sides.
The windshield shatters as the door-posts buckle in.
Metal and glass shower in through the side windows.
The frame twists and buckles. John feels like the fillings are being shaken right out of his teeth.
The wooden camper disintegrates, falling away as kindling behind them.

191C   INT. TANKER CAB

T-1000 holds the wheel hard over, mercilessly grinding the pickup. The whole rig jerks and shakes with the violence of the sustained hammering.

191D   INT. / EXT. PICKUP

Terminator slides toward the passenger side. Keeping his foot on the gas he lifts John over him and puts him in the driver's seat.

                              TERMINATOR
                    Drive for a minute.

                              JOHN
                    Where you going?!

Terminator slams the shattered windshield with the palm of his hand. Held together by the plastic laminate, the windshield flops out of its frame. It flies back over the top of the truck.

191E   Terminator pushes his upper body out over the dashboard and stands up. He turns and aims the M-79 one-handed.
191F   POOM! The grenade misses the T-1000 by less than a foot. It EXPLODES against the front bulkhead of the tanker, almost at the top. Liquid nitrogen pours from the opening, swept back by the 60-mph windstream.

191G   The big-rig swerves as T-1000 regains control. The tanker swings like a pendulum behind the cab.

191H   The pickup accelerates, getting back out in front by a few yards.
Behind it the big-rig is trailing a swirling comet-tail of nitrogen vapor. It is gaining again.

Terminator, still standing, opens the breech and starts to reload.
191I   John cuts across the highway and takes an OFF RAMP.

191J   T-1000 swerves the smoking behemoth across the lanes and down the ramp after them, still accelerating. It is twenty feet behind them and closing when Terminator closes the breech and FIRES.

191K   The grenade hits the front grill and EXPLODES.
The radiator is destroyed, along with half the hood. Steam blasts out, obscuring the whole front of the truck.

191L   The semi rams the back of the pickup again. Spewing smoke and vapor like some demon locomotive, the tractor-trailer pounds into the back of the pickup. Driving it right through the intersection at the bottom of the ramp, and straight toward---

EXT. STEEL MILL

The chase has led them to an area of heavy industry.

192   The GATES are blasted off their hinges as the semi rams the pickup right through them.
Terminator struggles to reload amid the chaos and impacts. He has THREE GRENADES LEFT
on the bandolier.

John isn't even steering. They are just being pushed. There's nothing he can do. They are
rocketing down the broad thoroughfare which leads directly to the MAIN BUILDING of the plant.

Various minor action changes were made in the tanker chase both to simplify the action and address
certain production concerns: Terminator leans out the open driver's door of the pickup rather than
smashing out the windshield and climbing out the dash, since with the windshield missing, the camera could
clearly see the stuntpeople doubling for actors Arnold Schwarzenegger, Linda Hamilton, and Eddie
Furlong; Terminator drops the last grenade out of reach in the bed of the pickup when the tanker rams it, so
he tosses the useless M-79 into the bed and takes his M-16 machine gun, crossing between the vehicles and
unloading the entire magazine through the driver's windshield into the T-1000. He then tosses the machine
gun away and reaches into the tanker's shattered windshield, throwing the steering wheel hard to the left,
intentionally swerving the tanker off the trail of the pickup. These latter two changes avoided the confusion
of keeping track of how many grenades are left and whether they're loaded in the M-79 or not.

192A   Terminator pulls himself onto the roof of the pickup.
He leaps to the bed, takes two powerful strides and--
Leaps onto the semi. He climbs rapidly onto the hood.

192B   And FIRES POINT BLANK THROUGH THE WINDSHIELD.
Right into T-1000's face.
The EXPLOSION blows out all the glass and fills the cab with smoke and fire. Terminator grabs
onto the air-horn as the truck starts to SHUDDER AND

192C   SCREAM. IT IS JACK-KNIFING.
Almost dream-slow the cab begins to swing sideways, until its tires are shrieking over the
pavement. The tractor is smashed back at right-angles to the tanker-trailer which begins to slide
broadside.

192D   The juggernaut bucks and shudders as the tires are smoke sideways across the pavement.
It begins to topple.
Terminator holds on as the side of the cab becomes the top.
With an unholy scream, like the unoiled hubs of Hell, the whole rig slides on its side at 60 mph
toward the steel mill. A sheet of sparks sixty feet wide trails behind it on the pavement.

192E   John sees what's behind him, then snaps around to see the building looming right in front. The
huge rolling doors are partly open.
No choice.
He steers right through them into the mill, as--

192F   Terminator, with one second to go, leaps from the cab--
He flies through the open doors as--
The tanker hits the building and--

193   INT. STEEL MILL / MAIN AISLE

Terminator slams to the floor of the mill and rolls, as--
The tanker-trailer smashes into a massive concrete support at one side of the doors. Thunderous
carnage of twisting metal.

193A   It splits wide open. A river of liquid nitrogen pours out at -230°.

193B   John hits the brakes, sliding out of control. He slows almost to a stop but hits a steel support column head-on. He and Sarah are slammed forward, hard.

193C   Terminator, still clutching the M-79 blooper, rolls and slides across the floor.
He smashes through a railing and slams up against the base of a massive machine.

193D   The semi cab swings about the trailer wreckage, into the building, and shudders to a stop. Liquid nitrogen sprays over the cab, flooding out around it in a HISSING WAVEFRONT OF ULTRACOLD.
Freezing vapor swirls everywhere, obscuring the wreck.

193E   TERMINATOR lies still. A beat. Then he rolls weakly, rising on one elbow to survey the scene.

193F   IN THE WRECKED PICKUP, John stirs. He is stunned, and blood runs from his nose. Dazed, he realizes he is in a steel mill. There are sirens, and he can see men running... shouting. He turns and sees what they are running from...

193G   The wall of nitrogen vapor spreads from the demolished tanker. It is a strange vista of fire and ice. The huge SMELTERS pour out orange light and fire from the sides of the huge gallery, while the freezing vapor rolls down the center.

193H   TIGHT ON THE WRECK. A billowing gray cloud. Deep inside, the shape of the cab is visible. A FIGURE emerges, pulling itself out. It drops to the floor. The hissing, boiling river of liquid nitrogen flows around its feet.

194   The T-1000 staggers, moving slowly, painfully. It has finally been affected by something. Its feet are freezing to the ground as it walks...

194A   CLINK! One of its feet breaks off at a glassy ankle. It stumbles forward, and--
194B   Its other foot snaps off. As it catches its balance on the stump of its other ankle, the whole lower
194C   leg shatters at the impact. It topples forward to its knees.
Catches itself on one hand. Liquid nitrogen flows around the hand.

Now the hand is stuck to the pavement.
194D   The T-1000 pulls and... CLINK! The hand snaps off at the wrist.
It looks stupidly at the glassy stump of a wrist. For the first time we see an expression on its face we know to be a true one...
The expression is pain. Agony. Its mouth opens in a soundless scream as the hoar-frost races up its legs, across its body.
194E   And that's the position it freezes in.
It has become a statue, kneeling in the frozen vapor, that surprised look of agony frozen on its face.

The liquid nitrogen stops flowing and begins to evaporate.
194F   Terminator, just beyond the boundary of the cold, can see the T-1000 clearly.
He draws his .45 and aims.

TERMINATOR
Hasta la vista, baby.

194G   K-POW! The single shot blows the T-1000 into a million diamonds spraying up into the air. They shimmer across the ground for twenty feet in all directions.
Terminator lowers the gun, satisfied.
He looks like he needs a vacation.

195   JOHN AND SARAH have seen it from the pickup. She is in bad shape.
Conscious but very weak. He tries the door. It's jammed. He kicks it open.

JOHN
Okay, Mom, we gotta get out now, come on. That's it.

He helps her slide down from the seat of the truck. Her knees give way. John has to take a lot of her weight. He reaches in and picks up the riot gun off the seat. They hobble toward--

195A   TERMINATOR. On his knees, he looks into the dissipating cloud of vapor.
The heat of the furnaces has evaporated all the liquid nitrogen.

196   INSERT, TIGHT ON THE FLOOR-- the T-1000 shards are melting, liquefying.
Hundreds of drops of mercury, spattered across the floor. Orange light of the enormous blast-furnaces dances on liquid metal.

197   TERMINATOR struggles to rise. One arm is shattered, the hand smashed and nearly useless.
And some leg-servos are damaged. He can barely stand. John and Sarah arrive.

TERMINATOR
We don't have much time.

JOHN
What?

Terminator points. John and Sarah watch as--

198   INSERT, T-1000 DROPLETS are creeping together. Fusing into larger blobs.
These pools shiver and run together, soon forming a central mass.

199   ON JOHN AND SARAH, realizing it's not over.

JOHN
Come on! Let's go!

Terminator gets one of Sarah's arms over his shoulder and they go.
BEHIND THEM, something is moving.

200   A HEAD is forming up out of a pool of mercury. It rises, as shoulders form, hunching up from the liquid mass. Half-formed, it turns to look straight at them.

John looks back in new terror as--

The T-1000 rises to man-height. It is still the mercury form, but its features are forming rapidly.
It takes its first step after them.
Sarah stumbles and they pull her up.

201   Terminator himself has a pronounced limp, dragging one leg with a shattered ankle joint. John's the one pulling, straining, driving them forward. They round a corner into--

202   INT. AISLE BETWEEN FURNACES

It is a maze of monstrous machinery. The heat is tremendous.
The air shivers with a pounding roar.
Sarah cries out in pain and stumbles again.

JOHN
Come on, Mom, you can do it! Come on!!

They drag her up, and stagger on. Her leg is bathed in blood and she is deathly pale. He looks back.

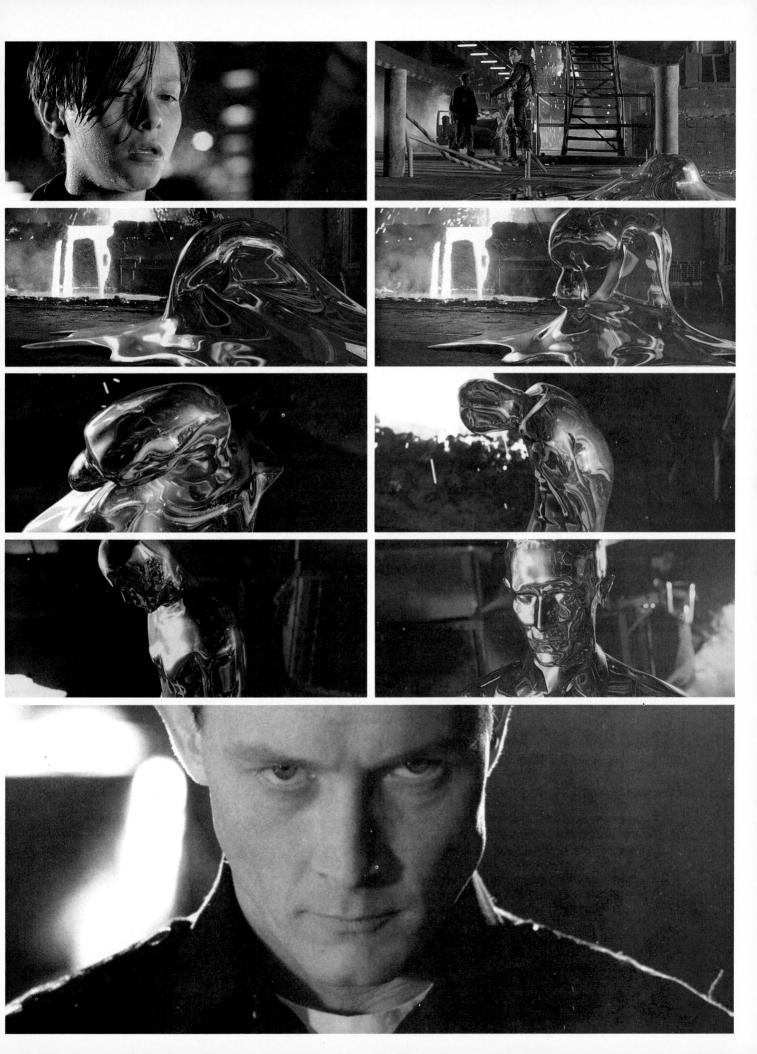

203   INT. MAIN GALLERY

The T-1000 steps INTO FRAME. Fully formed. The hell-fire light glints on its impassive cop face. It walks forward.   At first it seems unaffected by its crystallization but--

203A   ANGLE ON ITS HAND as it touches a railing in passing. The railing is covered with O.S.H.A. yellow-and-black safety tape.
The hand turns yellow and black, the color fading to normal by about the elbow. It rips the hand from the railing with difficulty. There is a sound like adhesive tape ripping off a surface.

203B   The T-1000 looks at its yellow-and-black striped hand. It wills the hand back to normal. We see ripples of "static" or system noise moving subtly over the surface of its body. It's starting to "glitch".

203C   TRACKING WITH THE T-1000'S FEET. With each step, the pattern of the tile floor "invades" its lower legs. Fades as the foot is lifted. Returns as it is set down. The foot is trying to meld with the floor. The chameleonic function is out of control.
The T-1000 is losing it. It moves forward, searching. It rounds the corner, entering the aisle between the furnaces.

Although technically superb and conceptually intriguing, all the featured shots of T-1000 glitching --of which there were three-- were completed but omitted for length, pacing, and narrative reasons. The first glitch shot, "OSHA hand," interrupted the pace of the chase, stopping it dead in its tracks as T-1000 dealt with the glitch; the second shot, of its feet sucking up the floor pattern (shot as metal diamondplate), was so bizarre an image that it was hard to grasp the concept, even seeing it; and the third shot, of a chrome glitch line crossing T-1000's face, was again difficult to understand. After having seen T-1000 do amazing transformations, it became increasingly tough to convey the idea that now its spontaneous morphs are malfunctions; to eliminate confusion and to preserve the suspenseful pacing of the sequence, the glitch idea was dropped. The only surviving hint of it is in the shot where T-1000, having pinned Terminator's arm in the chain drive gear, turns to look for John as a chrome glitch wipes across its face.

204   INT. AISLE

Terminator sees the SILHOUETTE closing on them through the smoky gloom. The T-1000 breaks into a loping run when it sees them.
Terminator turns Sarah over to John.

                    TERMINATOR
            Keep going.

John shakes his head no. The T-1000 is almost on them.

                    TERMINATOR
        RUN!

In the final film, Terminator stays back to fight T-1000 as John and Sarah flee deeper into the steel mill maze, not hanging around to watch the fight as scripted. John does not want to leave Terminator ("No, we gotta stick together!") until Terminator demands that he run ("Go! NOW!"). Not only is narrative logic preserved --it makes more sense for them to split up-- but the sense of Terminator's human character is shown in that he first suggests to John to leave, then orders him to do so. A TermoVision shot was also added here to show that Terminator is unable to acquire T-1000 with his infrared vision due to the heat of the billowing steam all around, thus giving T-1000 a chance to sneak up on him. In the fight, Terminator's M-79, already loaded, is knocked away in the general direction of the chain drive to set up its location where Terminator finds it later in the sequence. These small revisions not only help to simplify and clarify the action and suspense, but also to avoid relying on questionable logic and coincidence at pivotal points in the story.

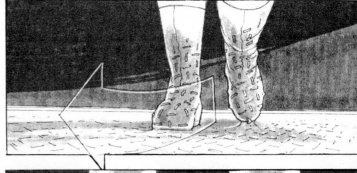

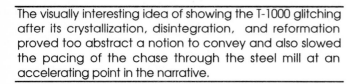

The visually interesting idea of showing the T-1000 glitching after its crystallization, disintegration, and reformation proved too abstract a notion to convey and also slowed the pacing of the chase through the steel mill at an accelerating point in the narrative.

One manifestation of the T-1000's malfunctoning chameleonic abilities is the random glitching on its surface, where the texture-mapping functions that maintain its colored surfaces suffer the T-1000 equivalent of video dropout, resulting in scan lines of chrome moving across its features.

TARGET NOT ACQUIRED
SCAN MODE 34303
73477
23922
56435
34593

SEARCH MODE

CAUTION
HEARING
PROTECTION
IN THIS

CAUTION
HEARING
PROTECTION
IN THIS

John runs, dragging, half-carrying Sarah as best he can.
She can barely stay conscious. Half-running, delirious, she stumbles and drops to her knees.
John pulls but she can't rise.

> JOHN
> (crying, shouting)
> Come on, you gotta try... please, Mom. Get up!

John looks back to see--

204A   TERMINATOR trying to load the M-79. With his shattered hand, he can barely maneuver his last grenade into the breech.
T-1000 smacks the weapon out of his hands. It clatters to the floor.

The grenade spins across the floor, rolling under some machinery.
Terminator lunges, slamming the T-1000 against a wall with all his weight. The battle is joined.

204B   JOHN AND SARAH have reached the back of the aisle. It is a cul-de-sac, blocked on the end by the base of an IMMENSE SMELTER CRUCIBLE. They turn to watch the titans battle in silhouette, backlit by the molten sparks falling from the furnaces above. The battle which will decide their fate.

204C   Terminator grabs the T-1000 and hurls it with awesome force against the opposite wall of the narrow alley. In less time than it would take to turn, the
204D   T-1000 morphs through itself, from front to back... face emerging from the back of its head.
204E   It comes off the wall straight at Terminator, who smashes his good fist into its face. The pile-driver blow buries Terminator's fist almost to the elbow.

204F   But the T-1000's head morphs in a split-second into a hand which grips Terminator's wrist, and the head "emerges" somewhere else, the geometry shifting faster than we can follow.
204G   The T-1000 slams Terminator into a large machine, jamming his arm into the moving works. A massive sliding bar SCISSORS HIS ARM, smashing it into junk at the elbow, pinning him in the machine.

Terminator strains against the machine pinning him. We hear his servos whining with overload. The T-1000 turns and lopes toward Sarah and John.

Sarah screams and hurls John into a gap between the machines. He falls into a maze of pipes and girders.

In the final film, Sarah lowers John down a chainfall and onto a conveyor belt, which carries him away into the bowels of the mill as Sarah prepares to take a stand against the approaching T-1000. John is carried away against his will, calling for Sarah to join him. T-1000 notes John's exit and prepares to use Sarah as a hostage to force John to come back. Meanwhile, Terminator frees himself from the chain drive gear more heroically by using the steel bar to wrench his crushed arm off at the elbow.

---

205   INT. MAZE OF MACHINES

JOHN turns to see her in the entrance of the narrow gap. She could follow him but she doesn't.
SUDDENLY a dark mass moves toward him. John gasps as a huge steel counterweight, driven by a chain 6 inches thick, slides toward him. He rolls out of its way. When he looks back, he cannot see the opening.

> JOHN
> Mom! MOMMM!!

206   INT. AISLE BETWEEN FURNACES

TERMINATOR strains to reach a 6-foot steel bar lying near him. Steel workers use them to move the red-hot ingots around. He gets hold of the end and uses it as a lever. With titanic effort he spreads the massive components which are holding him, and withdraws his arm, which is severed at the elbow. Dangling junk hangs from the crushed joint.

207   SARAH has lost sight of John. It is as much of a goodbye as they will have.
She turns as the T-1000 closes on her. She is half-slumped against the sooty machines, looking barely conscious. She struggles to load a shell into the empty weapon. At the last instant she whips up the RIOT GUN and FIRES.

A207   T-1000's face is blown open, but quickly reforms as it closes on her. She fumbles to get another shell into the magazine but--
A208   THUNK! A steel needle slams through her shoulder, pinning her.
The polymorphic killer cocks back its other hand. The index finger extends as a gleaming needle, toward her eye...

T-1000
Call to John. Now.

Being a somewhat more sadistic terminator ("I know this hurts..."), T-1000 patiently toys with Sarah rather than simply killing her and imitating her form at this point; the main reason for this is of course dramatic --to draw out the moment of suspense and to give Terminator time to come to her rescue, which is part of his burgeoning humanity: his protection of John now fully extends to those whom John loves as well.

207C   WHAM!! SOMETHING whistles down on the T-1000 with such force that it cleaves its head and body in two down to the navel. The 6-foot steel bar is imbedded in its body. Terminator hurls the killer off Sarah.

207D   The T-1000 pulls the steel shaft out of itself and attacks him with fury.
Swinging again and again. Hammering Terminator back. Terminator falls back against the wall.

Behind the T-1000 is an enormous I-beam, hanging from two chains. It is used to lift ingots into the smelters, and it runs on a linear track.
207E   The T-1000 grabs the I-beam and rolls it down the track. Straight at Terminator. The two-ton girder smashes into his chest, crushing the armor.
The T-1000 pulls the I-beam back, and then heaves it forward again. Terminator turns and takes the second blow on the shoulder. We hear metal crush and break inside him. He sags, turning to grip the wall...
The third blow slams into his back, smashing his spine and pelvis. We hear servos ratcheting and failing. He drops to his knees, crucified on a wall of machinery.
The fourth blow is centered between his shoulder blades. Sound of crushing metal. His skull is partially caved in.
He slides to the floor.

207F   ON THE T-1000, emotionless as it walks forward.

207G   TERMINATOR is a pathetic shape on the floor. He is trying to crawl, feebly.
Dragging his malfunctioning legs behind the crushed spine. His arm stump screeches on the tile floor as he inches himself forward. His exposed machine eye burns red with determination.

We see his prize. He has the M-79, with the breech still open, cradled in the crook of his ruined arm. His good hand, the exposed steel one, is reaching for the last grenade, which is visible under the skirt of the massive smelter base. His metal fingers reach out for it as--

207H   The T-1000 raises the heavy steel bar over his head and stabs it down with unbelievable force. It punches into Terminator's back, through a gap in the shattered armor. The T-1000 levers it back and forth, widening the hole. Then it raises the pointed bar again and slams it down.
It punches right through. Emerging from Terminator's chest.
And into the floor. He is pinioned. The cyborg sags face down and stops moving. The light goes out of his eye.

In the film, it is in this fight scene that Terminator receives the majority of his damage, including the exposure of his right eye servo and crushing of his skull and chest. Again, since the M-79 was established earlier as having been knocked in this direction, lost but already loaded, Terminator has a logical goal in trying to reach it. The substitution of whole gun for grenade clarifies the action. Most of the steel mill upper levels are floored with steel grating rather than tile as scripted, not only for logic but also because it allowed for both camera angles and interesting lighting to be set up from underneath the floor. The electrical discharge in the shots of Terminator being speared through the chest echo the final destruction of the terminator in the first film and is meant to make the audience believe that Terminator --his power cells ruptured and discharged-- is out of commission permanently.

In the film, there is an additional scene establishing the wounded Sarah painfully reloading her shotgun that comes right after Terminator is "terminated"; this short scene, intercut with shots of John moving furtively through the mill machinery, not only shows her heroic determination but also logically places her as John's protector now that Terminator seems dead.

CUT TO:

208   INT. MAZE OF MACHINERY

John scuttles like a rat through the guts of the smelter. Above him, vast machines churn untended.
He hears a voice... SARAH'S.
Calling low and urgent to him.

SARAH
John? John? Can you hear me? Where are you?

208A   He crawls out of the shadows.
Onto a landing next to one of the SMELTER CRUCIBLES. Molten steel glows bright orange in the crucible of the furnace. Heat shimmers the air, giving everything a hallucinatory quality.

John sees Sarah nearby, limping toward him. She can barely move, her leg bathed in blood. He runs toward her.

SARAH
(gasping)
Help me, honey...

TIGHT ON SARAH, her stoic face, as she hobbles forward, reaching out to him. <u>Something</u> rises behind her, OUT OF FOCUS.

209   ANOTHER, IDENTICAL, SARAH... but this one has a shotgun.
Aimed right at us.

209A   JOHN freezes. Which is which? He looks down. The first Sarah's feet are melding with the floor, sucking and fusing with the tiles as she walks. They have the color and pattern of the tiles up to the knee.

SARAH
<u>John, get out of the way!!</u>

ALTERNATE POWER

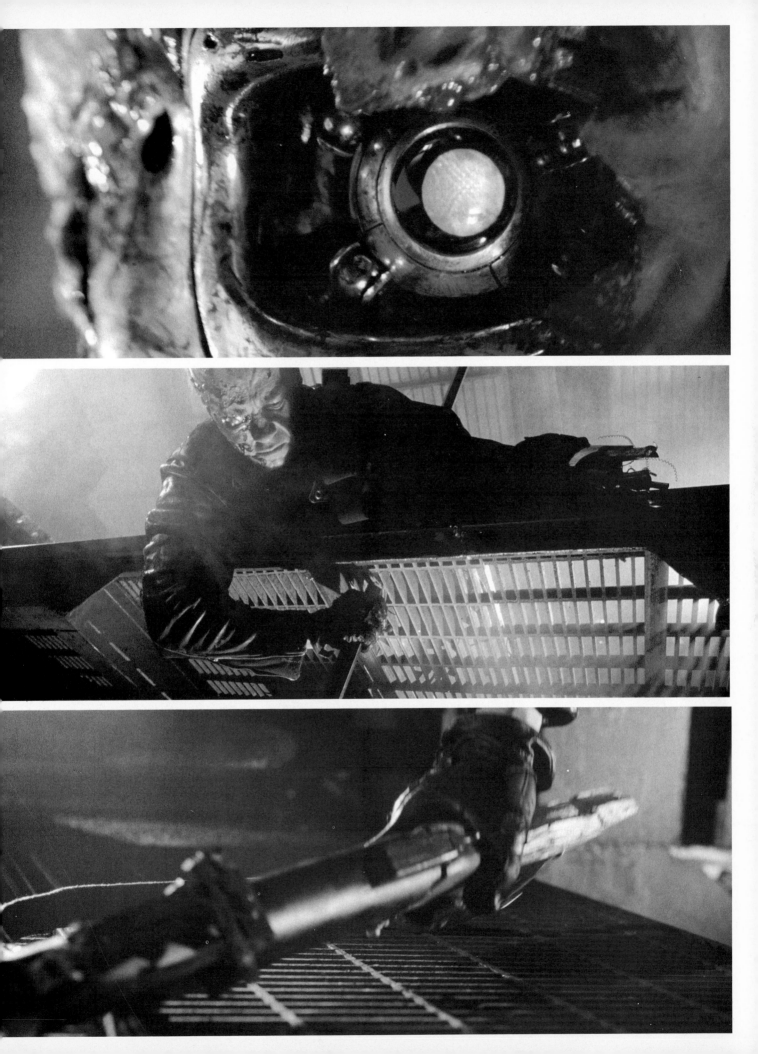

JOHN
(screaming)
SHOOT!!!!

With the omission of the T-1000 glitching motif in the earlier steel mill scenes, the pivotal moment when John recognizes which Sarah is which by seeing one of the Sarah's feet melding with the floor became both confusing and unnecessary and was cut from the film. Having seen Sarah with the shotgun in a previous scene, the audience is already clued in on which Sarah is which, and John figures it out because he knows T-1000 wouldn't hesitate to shoot at *him* first, rather than yelling for him to get out of the way. Again, the "fusefeet" effect was filmed with the faux Sarah's feet melding with the steel grating floor rather than tile as scripted.

209B   John dives aside. The Sarah-form spins, changing into you-know-who. Sarah starts unloading the shotgun into it. BOOM! It staggers back. K-CHAK. She chambers another round. BOOM! It staggers again. K-CHAK. BOOM! And again. And again.

209C   The T-1000 is blown back a step and Sarah advances a step with each shot. The craters in the T-1000's body "heal" slowly. Its power is waning. She FIRES again. And again. Her eyes blazing with feral intensity. She walks it back, right to the edge of the pit of MOLTEN STEEL.

K-CHAK... CLICK. She's empty. The T-1000 is right at the edge. In a second it will recover its composure, as its crater hits close slowly. She has failed. Now it will kill them both.
Except...

210   CLOSEUP TERMINATOR, as the chain drive brings it into view.
Half human flesh, half chrome skull.
His red eye gazes right at us as he--
FIRES.

In the final film, Terminator is seen rerouting his internal power (via another TermoVision POV shot) and coming back online, pulling out the steel bar that pins him to the floor and retrieving the loaded M-79. In the script, the narrative omission was intended to create greater suspense after Sarah runs out of ammunition on the verge of blowing T-1000 into the molten steel pit, but it was decided to show Terminator's return to life rather than simply implying it not only to avoid any question of *deux ex machina* but to reiterate the heroic dichotomy of Terminator's character, part man and part machine. This machine cannot be "killed," and also has learned human loyalty in his devotion to John; the unstoppable killer has become the unstoppable savior.

210A   The T-1000 takes the round in the belly. The grenade EXPLODES inside its body. A huge hole is blown clean through it, and it is ripped open and peeled back, half inside-out. It topples into the molten steel and--

211   The T-1000's head and upper body reappear above the molten steel.
It is screaming. A terrifying, inhuman siren of a scream.
It is changing, morphing, transforming into anything and everything it's ever been so rapidly the eye can barely follow...
We catch a glimpse of Janelle Voight checkered with linoleum tile colors, Lewis the Guard with knives exploding from his face, other faces, switching at a stroboscopic rate now... a face every two frames until they merge into one face--

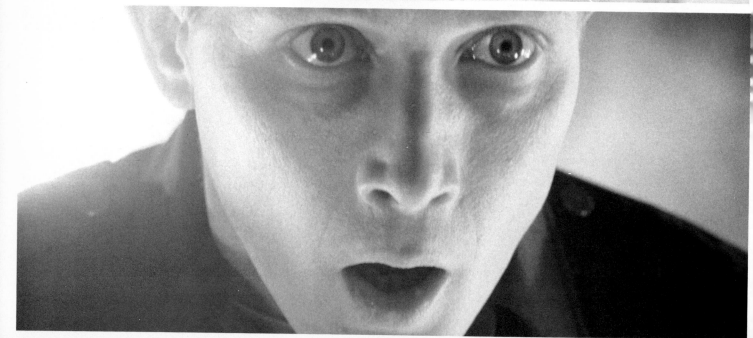

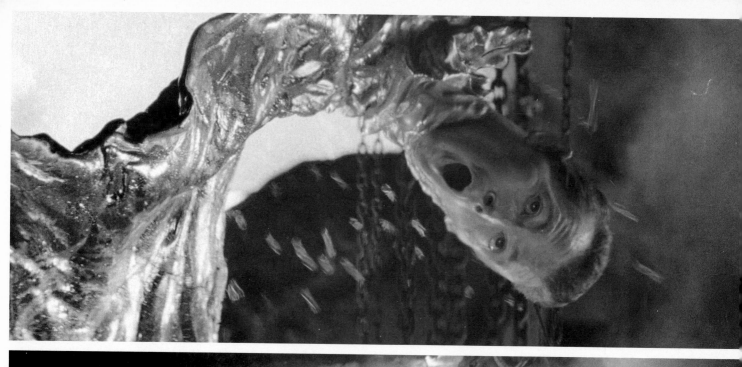

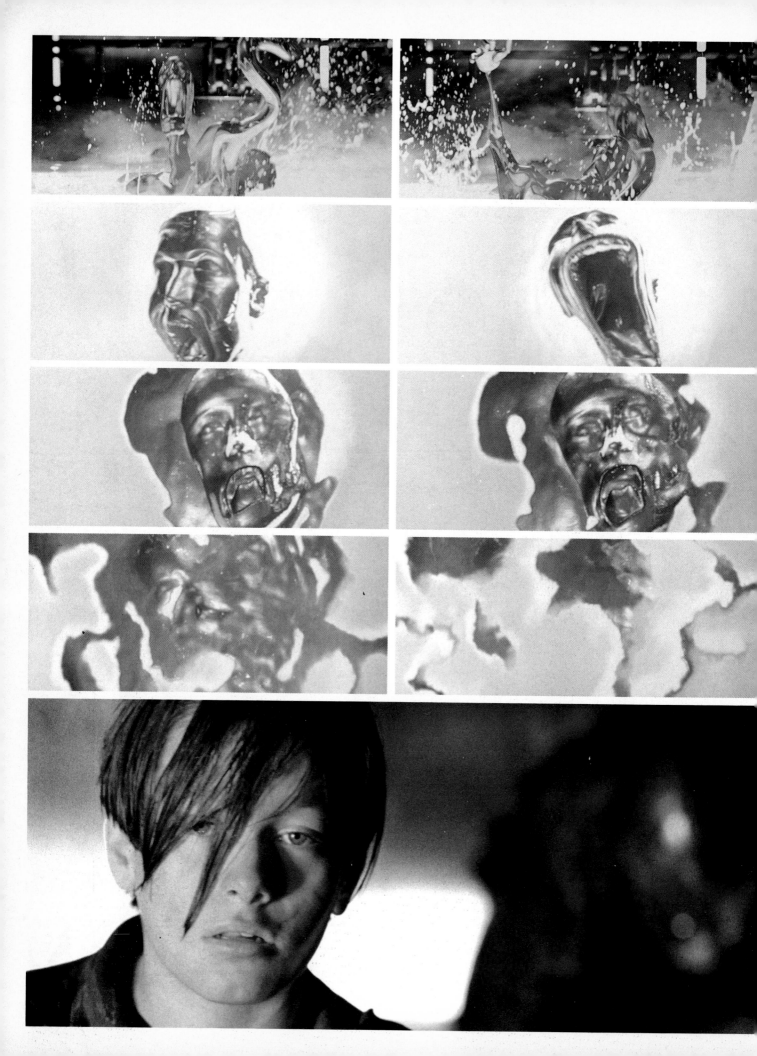

The T-1000 screams and slips beneath the surface of the molten steel. We see liquid silver running in dissipating whorls over the superheated surface... until it vanishes, swirling into nothing.

In the finished film, the destruction of the T-1000 is a simpler but bolder sequence as the disintegrating polymorph only manages to imitate a few of its previously sampled forms before it loses the ability to form coherent shapes. In light of production considerations (such as how in the world do we do this sequence? Submerging the actors in some form of liquid? Puppets? Bluescreen?) and the computer graphics costs of realizing the sequence, the original intention of showing a kinetic, stroboscopic demise proved both unfeasible and undesirable. A concern, too, was the fact that the faster the T-1000 morphed from character to character, the more it looked like an optical dissolve; the greatest difficulty lay in creating an impressive change that did *not* simply look like an optical effect. In the end, fewer and more definitive transformations were used, from T-1000 cop to Janelle with blade arm, to Lewis the Guard, to a chrome motorcycle cop, to a chrome figure with hooks and blades, to a melting, softened chrome figure (referred to by the effects team as "Giacometti spaghetti"), to the final shot of it screaming inside out before dissipating into the molten steel. The low choir music used in this scene also echoes the finality of the music used during the destruction of the terminator in the first film.

---

212   JOHN runs to Sarah. She stands staring into the pit. The empty shotgun slips from her fingers. Clatters to the floor. He sees that she's okay and he runs to the fallen Terminator.

212A   The crippled cyborg is trying to rise. Its servos whine and stutter. It pathetically lifts itself to a kneeling position, collapses... tries again.
John lifts for all he's worth. Sarah joins them, helping.
They help the crippled machine get on its feet. It can barely stand.

                    TERMINATOR
            I need a vacation.

They walk to the edge of the pit. Terminator looks down and sees that it is over.

                    JOHN
                (to Terminator)
            Is it dead?

                    TERMINATOR
            Terminated.

John unzips Sarah's backpack and takes out the hand of the first terminator.

                    JOHN
            Will it melt in there?

                    TERMINATOR
            Yes. Throw it in.

He does. It sinks in the lava. Vanishes.

                    TERMINATOR
            And the chip.

John takes it out of his pocket. Looks at it. Tosses it into the smelter.

                    SARAH
            It's finally over.

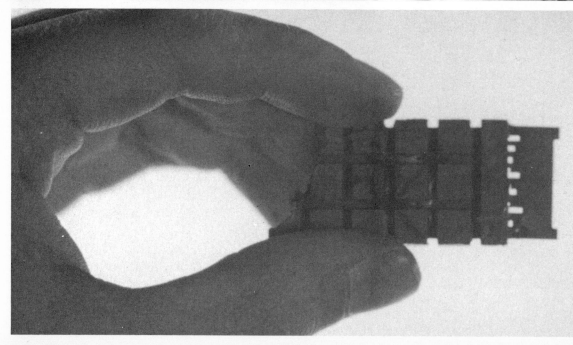

                    TERMINATOR
No. There is another chip.

He touches a metal finger to the side of his head.

                    TERMINATOR
And it must be destroyed also.

John suddenly understands what he means.
Terminator looks at Sarah. They both know what must be done.
John shakes his head.

                    JOHN
No!

                    TERMINATOR
I'm sorry, John.

                    JOHN
No, no no!! It'll be okay. Stay with us!

                    TERMINATOR
I have to go away, John.

                    JOHN
Don't do it. Please... don't go--

Tears are streaming down his face.

TIGHT CLOSEUP TERMINATOR, turning toward John.
The human side of his face is in shadow, so we see mostly the chrome skull and the red eye.

                    TERMINATOR
It must end here... *or I am the future.*

                    JOHN
I order you not to!

Terminator puts his hand on John's shoulder. He moves slightly and the human side of his face
comes into the light.
He reaches toward John's face. His metal finger touches the tear trickling down his cheek.

                    TERMINATOR
I know now why you cry. But it is something I can never do.
                         (to both of them)
Goodbye.

Sarah looks at Terminator. Reaches out her hand to shake his.
They lock eyes. Warriors. Comrades.

                    SARAH
Are you afraid?

                    TERMINATOR
Yes.

He turns and steps off the edge.

213 They watch him sink into the lava.

He disappears... the metal hand sinking last... at the last second it forms into a fist with the thumb extended... *a final thumbs up*.

Then it is gone.

In the film, Terminator is lowered into the molten steel on a motorized chainfall by Sarah in order to draw out the moment and play a more dramatic descent than simply jumping in, as scripted. To explain the rationale for drawing out the scene narratively, a line was added in post-production for Terminator: "I cannot self-terminate. You must lower me into the steel." Other non-essential bits of dialogue, though filmed, were cut from the scene not only to keep the emotional focus of the scene on John and Terminator's relationship, but to address other considerations: Terminator's line "...I am the future" with his exposed chrome dramatically lit loses much of its impact due to the fact that the pivotal half-face look has already been established and seen for the last few scenes, and thus a big emphasis on it seems somewhat heavy-handed; and Sarah's question "Are you afraid?" no longer has any context after the earlier weapons cache scene in which John and Terminator discuss fear was omitted. Also added was a final TermoVision shot of Terminator's POV as he "dies," with glitching read image of readouts collapsing to nothingness like a television set, to counterpoint with a technological death the emotion of the "human" one.

---

214 HOLD ON JOHN AND SARAH, watching through the heat ripples as we--

DISSOLVE TO:

215 THE SUN, PURE IN A CLOUDLESS SKY.

Tilting down reveals that we are in a park, very green. People are casually dressed, having fun. Cycling, reading... children are playing in a playground.

Beyond the line of trees we see the skyline of Washington, D.C., with the Capital Building and the Washington Monument. The skyline is subtly changed, with a lot of new buildings, advanced high-rises.

A CARD APPEARS.

July 11, 2029

WE BOOM DOWN AND TRACK LATERALLY through a playground in the foreground. Children swinging on swings. Sliding down slides. Timeless things that 4 decades of technical advancement will not change. As we track we hear:

> SARAH (V.O.)
> *August 29th 1997 came and went. Nothing much happened.*
> *Michael Jackson turned forty. There was no Judgment Day.*
> *People went to work as they always do, laughed, complained,*
> *watched TV, made love.*

We pass a jungle gym, neither melted nor burned, but full of kids swinging and yelling raucously. Past it we drop down to see a boy pumping the pedals of a tricycle.

> SARAH (V.O.)
> *I wanted to run down the street yelling... to grab them all and*
> *say "Every day from this day on is a gift. Use it well!" Instead*
> *I got drunk.*

STILL TRACKING we come to rest on an elderly woman seated on a bench. It is SARAH, now 64 years old. The world has aged her, but she seems at peace in this moment. She speaks into a microcassette recorder.

The Future Coda sequence begins with a tilt-down from the sun to establi[sh] a park in Washington D.C. of 2029. The futuristic buildings were designe[d] by artist Steve Burg and incorporated into the skyline in a matte paintin[g] by Mike Pangrazio of Matte World.

SARAH (V.O.)
*That was thirty years ago. But the dark future which never
came still exists for me, and it always will, like the traces of a
dream lingering in the morning light. And the war against the
machines goes on. Or, to be more precise, the war against those
who build the wrong machines.*

There is a man in his forties playing with two small children nearby. He turns. It is John Connor. Though he has the same stern features in adulthood, there is no eye-patch, no scarring. He is far from the haggard man of grim destiny we saw in the world that might have been. But there is still penetrating intelligence, even wisdom, in his eyes.

SARAH (V.O.)
*John fights the war differently than it was foretold. Here, on the
battlefield of the Senate, the weapons are common sense... and
hope.*

A FOUR-YEAR-OLD GIRL runs to her to have her shoelace tied.

GIRL
Tie me, grandma.

Grandma Sarah smiles. It is the only time we have seen her smile so far. She bends as the little girl puts her foot up on the bench. She ties as we hear:

SARAH (V.O.)
*The luxury of hope was given to me by the Terminator. Because
if a machine can learn the value of human life... maybe we can
too.*

Sarah ruffles the kid's hair as she runs off to play with her dad.

FADE OUT

In the released film, the image of Sarah and John at the steel mill dissolves to a shot traveling down a dark highway at night, with a final voiceover from Sarah: "The unknown future rolls toward us. I face it for the first time with a sense of hope, because if a machine, a terminator, can learn the value of human life, maybe we can, too." The original Future Coda ending was filmed and completed, but omitted for a variety of reasons: on an emotional level, the prospect of a definitive, happy ending felt somewhat out of context; on a visual level, the sunny park in Washington and the futuristic buildings felt again out of place; on a pseudo-narrative level, this ending effectively negated the storylines of both the first film and the first sequence in the second, raising to question the "grandfather paradox" of time-travel stories without the proper time to address it; and on a perceptual level of the characters, it was difficult to accept Sarah as a contented old observer after seeing her throughout the film as an intense, athletic heroine. (And then there was the small matter of how a juvenile deliquent like John, linked to a massive spree of destruction at age ten, could become a Senator...) The decision to maintain a sense of narrative ambiguity --to leave the future open-ended-- felt more in keeping with the tone of the film. Refer to Jim Cameron's introduction for more detail on the cutting of this scene.

"The unknown future rolls
toward us. I face it for the
first time with a sense of
hope, because if a machine,
a terminator, can learn the
value of human life, maybe
we can, too."

TERMINATOR 2
JUDGMENT DAY

Appendix of
Omitted Sequences

EXT. CITY RUINS - DAY

Same spot as the last shot, but now it is a frozen landscape in Hell. The cars are stopped in rusted rows, still bumper to bumper. The skyline of buildings beyond has been shattered by some unimaginable force like a row of kicked-down sandcastles. The sky glowers, dark as iron.

A freezing wind blows through the desolation, keening with the sound of ten million dead souls. It scurries the snow into drifts, stark white against the charred rubble. Fire and ice. The image is without color... lifeless as the moon. A TITLE CARD FADES IN:

LOS ANGELES, AUGUST 11, 2029

ANGLE ON a heap of fire-blackened bones. Skulls identify them as human. WE BEGIN TO TRACK, revealing beyond the mound a vast tundra of bones and shattered concrete. Skulls like eyeless sentinels. The rush hour crowds burned down in their tracks.
We hear a MAN'S VOICE, gentle, though rich in authority, and tempered by the pain of watching a world die.

> MAN (V.O.)
> *It all came down on a Tuesday in September of '99.*
> *Pretty normal day, except for the end of the world part.*
> *Somehow, I don't remember how, we started calling it*
> *Judgment Day. I was in Argentina that particular*
> *Tuesday. A good place to be, considering everything*
> *alive north of the equator stopped being alive....*

WE DISSOLVE TO a playground... where intense heat has half-melted the jungle gym, the blast has warped the swing set, the merry-go-round has sagged in the firestorm. Small skulls look accusingly from the snow-drifts. WE HEAR the distant echo of children's voices... playing and laughing in the sun. A silly, sing-songy rhyme as WE TRACK SLOWLY over seared asphalt where the faint hieroglyphs of hopscotch lines are still visible.

> MAN (V.O.)
> *Afterward it got cold. Real cold. Nuclear winter they*
> *called it. The few that survived, starved...*

CAMERA comes to rest on a burnt and rusted tricycle... next to the tiny skull of its owner. A metal foot crushes the skull like china.

> MAN (V.O.)
> *The few that survived <u>that</u> saw the Machines rise up...*
> *machines of many types but with one purpose... to hunt*
> *us down and kill us all like a bunch of cockroaches....*

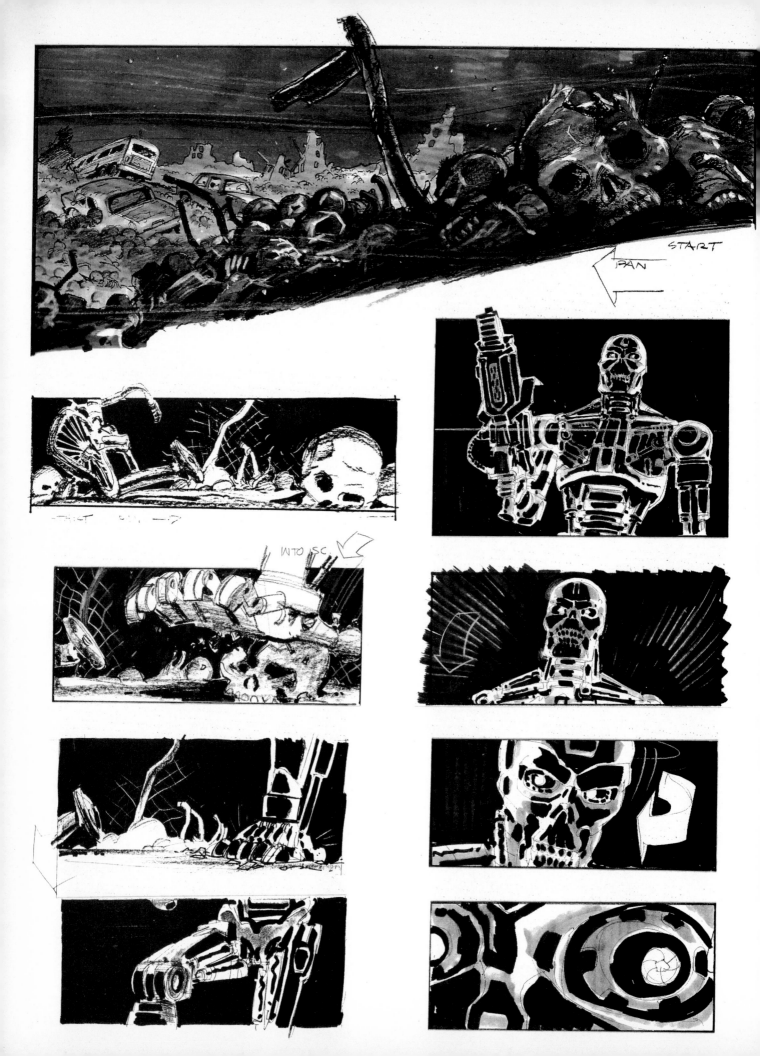

TILT UP, revealing a humanoid machine holding a massive battle rifle. It looks like a hydraulically-actuated CHROME SKELETON. A high-tech Death figure. It is a combat chassis, the underlying component, or endoskeleton, of a Series 800 terminator. An anti-personnel weapon controlled by Skynet, a computer which is threatening the human survivors of the war with final extinction.

The endoskeleton's glowing red eyes compassionlessly sweep the dead terrain, hunting. Then suddenly snap toward CAMERA.

ENDOSKELETON POV (DIGITIZED) as it tracks a RUNNING FIGURE across the desolate landscape. Through these eyes we see the world as a computer-generated image. Symbols and graphics rapidly appear on the center display as the machine acquires its target.

THE ENDOSKELETON swiftly raises its rifle, a phased-plasma-pulse energy weapon. Fires. A compact burst flashes from the barrel.

THE FIGURE, a young boy in rags, is centerpunched by the deadly round. He sprawls to a smoking heap on the blackened sludge.

ANOTHER FIGURE, a guerrilla soldier hefting a battered RPG rocket launcher, suddenly rises behind the endoskeleton.

THE ENDOSKELETON turns, too late. The rocket vaporizes the top half of it. Its bottom half takes a few uncertain steps, then topples to the earth.

> MAN (V.O.)
> *Our stubbornness makes no sense to their machine*
> *minds. We fight when logic tells us we are beaten. But*
> *we have a saying... it's not over 'till its over. It keeps us*
> *going. The war against the Machines is in its thirty -*
> *first year...*

The figure quickly takes cover at the approaching SOUND of ROARING TURBINES. A shadow blackens the sky as a formation of flying HK (Hunter-Killer) patrol machines passes overhead.
PAN WITH THEM toward the jagged horizon, beyond which we see flashes, and hear the distant thunder of a pitched battle in progress.

CUT TO:

EXT. BATTLEFIELD - DAY

THE BATTLE. Human troops in desperate combat with the Machines for possession of the dead Earth. The humans are a ragtag guerrilla army, made up mostly of troops from Southern Hemisphere countries... Africans, South Americans, Australians. The survivors of the nuclear war between the Northern Hemisphere super-powers. This is the reality of the post-Apocalyptic world. North of the equator we all die.

We hear radio chatter in Spanish, interspersed with Swahili and other African languages. The occasional Aussie unit can be heard.
The humans use RPG launchers, plasma-pulse battle rifles, and home-built armored personnel carriers.

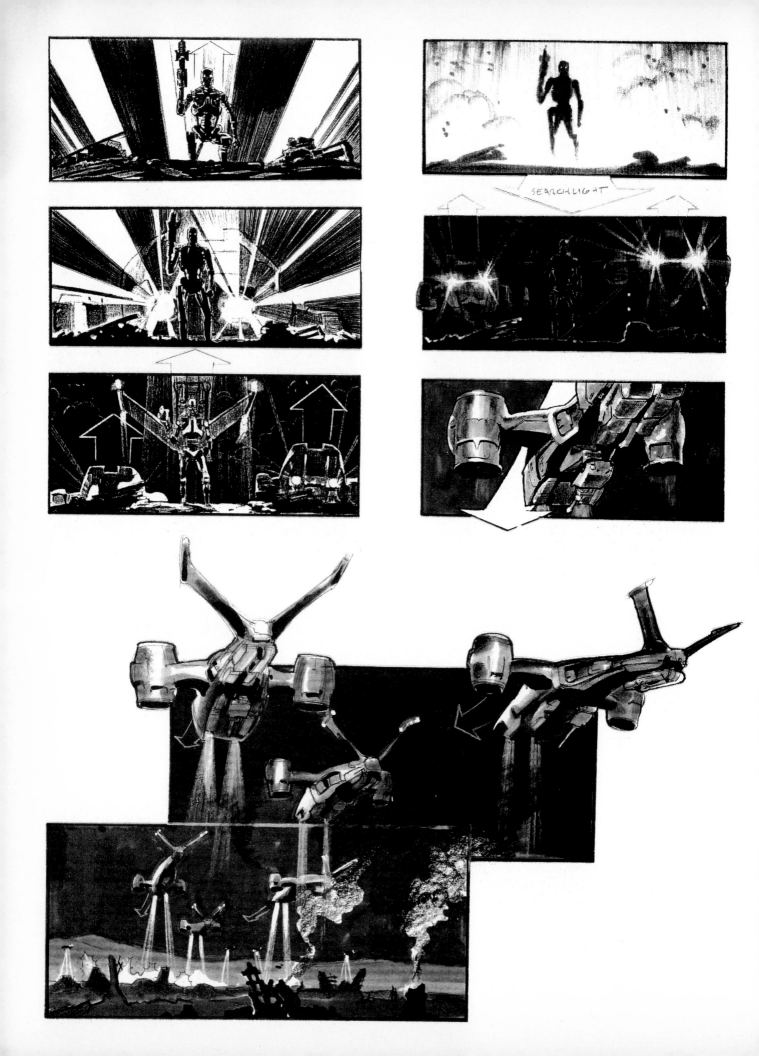

SEARCHLIGHT

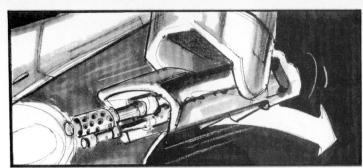

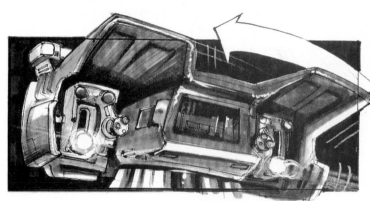

STEVE
BURG
4·90

THE LAST ARMY – LOS ANGELES, 2029

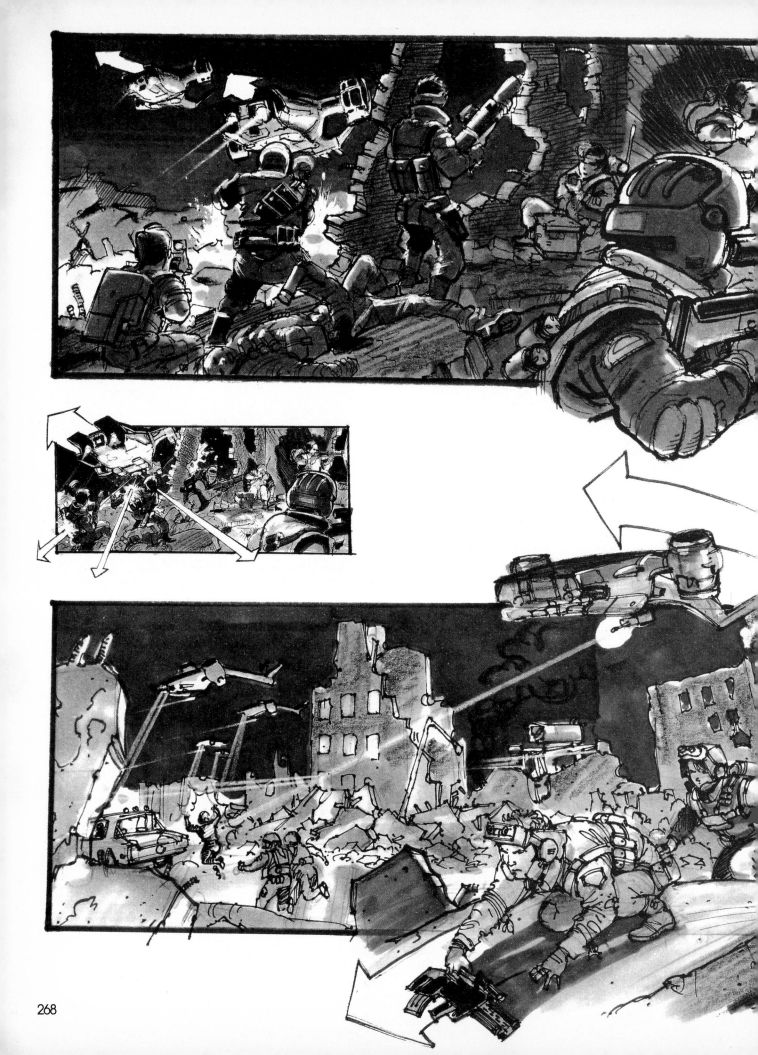

268

'SILVER FISH LAND TORPEDO

STEINBERG '4 90

LIVE   LASER

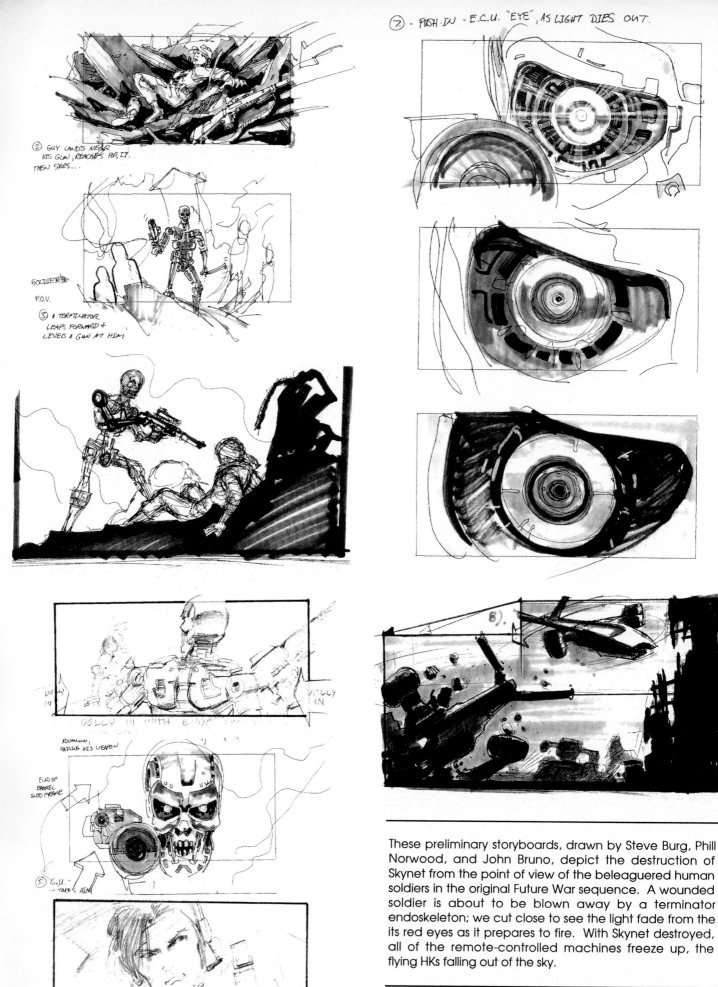

⑦ - PUSH-IN - E.C.U. "EYE", AS LIGHT DIES OUT.

② GUY LANDS NEAR
HIS GUN, REACHES FOR IT,
THEN SEES...

SOLDIER'S
P.O.V.

③ A TERMINATOR
LEAPS FORWARD &
LEVELS A GUN AT HIM

DOLLY
IN

DOLLY
IN

DOLLY IN WITH E.C.U.

ADVANCING,
RAISING HIS WEAPON

END OF
BARREL
INTO FRAME

⑤ C.U.
-- TAKES AIM

⑧

ON INJURED GIRL

These preliminary storyboards, drawn by Steve Burg, Phill Norwood, and John Bruno, depict the destruction of Skynet from the point of view of the beleaguered human soldiers in the original Future War sequence. A wounded soldier is about to be blown away by a terminator endoskeleton; we cut close to see the light fade from the its red eyes as it prepares to fire. With Skynet destroyed, all of the remote-controlled machines freeze up, the flying HKs falling out of the sky.

Skynet's weapons consist of the massive ground HKs (tank-like robot weapon-platforms), flying HKs, medium weight four-legged gun-pods called Centurions, the humanoid terminators in various forms (600, 700, and 800 Series), and small, fast-crawling kamikaze units called Silverfish that look like 5' long chrome centipedes. The Silverfish snake into your gun emplacements and explode.

SEQUENCE OF RAPID CUTS

Explosions!
Beam-weapons firing like searing strobe-lights.
Energy bolts crisscrossing frame.
Hand-launched Stinger missiles blowing an aerial HK out of the sky.
A Sapper team tries to disable a ground HK.
They get riddled by its rapidly tracking gun turret.

A TEAM OF GUERRILLAS is being overrun by terminator endoskeletons in the ruins of a building. One by one, the soldiers fall in desperate hand-to-hand combat. One of the terminators looms over a wounded soldier, its battle rifle's barrel swinging down toward the guerrilla's head. The man stares defiantly into his death. Then...
Suddenly, amazingly, the terminator stops, freezing in place...

Aerial HKs tilt slowly, out of control, and crunch to the ground. All the terminators stand frozen, unmoving, like a bunch of toy soldiers.

The sudden silence takes the humans by surprise. They slowly emerge from their rat-warren emplacements and approach the frozen machines. We hear a voice speaking over a radio headset. It is filled with awed emotion.

HEADSET VOICE (O.S.)
...The Colorado Division confirms that Skynet has been
destroyed... The war is over... I repeat, Skynet has--

CAMERA TRACKS along the soldiers, bleeding, frostbitten, wrapped in rags... Valley Forge with better weapons.
The wounded soldier in the ruins of the building cautiously approaches the chrome skeleton before him. He pushes against its chest with one finger. It topples with a crash and lies still.
The soldier turns to his comrades with an idiot grin. Tears are streaming down his face.
A mighty cheer goes up from the men and woman of the Last Army.

INT. TIME-DISPLACEMENT COMPLEX - L.A. - LATER

A STAINLESS STEEL ELEVATOR SHAFT, going deep into the bowels of the earth. Tiny figures stand on an open platform which descends rapidly, becoming a speck.

ON THE PLATFORM. An imposing man, surrounded by a team of guerrilla officers stands on the platform as it descends. He is JOHN CONNOR. Forty-five years old. Chiseled. Stern. The left side of his face is heavily scarred. A patch covers that eye. An impressive man, and clearly one forged in the furnace of a lifetime of war. The voice we heard before continues now.

> CONNOR (V.O.)
>
> *My name is Connor. It's my job to lead these people. My mother, Sarah, gave me the job... and she's not exactly someone you say "no" to. I wish to God I had. I've sent thousands to their deaths. But let me tell you about death in this world. We piss on the bones of a billion people. Death's not what it used to be. If there is a God, his love and 45 cents will buy you coffee...*

The platform reaches its destination. Connor and the officers step off. Begin moving down a long corridor.

INT. CORRIDOR

This place was designed by machines for machines. The architecture is alien, without aesthetics, without even such human basics as doorknobs and lights. Connor leads the team past more frozen terminator endoskeletons, deactivated like the ones on the surface.

> CONNOR (V.O.)
>
> *All these machines were controlled by a kind of God, a low-rent self-appointed God called Skynet. Skynet was a supercomputer built for strategic defense back in the Nineties. Today we destroyed it in its fortress in the Colorado Rockies, and all its toys stopped...*

As they continue on, they pass other teams of guerilla soldiers,

> CONNOR (V.O.)
>
> *This place is one of Skynet's toys. A machine built by machines. It is like nothing which has ever existed before... the first tactical time weapon. Before today, no human had seen this place, but I've been here in my dreams many times. All my life I've tried to imagine what it would look like. Now I'm actually here....*

INT. TIME DISPLACEMENT CHAMBER

Vault-like doors open. Connor strides through with authority and purpose. He is saluted smartly by everyone he encounters, though he wears no insignia of rank.

There is a bustle of hurried activity here. The chamber is the size of a high-school gym and consists totally of machine surfaces. Nothing in the design makes any sense. We can't tell what anything does. It is a technology we cannot imagine.

> CONNOR (V.O.)
>
> *Skynet, being almost infinitely smart, was also infinitely tricky. It knew it was losing, so it thought of a way to rig the game...*

Technicians have pulled up floor panels and tapped directly into the cabling of the machine, using portable terminals that they have wheeled in. Many of the soldiers in this war against machines are technical specialists... you have to fight fire with fire.

CONNOR (V.O.)
And now, though we've won the war, there is still one
battle left to fight. The most important one. It will be
fought in the past, almost four decades ago... before all
this began... See, the only problem with time travel is...
it ain't over even when it's over.

At the far end of the room, a young soldier stands surrounded by a team of technicians. KYLE REESE. Sarah Connor's defender, teacher, and lover in the first film. A simple soldier who is about to walk point into the gaping maw of history. At the moment, he is the center of activity. As he finishes stripping off his battle uniform, the techs begin smearing his body with a conductive so the time-field will follow his outline.

Reese looks around at all the activity. Battle and the prospect of death have never scared him. But the importance of what he is about to do terrifies him.

The techs move aside and suddenly John Connor is standing beside him. Connor... their grim messiah. Their leader. He fixes Reese with an intense gaze. There is so much he wants to say, but cannot bring himself to. Finally Reese speaks.

REESE
Did you know I'd be the one who volunteered?

Connor nods.

CONNOR
I've always known. Sarah told me.

Reese nods. Suddenly understanding everything.

REESE
That's why you moved me to your unit? Kept me so close.

Connor shrugs enigmatically.
One of the techs interrupts them.

TECH
We're ready, Sergeant.

THREE ENORMOUS CHROME RINGS, one inside the other, are suspended in a circular hole in the center of the room's floor. John and Reese approach them.

Reese steps onto the first ring. It bobs slightly under his weight. We see that the rings are freely floating in a magnetic field. Reese steps to the inner ring and looks into the hole. A vast echoing darkness below. He looks back at John. The messiah is waiting for him to step into the bottomless pit.

CONNOR
Sometimes you have to put your faith in the machine.

Reese takes a breath, then steps into open space and is buoyed up by an unseen field of force. He floats in the middle of the rings. The techs start the time displacement sequence.

THE RINGS BEGIN TO MOVE, slowly rotating around each other on different axes like some complex gyroscope.

THE FLOOR BEGINS TO SPLIT OPEN, like wedges in a pie which begin to pull back from the center. The rings are spinning faster now, suspended in space in the middle of the receding floor wedges. The rings begin to descend.

JOHN AND REESE LOCK EYES as they move apart. Reese is dropping into an unbelievably vast circular space... the time-field generator. John watches him go, until Reese is a tiny figure. The rings are spinning so rapidly now they almost disappear, becoming a sphere of whirling steel. Technicians pull John back from the edge.

LIGHTNING BEGINS TO ARC across the vast room below. A huge charge of energy is building up. Everyone takes cover behind blast walls they have set up. They put on goggles like they used to do at A-bomb tests. This is going to be big.

The chamber below has become a Hell of energy with Reese at its center. The drone and crackle of the machines builds to thunder, there is a BLINDING FLASH OF LIGHT!

When the glare fades the floating rings are empty. They slow to a stop, seared and smoking. Reese is gone.

FUENTES, one of the officers, turns to Connor.

> FUENTES
> Now what happens to Reese? I mean, what *did* happen?"

Connor's gaze seems far away from this time and place.

> CONNOR
> He accomplishes his mission and in doing so, he dies.

> FUENTES
> He is a good soldier.

Connor solemnly nods.

> CONNOR
> Yes. He's also my father.

> FUENTES
> Madre de Dios!

Fuentes stares at Connor in amazement. He has just been given a glimpse into his leader's private Hell. Connor turns from the smoking chamber. He seems suddenly ten years older as his features drain of strength, shoulders sagging.

Fuentes shouts an order in Spanish to a waiting Sapper team.

> FUENTES
> (in Spanish)
> Sapper team. Set your charges. Let's blow this place
> back to Hell.

Connor shakes his head no. Mustering his strength.

> CONNOR
> Not yet. There's one more thing we have to do.

276

TIGHT ON MASSIVE DOORS OF STEEL, covered with a thin sheet of ice. Locking bolts slam back. Ice shatters like glass as the doors begin to open. We are in--

INT. COLD STORAGE FACILITY

Connor walks into the darkness, followed by a few technicians. They are in a vault-like cold-storage room. Hanging in steel racks from ceiling tracks are hundreds of what appear to be men. They are in rows of ten. Within each row, each of the bodies are absolutely identical.

Connor signals the techs to remain by the door and walks out among the dark bodies. They are UNACTIVATED TERMINATORS. He stops at a row in which they are identical to the terminator which was sent to kill Sarah (the Arnold model).

He walks to the end of the row. There is one empty rack. He faces the terminator in the next rack. Its eyes are closed.
John seems distant as he studies that face.
Fuentes enters the chamber, pushing past the technicians. Calls for his leader in the darkness.

                    FUENTES
        John?... John?...

TIGHT ON CONNOR, his face pensive as Fuentes calls his name. Fuentes voice slowly dissolves to ANOTHER VOICE. A woman's. Echoing as though from a great distance....

                                        CUT TO:

This audio segue thus takes us directly to the scene of young John Connor in the Voights' garage in the present-day. The use of a sound dissolve between two voice calling John's name while holding a tight shot on his face works as a flashback-style transition to bridge the future and the present.

CONCEPT FOR AREA AROUND HEAD

277

NORWOOD

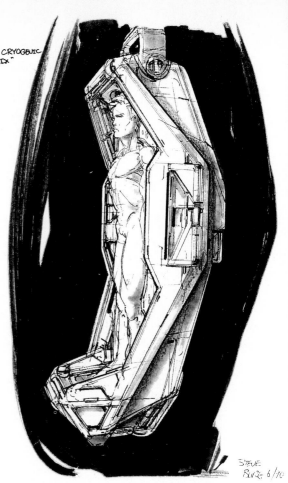

STEVE
BURG 6/10

STEVE BURG

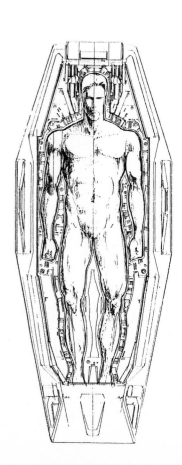

278

INT. HOSPITAL CORRIDOR

Sarah, strait-jacketed and strapped onto a GURNEY, is being wheeled down the corridor by Douglas and the other orderlies. Silberman is right behind her with the interns. Sarah's eyes are full of suppressed rage as she stares up and back at him.

> SILBERMAN
> (to the interns)
> What's fascinating about her case is that the architecture
> of the delusion--

> SARAH
> Don't talk about me like I'm not here. I'm right
> goddamn here!

> SILBERMAN
> We know where you are, Sarah...
> (continuing to the interns, as before)
> ... the delusion seems to have begun with the boyfriend
> and then been adopted by the patient. He believed he was
> a soldier from the next century, sent to protect her from a
> killer machine called a "terminator".

Frustrated, Sarah begins struggling against her restraints. Douglas, blocking the action from the doctors, casually smacks her solar plexus with his baton. Sarah gasps for air. Douglas winks at her.

> SILBERMAN
> You see, it's all about machines, for her. We're seeing
> more and more of this new syndrome, a sort of acute
> phobic reaction to technology. It's a defensive response
> to the dehumanization of relationships in a high-tech
> world.

They sweep through a set of double doors. The doors swing closed into CLOSEUP. Big block letters stenciled across them read:
ELECTRO-CONVULSIVE THERAPY.
Yes, they still do this shit to people.

INT. E.C.T. ROOM

Sarah's eyes go wide, clocking the sign on the door as she is wheeled in to a room full of ominous machines. Aging shock therapy equipment.

> SILBERMAN
> Sarah, today we're going to be trying ECT... electro-convulsive therapy--

> SARAH
> No! Don't do this. Okay, look, Silberman-- hey! Don't put that-- HEY!

She struggles vainly against the gurney straps as a NURSE tapes electrodes to her head. Silberman leans down to Sarah. The interns and the orderlies watch from near the door.

> SILBERMAN
> Now relax, we've found this very helpful with problems like yours. Such as this feeling that you're being persecuted--

> SARAH
> I'm not being persecuted, you fucking moron! I'm not a threat to them anymore. I told you. It's my son who's the target!

Silberman sighs. They finish placing the electrodes on her temples.

> SARAH
> You've got to let me go so I can protect him! He's naked if they come for him now! Please! Why won't you listen? You know how important this is!

The nurse sets the dials on the machine. Sarah starts to thrash now, becoming irrational. Starts shrieking at everyone in the room. She sounds exactly like what they say she is-- a whacko

> SARAH
> Goddamnit. Let me go!! I'll kill you, FUCKER!!

She screams incoherently as they jam the rubber biscuit down between her teeth so she won't bite through her tongue when the voltage jumpstarts her brain. Silberman is smooth and cheerful as he turns to the interns.

> SILBERMAN
> ECT is coming back into favor lately, and we've had good results with it. It looks worse than it is. As soon as the current hits her brain, she's out. It's a bit like punching the restart button on a computer when the program crashes.

He nods to the nurse and the current blasts through Sarah's brain, locking every muscle in her body into a painful contortion. It triggers an epilepsy-like seizure and she bucks and flops on the gurney.

SILBERMAN
She's not feeling anything right now.

TIGHT ON SARAH'S FACE, contorted, jerking spasmodically.   Then...

STROBOSCOPIC FLASH CUTS speeding up in rhythm, images coming at us like a
roaring freight-train:

TERMINATOR'S STEEL HAND lunging for her in the punch press.
A CHROME SKULL, eyes burning red, a demon after her soul.
STEEL FINGERS closing on her throat. Then...
SARAH'S FINGERS groping endlessly for the switch to the press. Then...

TERMINATOR'S RED EYES filling frame. Lightning arcing all around as the press
crushes the hideous machine. But even as it dies it has her by the throat. Even now, long
after it's dead, it still has her by the throat. The lightning gets brighter and brighter...
WHITING OUT FRAME

CUT TO:

This ending lightning and whiteout then cuts direstly to the lightning arcing outside the
trucker bar at night, heralding the arrival of Terminator through time. The stroboscopic
flash cuts in the moments immediately preceding this transition were to be shots from
the climax of the first film, as Sarah in the throes of her electroshock therapy relives the
arcing destruction of the first terminator, a nightmare that is still ever-present in her mind.

A117   SARAH'S HEAD droops. She closes her eyes.

118   *TIGHT ON small children playing. Different ones.*
Wider now, to reveal a playground in a park. Very idyllic. A dream playground, crowded with laughing kids playing on swings, slides, and a jungle gym. It could be the playground we saw melted and frozen in the post-nuclear desolation of 2029. But here the grass is vibrant green and the sun is shining.

118A   *Sarah, short-haired, looking drab and paramilitary, stands outside the playground. An outsider. Her fingers are hooked in a chain-link fence and she is staring through the fence at the young mothers playing with their kids. A grim-faced harbinger.*

118B   *Some girls play skip-rope. Their sing-song chant weaves through the random burbling laughter of the kids. One of the young mothers walks her two-year-old son by the hands. She is wearing a pink waitress uniform. She turns to us, laughing.*
It is Sarah. Beautiful. Radiant. Sarah from another life, uncontaminated by the dark future. She glances at the strange woman beyond the fence.

118C   *Grim-faced Sarah presses against the fence. She starts shouting at them in SLOW MOTION. No sound comes from her mouth. She grabs the fence in frustration, shaking it. Screaming soundlessly.*
Waitress Sarah's smile falls. Then returns as her little boy throws some sand at her. She laughs, turning away, as if the woman at the fence were a shadow, a trick of the light.

118D   *Behind her the earth splits open.*
In a wide shot we see everyone stop and stare as the ground heaves upward all around them. As far as the eye can see the monstrous caps of missile silos are hingeing up, ripping up through the grass and soil. Now the mothers are screaming, pulling their children to them... but it is too late to run. The silo caps are open, rows of them marching to the horizon. As if a tranquil reality has split open to reveal another horrible reality which has always been there, hidden beneath it.

118E   *Thunder shakes the earth. We see the obscene heads of the missiles thrusting up out of the holes in the ground. Walls of fire erupt as the fat cylinders rise like awakened monsters from the earth.*

118F   *Sarah stares in numb horror as the tail-nozzles clear the silo rims, and a wall of flame roars out, devouring the cowering mothers and children. Incinerating them and rolling on, toward her.*
She screams and we hear it now, shrill and terrifying, mixing with the thunder as the flames wrap around her, blasting her apart and she...

119   Wakes up.

SALCEDA'S DEATH SEQUENCE - 9/10/90 draft

Salceda's Death sequence from 9/10/90 draft was scheduled but never filmed due to both scheduling and cost considerations; scheduled for the first week of principal photography, the scene would have involved a great number of mechanical makeup and pyrotechnic effects, not to mention a fair number of complicated visual effects plates for computer graphics shots. Since its only narrative purpose was to show how T-1000 follows them to Dyson's house and a number of the T-1000 gags in the scene were reprised more effectively elsewhere, it was deemed redundant to the plot and unnecessarily complicated for the first week of shooting.

A125   EXT. SALCEDA'S CAMP - NIGHT

SALCEDA'S DOG, teeth bared, barks a furious warning. The SOUND of machine gun fire erupts, drowning him out.
YOLANDA, clutching a .45 Officer's Colt, sweeps Paco and Juanita up in her arms and races away.

SALCEDA is firing an MP5K on full auto, its strobing barrel flash lighting up the camp.
CAMERA PUSHING IN ON HIM AS...

A125A THE T-1000 calmly walks toward him, unbothered by the stream of bullets.
Unhurried. Salceda, amazed, is backing toward his truck, and the stacks of crated grenades and ammo boxes beside it.
The T-1000 keeps coming. Steps right up to Salceda, knocks the weapon away and slams him to the ground.

A125B Salceda sprawls against one of the open wooden crates.
T-1000 kneels before him. Points its finger. THUNK. Salceda screams, pinned to the crate by a two-foot steel needle through his left lung.

                         T-1000
                Where is John Connor?

                         SALCEDA
            John who?

A125C THUNK!! Another needle slams through him. Salceda struggles to breathe against the excruciating pain.

A125D   T-1000
                   (almost soothingly)
            I know this hurts. Where is John Connor?

Salceda's hand gropes in the open crate of grenades behind him. He clutches one. Then apparently ready to cooperate he clutches T-1000's shoulder and struggles to pull himself closer, up along the impaling spikes.

Behind the T-1000's neck, Salceda pulls the grenade's pin with his free hand. The spoon flies off... CLINK.

                         SALCEDA
            FUCK YOU!!

A125E The truck, Salceda, and the T-1000 vanish in a MASSIVE EXPLOSION as the grenade sets off the other munitions. A huge ball of fire ascends into the night.

PAGE ONE

HARD CUT - C.U.
MP5K FIRING -
JUMPING AWAY
FROM CAMERA.

JIM
WHEN YOU HAVE
FREE TIME (LIKE
TAKING A DUMP)
LOOK THESE ROUGHS
OVER. PHILL

CONTINUES BACKING AWAY FROM CAMERA.

T-1000 ENTERS FRAME.

SALCEDA REFLECTED
IN MIRROR SHADES.
TRACK BACK WITH
T-1000

PAGE TWO
SALCEDA TRIPS
AGAINST CRATES.

... AND FALLS BACK
AGAINST 4 by 4 ...
... T-1000
WALKS INTO FRAME

UPSHOT T-1000
WALKS INTO SHOT...

... CONTINUES FORWARD
HIS BULLET RIDDEN
CHEST IN FRAME.

SALCEDA LOOKS
UP AT THE RE-HEALING
T-1000 WHO
STARTS TO KNEEL

PAGE 3
T-1000 KNEELS
NEXT TO SALCEDA
POINTS HIS RT.
HAND AT HIM...

THUD!

T-1000
WHERE IS JOHN
CONOR?

SALCEDA
JOHN WHO?

T-1000
STICKS HIM
WITH THE LEFT
HAND

PAGE 4
C.U. SPIKE COMING
THROUGH SALCEDA'S
BACK INTO 4 by 4.

THUD!

THUD!

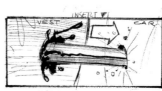

T-1000
I KNOW THIS HURTS

TILT
DOWN

PULLS OUT
GRENADE ....

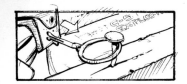

HOOKS PIN RING
ON NAIL - AND
PULLS RING

SALCEDA GRABS
T-1000 SHOULDER
AND TRIES TO

SALCEDA
AAAHHHH....
PUSHES HIMSELF
ALONG SPIKES

CONT

CONTINUES.

SALCEDA
CONTINUES TO
MOVE FORWARD

GRENADE
EXPLODES

WIDE SHOT   AMMO CATCHES
            ALSO

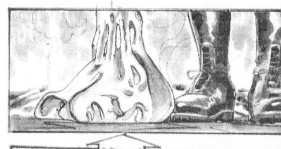

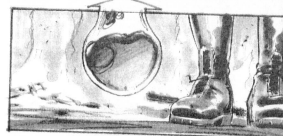

A125F YOLANDA, huddled with her children, the .45 held before her in a combat grip, screams
as—

A125G A CHROME HEAD rolls out of the inferno and comes to rest in the dirt, the liquid metal
mouth gulping like a gaffed fish.

A125H A figure appears, silhouetted by the fire... or most of a figure.

A125I We TRACK WITH the polished black cop shoes toward the head lying in the dirt. A hand
enters frame. The head dissolves and fuses with the hand, like two blobs of solder running
together.

A125J IN CLOSE-UP, the T-1000 rises into frame, whole again. It trains its gaze on Yolanda and
the children.

A125K She stares in shock at the thing approaching. She slowly lowers the useless pistol. The T-
1000 walks right up to her. It reaches down and picks up little Juanita. Gives her a friendly
smile.

> T-1000
> Do you know where John Connor is?

The child mutely shakes her head no. T-1000 nods, unperturbed. Points toward the road.
Juanita follows with her eyes.

> T-1000
> When they reached the main road, did they go north...
>> (indicating)
> ...or south?

She points north. T-1000 smiles. Sets her down, unharmed.

> T-1000
> Thank you for your cooperation.

With that, T-1000 turns and strides to its motorcycle parked a few yards away. Yolanda
and her children silently watch as the Cop from Hell climbs onto the bike and and roars off
into the night.

> CUT TO:

The reabsorption of T-1000's gulping head was one of the favorite moments that was
reluctantly lost when the scene was cut; it served no narrative purpose and was merely
a variation on the reabsorption of the chrome hook hand in Scene 801, just as the
skewering of Salceda is a less involving take on the skewering of Sarah at the steel mill
later on. In a very telling moment at the end of this sequence, T-1000 demonstrates the
subtlety with which it goes about its mission, shifting gears from the brutal interrogation of
Salceda to the gentle questioning of Yolanda and the kids. Compare this to the same
point in the following Gant Ranch sequence.

100   EXT. DIRT ROAD - DAY

The desolate hills southwest of Brawley.
TERMINATOR steers the pickup along a narrow dirt road which winds precariously through the hills. It is designed to discourage casual visitors.

101   They approach a heavy metal gate which blocks the road.
It is flanked on both sides by a high chain-link fence topped with razor-wire. There is no call box or phone. Only a NO TRESPASSING sign with a bunch of dried rattlesnake heads decorating it, their jaws wide, fangs gleaming.

> SARAH
> Don't get out. They saw us coming three miles back.

101A   On cue, a jeep rounds the bend beyond the gate and roars toward them. They hear a thundering whop-whop of rotors and a Vietnam-era Huey roars over the hill next to them and hovers overhead, blasting them with its rotor wash.
Three men dismount from the jeep and walk forward. One carries a shotgun, the other two M-16s. Above them, in the door of the Huey, another guy has an AK-47 trained on them. Terminator steps out with the shotgun.

Sarah gets out and goes to the gate, waiting for the sentries to reach her. She speaks to the lead man, SALCEDA, through the gate in perfect, almost unaccented Spanish.

> SARAH
> (subtitled)
> Tell Gant I'm here.

Salceda, a Mexican wearing jeans, cowboy boots, and a flak vest, grins at her.

> SALCEDA
> (Spanish / subtitled)
> He doesn't want to see you.

> SARAH
> Just tell him, *pendejo*. And tell him I have John with me.

The sentry speaks into a walkie-talkie. We hear her name mentioned, but not much else. John waits at the truck with Terminator.

101B
> JOHN
> This place is run by a guy named Travis Gant. An ex-Green Beret. A total wild man... he's got connections all over Mexico and Central America.

101C   The sentry is nodding, holding the walkie up to his ear. We don't hear the other end of the conversation over the helicopter. He looks at Sarah and shrugs. The sentries open the gate, waving the chopper off.

                              SALCEDA
                         (to Terminator)
                    Put the shotgun back in the truck.

Sarah nods to him to comply.

                              SALCEDA
                    You ride with me. Enrique will bring your truck.

One of the sentries walks past them to their truck as they move to Salceda's jeep.

                                                        CUT TO:

102   EXT. DIRT ROAD

IN THE JEEP, bumping along the winding road. Sarah, John, and Terminator jammed in the back, holding onto a roll bar.

                              JOHN
                    What makes you think he'll help us?

                              SARAH
                    He'll help us.

                              JOHN
                         (to Terminator)
                    The last time Gant and Sarah were in the same room he
                    was in a drunken rage and coming after her with a
                    sheepskinning knife.

                              TERMINATOR
                    Why?

                              SARAH
                    We were breaking up at the time.

103   EXT. GANT'S RANCH / COMPOUND - DAY

The jeep passes through an arched stone gate and enters the courtyard of Gant's run-down hacienda. The place might have been nice once, but it's a dump now. A lot of military-surplus jeeps and other vehicles are parked around, and we see surveillance cameras, razor wire, and other styling touches which make the place look more like a military compound than a ranch.

There are more men, mostly Hispanic. A few white guys. Dress varies from biker denims to military fatigues. There are women, children running, and dogs.

Terminator, John, and Sarah get out of the jeep.
The dogs do not dig Terminator at all. They are barking and whining, slinking around, keeping their distance.

Two men come out of the main house, one striding ahead of the other. In the lead is
TRAVIS GANT, followed by his first lieutenant, INGRAM. Gant is in his late thirties,
lean and muscular. He wears combat boots and cammo pants, no shirt, a denim vest, and
a greasy bandana rolled into a headband. He is tight lipped, no nonsense, and even though
his hair has grown out and he only shaves every other day, his bearing is utterly
military... no fat, no nonsense, no wasted movement. His eyes are concealed by dark
aviator-style shades, and he wears a Detonics custom .45 holstered at his hip.

Ingram is younger, an almost baby-faced ex-Marine punk with a bad attitude. Gant walks
up to Sarah, glancing once warily at Terminator, and plants himself right in front of her.

> GANT
> Man, you are one fuckin' section-eight crazy fucking
> bitch, coming here, you know that?
>> (changing tone)
> Hi John, long time.

> JOHN
> Hi, Travis.

Gant turns back to Sarah, talking lower. Very tense.
He leans close to her, so no one else in the compound can hear them.

> GANT
> Your picture's all over the TV, you know that? You and
> your psycho buddy, there. Man, I do NOT need this! I got
> a business to run. I can't afford any heat up here.

> SARAH
> So deal to us and we're on our way.

> GANT
> What do you need?

> SARAH
> Guns... heavy stuff. Explosives... and com gear, travel
> documents. And I need you to get us across the ditch and
> arrange for a trip south. Costa Rica. Peru. Whatever
> you can set up.

> GANT
> How about the fillings out of my fucking teeth?! Man,
> you are unbelievable!

John sees them standing close together and says to Terminator...

> JOHN
> This is going better than I thought it would.

ON SARAH AND GANT, TIGHT.

> GANT
> I can't believe you had the balls to come back here. And
> dragging that poor kid along. You still feeding him all
> that crazy shit about a nuclear war and how he's gonna
> be the savior of all mankind?

290

                    SARAH
He is.

                    GANT
Still a goddamn loony tune. You always were. A good
fuck, but a loony tune. Just get out of here, Sarah.

                    SARAH
I need your help, Gant.

                    GANT
Forget it. When the Ice Capades open in Hell, you call
me.

Gant turns to walk away, yelling to Ingram and the others.

                    GANT
Get her out of here!

                    SARAH
Wait!

Gant pauses. She gestures to Terminator to walk forward. Ingram and the sentries raise
their weapons.

                    SARAH
Tell him what you are.

                    TERMINATOR
Series 800 terminator. Model 101. Cyborg tactical
infiltrator.

                    GANT
Oh my God. A killing machine from the future. Watch
out, guys.

Gant snorts, shaking his head. Looks between Terminator and Sarah like they are a sorry
pair of losers.

                    GANT
Man, you two deserve each other.

                    SARAH
            (to Gant)
Give me your .45. I need to show you something.

Gant looks at her warily. But there are ten of his people around with automatic weapons, so
he unholsters the pistol and hands it to her. Sarah shows it to Terminator.

                    SARAH
Can I shoot you in the head with this?

                    TERMINATOR
If it will help.

                    SARAH
Turn around.

He does and she levels the pistol in a two-hand grip at the back of his head, point blank. Sarah clicks off the safety. Gant can't believe what he's seeing here. She's really going to do it...

                         GANT
         Bullshit!!

POW! POW!
Terminator's head jerks a little with each hit. John winces. The cyborg turns to them, calm and unhurt.

                         TERMINATOR
         No problemo.

Gant just stares, his mouth hanging open. He slowly goes up to Terminator. Gets right up to his face. He looks right into the eyes. Touches the skin of the cyborg's cheek.
Walks slowly behind him, not knowing what he expects to see.
It all comes crashing in on him. We see it in his face. He believes. Gant turns to Sarah.

                         GANT
                  (weakly)
         Come inside.

John winks at Terminator. Gives him a BIG THUMBS UP.
Terminator imitates the gesture, then *tries* a wink. It needs work.

104   INT. GANT'S HACIENDA - DAY

Gant leads them into the kitchen, yelling to the house in general.

                         GANT
         Yolanda?! We got company!

He is in shock, going to one cupboard then another, then back to the first. His body moving while his brain reels.

                         GANT
         Where's the fucking tequila?

He pulls a bottle out of the cupboard and grabs more glasses than he can carry, gets them to the table. Sarah helps him.
A WOMAN comes to the doorway... Hispanic, about 25, and seven months pregnant. She looks stonily at the scene, wary of the strangers. A two-year-old boy toddles up behind her, hand jammed in his mouth.

                         GANT
         That's Yolanda. <u>Mrs</u>. Gant.
                  (he arches his eyebrow at Sarah)
         Go figure, huh?

                         JOHN
                  (in Spanish/ subtitled)
         Hi. Nice to meet you. I'm John, this is Sarah, and this
         is--
                  (indicating Terminator)
         Uh... my uncle. Bob. Uncle Bob.

Yolanda smiles. John has broken the ice. He has a way of controlling situations, understanding people.

Gant is ripping the cap off the tequila bottle. The two-year-old toddles to him and grabs his cammo pants, sliming them with drool.

Terminator watches the tiny kid, fascinated. What is it?

> GANT
> And this is Paco. Honey, take Pacolito. Thanks, baby.

She takes the child and retreats. Wife as domestic slave. After Sarah, the guy obviously wanted somebody more tame.

Gant sits heavily at the table, moving like the breath is knocked out of him. He pours himself a tall shot and downs it in one gulp.

> GANT
> So ... everything you always said. The war... the future... it's all real?

He looks at Terminator, who nods "yes".

Gant grabs the other glasses, pouring while he talks.

> GANT
> Wheww! Damn. I feel like I been kneed in the balls here. This is big.
> (to Terminator)
> Drink?

Terminator gestures "no" at the proffered glass.

Gant realizes his mistake. This cyborg shit takes getting used to.

> GANT
> Yeah, right.

Sarah pours for herself. A straight shooter. She tosses it back.

> SARAH
> I tried to tell you.

> GANT
> I know. You did. Many times.

John signals to Terminator "let's go". He wants to leave Sarah and Travis alone to work this out. As always, his instincts are solid. He takes Terminator by the sleeve of his jacket and they drift away. John calls from the front door...

> JOHN
> Any place I shouldn't go?

> GANT
> Su casa, John. You know that. Anything I got's yours.

105   EXT. MAIN HOUSE

Terminator and John walk out on the porch. Ingram, standing just outside the door, eyes them coldly. He has heard Gant's shouted carte-blanche but he doesn't like it.

As they walk down the steps Terminator looks at John...

TERMINATOR
Uncle Bob?

106   INT. HOUSE

Gant and Sarah, alone at the kitchen table. He takes off his dark glasses and his eyes are somehow appealing, not hard like we might have expected.

                    GANT
          When you first laid that shit on me, about John, I thought
          you were section-eight for sure. Psycho waitress that
          thinks her kid's fucking Napoleon.

                    SARAH
               (she smiles)
          You didn't exactly throw us out.

                    GANT
          Naw. I start cuttin' people off just cause they're crazy
          an' I'd lose *all* my friends. Now I see why you were
          always serious as a heart attack. Carrying that kind of
          shit around, by yourself, year after year. I'm impressed
          kid.

                                             CUT TO:

107   EXT. COMPOUND

John and Terminator walking across the compound.
John calls to some guys he knows, yelling in fluent Spanish.
They wave to him.

                    TERMINATOR
          How long did you live here?

                    JOHN
          Four years. But we spent a lot of time in Nicaragua,
          Costa Rica... places like that. Wherever Travis had
          business. I thought this was how people lived. Like
          everybody grew up doing weapons training. Riding
          around in helicopters. Learning how to blow shit up.

                    TERMINATOR
          Gant taught you?

                    JOHN
          My mom and him, yeah. When she got busted I got put in
          a regular school. The other kids thought I was a *little*
          weird.

108   INT. HOUSE/ KITCHEN

Gant stares at her, thinking back. It's one of those moments where someone is utterly familiar and yet somehow suddenly a total stranger.

                    GANT

Yeah... now I look back I can see your whole plan. Find
some guy that knows weapons and tactics, some dumb
bastard, and get him to teach you how to run a military
operation... so you could pass it on when the kid was old
enough. Brilliant. And I was the dumb bastard.

                    SARAH

Travis...

                    GANT

Everything had a purpose. Coming on to me, getting me
to teach you, take you out on runs. Christ, I didn't care.
Long's you wrapped them legs around me, I'd a done
anything. Damn, you didn't give one shit for me really,
did you?

In her expression, her contained sadness, we see that she did not.

                    SARAH

I'm sorry, Travis.

                    GANT

You took me for a ride, got what you needed, and got off.

We can see his pain. He thought they had something. Even though it ended badly, he
remembered good moments. His new knowledge has led to a bitter re-evaluation. Now he
knows those moments were hollow even then.

                    SARAH

I did what I had to do.

                    GANT

Yeah. I guess you did. You wanna know what's crazy
about it?

                    SARAH

What?

He pours again, for both of them. Tall.

                    GANT

You did it exactly right. You knew what you had to do
and you did it. You got nerves of fucking stainless steel,
baby. I'm proud of ya. I really mean that.

They lock eyes... a moment of connection.
She is forgiven, although it is a painful forgiveness.
He grins at her, suddenly, a crazy kamikaze grin.
Clinks her glass.

                    GANT

<u>To the future! Fuck it if it can't take a joke! Right?</u>

He tosses back the tequila.

109   EXT. COMPOUND

John and Terminator pass some stripped Hueys, rusting on blocks. The functional Huey
sits on the grass beyond. Salceda is supervising the unloading of some crates from the
chopper.

                              JOHN
                 It's sad, my mom and Travis. She won't let anybody
                 take the place of my real dad.

                              TERMINATOR
                 Kyle Reese.

                              JOHN
                 Yeah. He's dead.
                      (brightening suddenly)
                 Hey! Did you ever meet him? Up in the future, I mean.

                              TERMINATOR
                 No. Sorry.

John shrugs. He thinks he's being casual, but his longing for some kind of parental
connection is obvious.

                              JOHN
                 I wish I coulda met him. I guess I will, when I'm older,
                 cause I send him back through time and all. He hasn't
                 even been born yet. Man, it messes with your head.

                              TERMINATOR
                      (remembering the phrase)
                 It messes with your head.

                              JOHN
                 Yeah. My mom and him were only together for one
                 night, but she talks about him every day. She still loves
                 him, I guess. I see her crying sometimes. She denies it
                 totally, of course. Says she got something in her eye.

109A   They reach a bunker-like concrete building. There is a combination lock on
       the heavy steel door, like a bank vault. John starts twiddling the dial on the lock.

                              TERMINATOR
                 Why do you cry?

                              JOHN
                 Left 3 to 48.
                      (looking up)
                 You mean people? I don't know. We just cry. You
                 know. When it hurts. *Right 2 to 90.*

                              TERMINATOR
                 Pain causes it?

                    JOHN
Uh-unh, no, pain is like a... like an alarm that tells you
when there's damage. This is different... *And left one
to 20.* It's when there's nothing wrong with you but you
hurt anyway. Because you love somebody, and they're
gone or whatever. You get it?

                 TERMINATOR
No.

John completes the combination and tries the latch. It unlocks with a CLUNK.

                    JOHN
He should change this combination.

110   INT. ARMORY

John precedes Terminator into Gant's armory. A long concrete room lined with every
imaginable kind of weapon. Racks of rifles, pistols, rocket launchers, mortars, RPGs,
radio gear. At the far end boxes containing ammo, grenades etc. are stacked to the ceiling.
Terminator gets real alert. Scanning the walls, wondering where to begin.

                 TERMINATOR
Radical.

                    JOHN
Yeah, I thought you'd like this place.

Terminator picks up a MAC 10 machine pistol. Slaps in a magazine.
John grabs an AK-47 and racks the bolt with a practiced action. Inspects the receiver for
wear. Doesn't like what he sees. Puts it back. His movements are efficient.
Professional. Uninterested.

                    JOHN
Hey, do you feel any different yet? Like you're learning
stuff?

                 TERMINATOR
I don't know. I feel the same.

                    JOHN
Have you figured out yet why you can't go around
killing people?

Terminator is still stumped. He takes a shot in the dark.

                 TERMINATOR
Because it hurts them?

                    JOHN
Nooo. Because it hurts the people who love them. Get it?
That's the value of human life... we have feelings,
people love each other.
        (a beat, then--)
Are you afraid of dying?

Terminator pauses a second. The thought never occurred to him. He searches his mind for the answer...

> TERMINATOR
> No.

Terminator has found a Vietnam-era "blooper" M-79 grenade launcher. A very crude but effective weapon. He opens the breech and inspects the bore.

> JOHN
> You don't feel any emotion about it one way or the other?

> TERMINATOR
> No.

Terminator slings the M-79 and starts looking for the grenades.
John is idly spinning a Sig Saur 9mm pistol on his finger... backwards and forwards like Bat Masterson.

> JOHN
> See, that's the problem. You don't care if you live or die,
> and so you think everybody's like that.

> TERMINATOR
> I have to stay functional until my mission is complete.
> Then it doesn't matter.

John picks up a 2nd generation Starlite scope. Switches it on. Twiddles the gain. Looks through it.

> JOHN
> Yeah. I have to stay functional too.
> (sing-songy)
> "I'm too important".
> (he puts the scope down)
> She won't even let me play football. It's a drag.

111   EXT. COMPOUND - DAY /LATER

Sarah has changed. Boots, black fatigue pants, T-shirt. Night patrol jacket. Shades. She looks hard. She and John have their weapons and supply selections laid out for cleaning and packing.
Maps, radios, documents, explosives, detonators... just the basics.
Gant strides up.

> GANT
> It's set. Soon as it's dark we'll cross the ditch in the
> Huey, and I've got a Citation meeting us at that strip in
> San Lupe.

> SARAH
> Thanks.

Sarah eyes the preparations one last time and walks away.

                                        CUT TO:

298

112   INT. T-1000'S POLICE CRUISER - DAY

The T-1000 sits as before. Monitoring the police radio. Listening to Sarah's tapes.
Scanning John's letters and papers.

                        SARAH (VO)
            ...if we're ever separated, go directly to Gant's ranch.
            Travis will take care of you until I get there...

T-1000 stops scanning the letter in its hand. It zeros in on the sentence it just heard. Stops
the cassette recorder. Reaches to the computer terminal on the dash. Types "Travis Gant"
with a KNOWN ACQUAINTANCES cross-reference to "Sarah Connor".

112A   TIGHT ON THE COMPUTER SCREEN. Gant's vital statistics come up. Date
of Birth. License. Number of arrests. And an address out in Imperial Valley, near the
Mexican border.

112B   TIGHT ON T-1000 staring at the screen.
Suddenly, the barrel of a REVOLVER appears through the open window beside it. It's
aiming right at its head. The owner is a helmeted C.H.P. OFFICER.
                        CHP
            Freeze! Police!

The T-1000 calmly complies.

112C   ANGLE ON CRUISER from a few yards away. The motorcycle cop stands outside the
cruiser's window, aiming his revolver. We see his motorcycle parked off to the side of the
empty road.

112D   A SECOND MOTORCYCLE COP pulls into shot, rolling into CLOSEUP.
He's wearing a headset/microphone under his helmet. We hear him calling in the report.

                        2ND CHP
            Roger, that's a positive I.D. on the vehicle. Suspect is in
            custody.

                                                CUT TO:

113   EXT. HIGHWAY - DAY / MINUTES LATER

The T-1000 thunders along on a CHP Kawasaki 1100, doing about a hundred and twenty.
PAN WITH IT until it recedes toward the horizon.
                                                CUT TO:

114   EXT. GANT'S RANCH / COMPOUND -DAY

Sarah seems to have the weight of the whole world on her shoulders. She sits at a picnic
table. Draws her boot knife.
Starts to carve the words... "There is no--"

115   NOT FAR AWAY, JOHN is field-stripping and cleaning weapons, packing for the trip.

116   UP ON THE HUEY NEARBY, Gant and Terminator are flight-checking the aircraft,
Gant covered with grease, changing a part in the rotor-head. Terminator helps him install
the component.

                          GANT
So you're supposed to stay with the kid forever, and teach
him, protect him, and keep him out of trouble?

                       TERMINATOR
Correct.

                          GANT
Buddy, sounds like you just got yourself elected father.

                       TERMINATOR
Father?

                          GANT
Women'll do that.

                       TERMINATOR
I'm not even human.

                          GANT
No, it's fucking brilliant. Think about it. She knows
you'll never stop... that you'll always be there. And
you'll never hurt the kid. You'll never shout at him,
never get drunk and hit him. Never say you can't spend
time with him 'cause you're too busy. And you'd die to
protect him. You're the ultimate parent.

                       TERMINATOR
You're better suited. The boy likes you.

                          GANT
Naw. I ain't the guy. Forget it. She wrote me off a long
time ago. Too many bad habits.

Gant laughs and takes a long pull from the tequila bottle.
He looks at Terminator, the solemn cyborg from the future.

                          GANT
Anyway, considering what's ahead for that kid, you're a
better role model... God help him.

HOLD ON Terminator, thinking about what's been said.

                       TERMINATOR
You are a father. Do you have any advice?

                          GANT
Talk about the blind leading the blind. My advice?
Lighten up-- the kid's world is so goddamn grim-- smile
once in a while.

                       TERMINATOR
Smile?

> GANT
> Yeah. *Smile*. You know.
> (he whistles to one of his men)
> Hey, Enrique... your sister still sucking off donkeys in
> Tijuana?

> ENRIQUE
> (with a shit-eating grin)
> No man, she's cutting down. Your mother's taking all
> the business.

> GANT
> See. That's a smile.

116A TERMINATOR POV (DIGITIZED) The real-time image continues while a replay of Enrique grinning runs in a window. It expands, so that Enrique's mouth fills the window. Replays again in slow motion. A vector-graphic of lips smiling appears, along with an array of symbolic data.

117 Terminator tries it. The result is dismal. A rictus-like curling up of the lip.
Terminator's next effort is a marginal improvement.

> GANT
> I don't know, maybe you could practice in front of a
> mirror or something.

ON SARAH, AT THE TABLE, as she looks up from her carving, thinking. She watches some kids playing in a sprinkler nearby.
They are children of some of Gant's men... shrieking as the cold water hits them and loving it.

Sarah sees Yolanda walking Pacolito by the hands.
Backlit, stylized. Carefree, despite the para-military setting.
She looks over at John, cleaning guns... sees his future.

117A ANGLE ON kids playing.

117B TIGHT ON John inserting a part.

117C SARAH leans back against a tree trunk. Closes her eyes.

118 *TIGHT ON small children playing. Different ones.*
Wider now, to reveal a playground in a park. Very idyllic. A dream playground, crowded with laughing kids playing on swings, slides, and a jungle gym. It could be the playground we saw melted and frozen in the post-nuclear desolation of 2029. But here the grass is vibrant green and the sun is shining.

118A *Sarah, short-haired, looking drab and paramilitary, stands outside the playground. An outsider. Her fingers are hooked in a chain-link fence and she is staring through the fence at the young mothers playing with their kids. A grim-faced harbinger.*

118B *Some girls play skip-rope. Their sing-song chant weaves through the random burbling laughter of the kids. One of the young mothers walks her two-year-old son by the hands. She is wearing a pink waitress uniform. She turns to us, laughing.*
It is Sarah. Beautiful. Radiant. Sarah from another life, uncontaminated by the dark future. She glances at the strange woman beyond the fence.

118C *Grim-faced Sarah presses against the fence. She starts shouting at them in SLOW MOTION. No sound comes from her mouth. She grabs the fence in frustration, shaking it. Screaming soundlessly.*
Waitress Sarah's smile falls. Then returns as her little boy throws some sand at her. She laughs, turning away, as if the woman at the fence were a shadow, a trick of the light.

118D *Behind her the earth splits open.*
In a wide shot we see everyone stop and stare as the ground heaves upward all around them. As far as the eye can see the monstrous caps of missile silos are hingeing up, ripping up through the grass and soil. Now the mothers are screaming, pulling their children to them... but it is too late to run. The silo caps are open, rows of them marching to the horizon. As if a tranquil reality has split open to reveal another horrible reality which has always been there, hidden beneath it.

118E *A thunderous roar shakes the earth. We see the obscene heads of the missiles thrusting up out of the holes in the ground. Smoke geysers up, and walls of fire erupt as the fat cylinders rise like awakened monsters from the earth.*

118F *Sarah stares in numb horror as the tail-nozzles clear the silo rims, and a wall of flame roars out, devouring the cowering mothers and children. Incinerating them and rolling on, toward her.*
She screams and we hear it now, shrill and terrifying, mixing with the thunder as the flames wrap around her, blasting her apart and she...

119   Wakes up.
All is quiet and normal. The children are still running through the sprinkler nearby. Less than fifteen minutes have gone by.

Bathed in sweat, Sarah sits hunched over the table. Every muscle is shaking. She is gasping.
Sarah struggles to breathe, running her hand through her short hair which is spiky with sweat. She can escape from the hospital, but she can't escape from the demon which haunts her.

She looks down at the words she has carved on the table, amid the scrawled hearts and bird-droppings. They are words Kyle Reese told her, which John Connor made him memorize before he came across time. They are:
"There is no fate but what we make."

Something changes in her eyes.
She slams her knife down in the table top, embedding it deeply in the words. Then gets up suddenly and we--

CUT TO:

120   INT. ARMORY

The door opens and Sarah walks in out of the afternoon sun.

120A   SERIES OF TIGHT SHOTS:
A big FN FAL .308 rifle is snatched from a rack.
A laser-designator is clipped onto the barrel.
A tritium-reticle night-scope is snapped into place.
Long .308 bullets are rammed one by one into a magazine.

120B   TIGHT ON SARAH, looking at the last bullet. She pushes it down into the magazine with her thumb. Sitting on top, it will be the first one fired. A 20 cent bullet which could save 3 billion lives.
She slaps the magazine into the rifle and chambers the first round.
Slinging the heavy weapon over her shoulder she exits.

121   LONG LENS on Sarah walking toward us. In the sunlight now, she pulls a pair of dark glasses from her jacket and puts them on. In her night-patrol fatigue pants, boots and glasses she is all business.
She strides across the compound with grim purpose.
Her face is an impassive mask, her lips set. She has become a terminator.

JOHN LOOKS UP from his work in time to see Sarah throw the rifle into the back seat of a hard-top jeep, jump in and start it. She slams it in gear.

122   GANT AND TERMINATOR look up as the jeep brakes hard alongside the Huey. They are up on top of the cowl, adjusting the cyclic linkage.

Sarah roars up in the jeep. She yells to them without getting out.

> SARAH
> Fly John out tonight as planned. Then come back and
> wait for me here. I'll be back by dawn.

> GANT
> Where you going?
> (she roars off)
> Hey!! Where-- god-DAMN-it.

MOVING WITH SARAH as she leaves the compound. We see John running after her... yelling. Can't hear his words. She looks in the rear-view mirror but doesn't slow down.

CUT TO:

123   EXT. COMPOUND - DAY / MINUTES LATER

John, Terminator, and Gant ponder the message carved into the top of the picnic table. Sarah's knife is still embedded there. Ingram looks on, wondering what the big deal is.

> JOHN
> "No fate but what we make." My father told her this... I
> mean, I made him memorize it, up in the future as a
> message to her--
> (he sees Gant's expression)
> Never mind. Okay, the whole thing goes "The future is
> not set. There is no fate but what we make for ourselves"

> GANT
> What's it mean?

> TERMINATOR
> It means she intends to change the future somehow.

John snaps his fingers as it hits him...

> JOHN
> Dyson!!!

                              GANT
          What?

                              JOHN
          Miles Dyson. She's gonna blow him away. Son of a
          bitch!

                              GANT
          Who's Dyson?

                              JOHN
                      (to Terminator)
          We gotta stop her.
                      (he spins to Gant)
          Travis, you stay here in case she comes back. Keep her
          here till we get back. We need a jeep.

Gant is amazed to be getting orders from a ten-year-old. Even more amazed to be
following them.

                              GANT
          Take that one.

He points at an open jeep nearby. John motions to Terminator and breaks into a run.

                              JOHN
          Come on. Let's get our stuff.

                                              CUT TO:

124   INT./EXT. SARAH'S JEEP - DUSK

Sarah speeds through the darkening desert. Her face is a mask. Grim and
expressionless. In her dark glasses, she looks severe. Pitiless as an insect.

                                              DISSOLVE TO:

125   EXT. HIGHWAY - NIGHT

TRACKING WITH A JEEP, Terminator and John heading into L.A.

                              TERMINATOR
          Why do you want to stop her, John? It may work.

                              JOHN
          I don't care!! Haven't you learned anything?! There's
          gotta be another way. Think!

PAN THEM BY as they pass, revealing the lights of the city ahead.

                                              CUT TO:

126   EXT. GANT'S RANCH

Gant, deep in thought, approaches the back entrance to the main house. He sees Enrique
asleep in a chair on the back porch, rifle across his knees. Gant works up to him like a cat,
and surprises him by swiping his cap.

Only Enrique doesn't surprise so well. His head lolls over and Gant sees the dilated pupils, the trickle of blood from the corner of one eye.

Gant gets a shot of adrenalin that revs him into hyper-alertness in two seconds. He drops into the shadows next to the chair and scans the surroundings rapidly. In the bushes, twenty feet away, another one of his men lies crumpled and motionless. Gant pulls his Detonics .45 and thumbs the safety off, then slips his walkie off his belt.
He cups his hand over it and whispers.

> GANT
> Main gate? Miguel? Don't talk, just key your walkie if
> you copy, over.
> > (there is no answer)
> Salceda? You copy? Franco? Come back.

His answer is static.
Not good. Gant takes a couple grenades from Enrique's harness and slips them in a vest pocket. He cat-steps to the house.

127   INT. GANT'S HOUSE

Gant enters the dark house. His radar is turned up all the way. He hasn't felt his heart pounding like this since Khe San. He crosses the living room. Pauses in the corridor. Silhouetted in the kitchen is a motionless figure... Yolanda.

He puts his finger to his lips and motions her to him.

127A   As she comes toward him Gant wonders at the last second why she doesn't look particularly afraid... an instant before Yolanda's hand snaps out into a two-foot steel needle which punches through his abdomen and pins him to a solid oak door with a THUNK!
He whips up the .45 but THUNK! His forearm is skewered, pinned to the door at his side. The pistol clatters to the floor.

127B   He stares, face to face, into the eyes of the T-1000 as it morphs into the cop-form. Maybe this is an acid flashback, except it hurts too goddamn much. He knows suddenly that very special fear, not just of death, but of an incomprehensible death in a deranged universe.

> T-1000
> Where is John Connor?

Gant squirms on the skewers like a bug, gasping with the pain.

> GANT
> John who?

127C   THUNK!! Another needle slams through him, sprouting directly from the cop's chest. It pins him through the left lung.

> T-1000
> Where is John Connor?

Gant struggles to breathe against excruciating pain.

> GANT
> Don't know... gone.
> > (THUNK. Another needle)
> Aaaarrgh!

127D

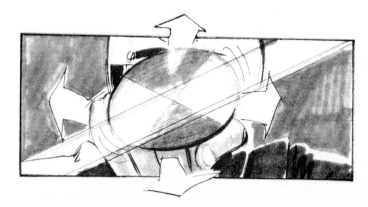

127E   THUNK. Another. Gant screams now, feeling rapier thrusts through shoulder and groin. He can't believe the pain. His hand fumbles into the pocket of his vest. Sweaty fingers find a grenade there. He pulls the pin. The spoon flies out and clinks on the floor. T-1000 looks down and looks back up, into Gant's eyes.

GANT

<u>FUCK YOU!!</u>

128   EXT. GANT'S HOUSE

    The front of the house EXPLODES in Ingram's face. He was running toward the front door with his MPK machine-pistol at ready. The blast knocks him on his ass. He sits up, slashed by flying glass, to see the inside of the house engulfed in flame. Then he sees something on the ground, just outside the shattered front door...

128A   A chrome head. Ingram's expression goes bugshit. The chrome mouth is moving, gulping like a gaffed fish.

218B   A figure appears in the doorway... or most of a figure.
       We TRACK WITH the polished black cop shoes toward the head lying in the dirt.

128C   A hand enters frame. The head dissolves and fuses with the hand, like two blobs of solder running together.

128D   IN CLOSE-UP, the T-1000 rises into frame, whole again.

128E   INGRAM snaps out of his stupor and crawls in a frenzy for his machine pistol. He starts screaming and firing, screaming and firing as we TRACK IN ON HIM.

128F   The MPK clicks empty. It is swatted out of his hands and a steel needle pins him to the dirt.

T-1000

Where is John Connor?

INGRAM

I don't know, man... aaaargh... they were talking about
some guy... Dyson or something like that...

INGRAM'S POV as the impassive cop face hovers above him.

T-1000

Thank you for your cooperation.

128G   The cop's hand comes into frame, the index finger pointing straight at us.
       RACK FOCUS to the tip of the finger as--
       SSSNICK! A flash of steel FILLS FRAME, then blackness.

CUT TO:

DYSON'S VISION SEQUENCE - 9/10/90 draft

Dyson's dying vision in the 9/10/90 draft was originally a much more stylized and lyrical death scene that emphasized the man's character making peace with himself and with his family at his sacrifice for the good of mankind. Although a powerful scene, it was ultimately never filmed as the exploration of Dyson's character and his relationship with his family became secondary to the main thrust of the narrative.

167   INT. LAB

Dyson is lying amid the ruins of his dream. Sprawled on the floor, he has his back propped up against the desk. He is bathed in his own blood, which runs out in long fingers across the tiles. His breathing is shallow and raspy. He still holds the book, trembling, above the switch.

In his lap is the picture from his desk. He has pulled it from the debris next to him. A tear trickles from his eye. His wife and children smile up at him through broken glass.

168   DYSON'S POV-- He sees only the picture. WE PUSH IN SLOWLY. The sounds from outside are fading... megaphones, the helicopter, distant sirens, all become fainter... replaced by a ROARING SOUND which swells as the image of the picture grows dark. Darker and darker, the blackness rushing at us now with the sound of thunder. It gets louder and LOUDER. Like a black train pounding at us, only it is a roiling cloud of red and black... blood-red fire boiling up through a cloud-mass black as iron. It is the cloud-column of a hydrogen bomb, FILLING FRAME, shaking our senses with its power.

And then--
It begins to recede. The thunder rolls away, dying into a wind which is like the last winds of a great storm, ebbing into a soothing breeze as the iron clouds swirl away, giving way to an image of gauzy light. As if behind a soft veil we see--

168A   *Danny and Blythe running toward us, laughing, in slow motion. Tarissa is behind them, smiling. They are in bright sunlight, an image of motion and life, a slice of memory so vivid and precious a man needs only this to face eternity. We see their hair blown by the wind, the wind which blows through history now, changing it...*

We tilt up into a pure blue sky until the sun comes into frame, spearing straight into the lens with pure light and we...

169   CUT TO THE PUPIL OF HIS EYE, the sun becoming a glint of light in that pupil, as we do a SNAP-PULLBACK to see Miles Dyson at the moment of death. His face is almost blank, his gaze fixed, seeing what we cannot see, seeing a future which is changed... there is the faintest hint of a smile, the instant the light fades from his eyes and he is gone--
His arm drops and the book hits the switch--

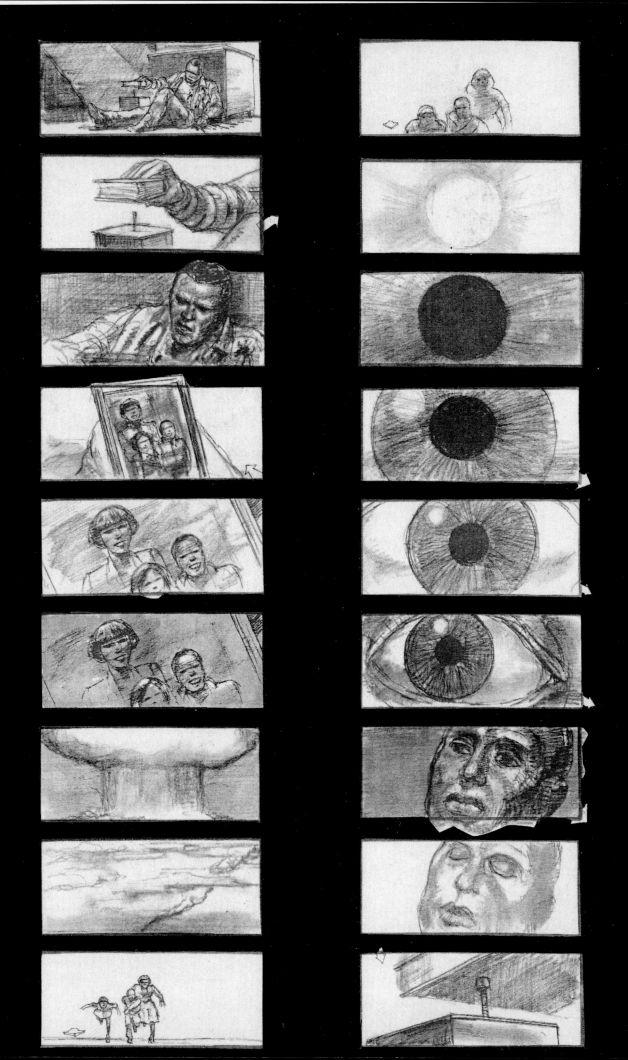

OPENING CREDITS:

MARIO KASSAR
PRESENTS

A
PACIFIC WESTERN
PRODUCTION

IN ASSOCIATION WITH
LIGHTSTORM ENTERTAINMENT

A
JAMES CAMERON
FILM

ARNOLD
SCHWARZENEGGER

TERMINATOR 2
JUDGMENT DAY

LINDA HAMILTON

ROBERT PATRICK

JOE MORTON

EARL BOEN
S. EPATHA MERKERSON

DANNY COOKSEY
CASTULO GUERRA

AND INTRODUCING
EDWARD FURLONG

CASTING BY
MALI FINN

COSTUMES DESIGNED BY
MARLENE STEWART

MUSIC BY
BRAD FIEDEL

INDUSTRIAL LIGHT AND MAGIC
VISUAL EFFECTS SUPERVISOR
DENNIS MUREN, A.S.C.

SPECIAL MAKEUP AND TERMINATOR EFFECTS
PRODUCED BY
STAN WINSTON

FILM EDITORS
CONRAD BUFF
MARK GOLDBLATT, A.C.E.
RICHARD A. HARRIS

PRODUCTION DESIGNER
JOSEPH NEMEC, III

DIRECTOR OF PHOTOGRAPHY
ADAM GREENBERG, A.S.C.

CO-PRODUCERS
B.J. RACK
STEPHANIE AUSTIN

EXECUTIVE PRODUCERS
GALE ANNE HURD
AND
MARIO KASSAR

WRITTEN BY
JAMES CAMERON
& WILLIAM WISHER

PRODUCED AND DIRECTED BY
JAMES CAMERON

END CREDITS:

Presented In Association With
LE STUDIO CANAL+ S.A.

Unit Production Manager	DIRK PETERSMANN
First Assistant Directors	J. MICHAEL HAYNIE TERRY MILLER
Key Second Assistant Directors	SCOTT LAUGHLIN FRANK DAVIS

CAST OF CHARACTERS

The Terminator	ARNOLD SCHWARZENEGGER
Sarah Connor	LINDA HAMILTON
John Connor	EDWARD FURLONG
T-1000	ROBERT PATRICK
Dr. Silberman	EARL BOEN
Miles Dyson	JOE MORTON
Tarissa Dyson	S. EPATHA MERKERSON
Enrique Salceda	CASTULO GUERRA
Tim	DANNY COOKSEY
Janelle Voight	JENETTE GOLDSTEIN
Todd Voight	XANDER BERKELEY
Twin Sarah	LESLIE HAMILTON GEARREN
Douglas	KEN GIBBEL
Cigar Biker	ROBERT WINLEY
Lloyd	PETE SCHRUM
Trucker	SHANE WILDER
Old John Connor	MICHAEL EDWARDS
Kids	JARED LOUNSBERY
	CASEY CHAVEZ
Bryant	ENNALLS BERL
Mossberg	DON LAKE
Weatherby	RICHARD VIDAN
Cop	TOM McDONALD
Jocks	JIM PALMER
	GERARD G. WILLIAMS
Night Nurse	GWENDA DEACON
Lewis, the Guard	DON STANTON
Lewis as T-1000	DAN STANTON
Attendant	COLIN PATRICK LYNCH
Hospital Guard	NOEL EVANGELISTI
Girls	NIKKI COX
	LISA BRINEGAR
Danny Dyson	DE VAUGHN NIXON
Vault Guard	TONY SIMOTES
Jolanda Salceda	DIANE RODRIGUEZ
Infant John Connor	DALTON ABBOTT
Pool Cue Biker	RON YOUNG
Tattoo Biker	CHARLES ROBERT BROWN
Gibbons	ABDUL SALAAM EL RAZZAC
Moshier	MIKE MUSCAT
SWAT Team Leader	DEAN NORRIS
Police Chopper Pilot	CHARLES TAMBURRO
Pickup Truck Driver	J. ROB JORDAN
Tanker Truck Driver	TERRENCE EVANS
Burly Attendants	DENNEY PIERCE
	MARK CHRISTOPHER LAWRENCE
SWAT Leader	PAT KOURI
Cyberdyne Tech	VAN LING
Mr. Schwarzenegger's Stand-In	PETER KENT
Ms. Hamilton's Stand-In	MARY ELLEN AVIANO
Mr. Furlong's Stand-In	RHONDA MILLER

Stunts

JANET BRADY	BILLY HANK HOOKER	BILL LUCAS
BOB BROWN	NORMAN HOWELL	COTTON MATHER
DOC D. CHARBONNEAU	THOMAS J. HUFF	BOBBY PORTER
GILBERT B. COMBS	LARRY JOHNSON	DAVID WEBSTER
JEFF DASHNAW	PETER KENT	GLENN WILDER
DEBBIE EVANS	LANE LEAVITT	DICK ZIKER

Stunt Coordinators
JOEL KRAMER   GARY DAVIS

Second Assistant Directors	TONY PEREZ DUSTIN BERNARD JAMES LANSBURY
Second Second Assistant Director	XOCHI BLYMYER

Art Director
JOSEPH P. LUCKY

Assistant Art Directors
CHARLES W. BREEN
GARY DIAMOND

Art Department Coordinator
CARLA S. NEMEC

Art Department Assistant
DUNCAN KENNEDY

Set Designers
WALTER MARTISHIUS
CAROLE L. COLE

Set Decorator
JOHN M. DWYER

Leadman
BARTON M. SUSMAN

On Set Dresser
R. PATRICK McGEE

Set Dressers
JOE PIZZORUSSO
WILLIAM DOLAN
CRAIG BARON

Chief Lighting Technican
GARY TANDROW

Electric Best Boy
STEVEN C. McGEE

Rigging Gaffer
KEVIN J. LANG

Rigging Best Boy
STEVE HASTINGS

Electricians
JAMES COX
DAVID DUNBAR
BRAD EMMONS
JASON GUNN
DAVID E. HENGSTELLER
FRANK KREJSA
JOE ROWAN
JOHN SMOCK
DONALD STANFORD
DARRIN PULFORD

Key Grip
ROBERT GRAY

Best Boy Grip
"SLICK" RICK RADER

Dolly Grip
DONALD L. HARTLEY

"A" Camera Operators
MICHAEL A. BENSON, S.O.C.
MICHAEL ST. HILLAIRE, S.O.C.

Lead Assistant Camera
DENNIS J. LAINE

First Assistant Camera
MICHAEL J. FAUNTLEROY

Second Assistant Camera
ALAN COHEN
GAVIN ALCOTT
DAN TEAZE

Film Loader
STEPHEN A. SFETKU

Extra Camera Operator
PAUL C. BABIN

Steadicam® Operator
JAMES MURO

Vista Vision Camera Technician
CHRISTOPHER DUDDY

Aerial Director of Photography
DAVID L. BUTLER

Aerial Coordinator
CHUCK TAMBURRO

Still Photographer
ZADE ROSENTHAL

Video Assist Operators
PETE MARTINEZ
SCOTT WARNER

Sound Mixer
LEE ORLOFF, C.A.S.

Boom Operator
NICHOLAS R. ALLEN

Cable
KNOX GRANTHAM WHITE

Property Master
CHARLES STEWART

Assistant Property Master
LINDA WAXMAN

Grips
RICHARD CROMPTON
HILARY KLYM
BRIAN LIBERMAN
TYRONE JACKSON
JOHN NASH, RYAN RUSSILL

Rigging Grip
RODNEY VELO

Special Effects Coordinator   THOMAS L. FISHER

Special Effect Assistants
SCOTT FISHER, BOB KING
JAY KING, TERRY KING
ROGER HANSEN, BRUCE MINKUS
MARK NOEL

Key Makeup Artist JEFF DAWN

Makeup Artists
STEVE LaPORTE
ED FRENCH

Script Supervisor
TRUDY RAMIREZ

Locations Managers
RICHARD KLOTZ
STEVE DAWSON
JIM MORRIS

Assistant Location Manager
ROBERT FOULKES

Location Assistant
MARC COHEN

Location Security
LAURA CATHLEEN SHERMAN

Costume Supervisor
BRUCE R. HOGARD

Set Costumes
GREG HALL, DAWN Y. LINE

Specialty Costume Manufacturing
CAROL DOBROVOLNY

Key Hairstylist PETER TOTHPAL

Hairstylist
ROBERT L. STEVENSEN

Production Accountant
CHRIS SILVER FINIGAN

Assistant Production Accountants
THOMAS A. DAVILA
TIMOTHY A. BURRIS
RICK SWEENEY

Acting Coach
MIKE MUSCAT

Teacher
PIA MEHR

Production Coordinator
JANE PROSNIT

Assistant to Mr. Kassar
KIM BALSER

Assistant to Ms. Rack
LISA ANN STONE

Production Assistants
JOHN DAVIS
JEFFREY D. NELSON
RACHEL OBERSTEIN
MICHAEL PITT
KRISTINE SPINDLER
LIAM PHILLIPS
MICHAEL VIGILIETTA

Transportation Coordinator
GENE JOHNSON

Transportation Captain
JERRY JOHNSON

Picture Car Captain
STEVE BONNER

Transportation Office
Coordinator
KENNETH NEWLAND

Construction Coordinator
STEVE CALLAS

General Foreman
MIKE WELLS

Steel Mill Consultant
MARV FREEMAN

Craft Service
JOHN MOY

Stand-by Painter
BILL K. HOYT

Catering
GALA CATERING

Assistant Production
Coordinator
DEAN WRIGHT

Assistant to Ms. Hurd
JOE EARLEY

Ms. Hamilton's Personal
Trainer
ANTHONY CORTES

Technical Advisor
and Trainer
UZI GAL

Coordinating Motor
Officers
JACK WOOD, L.A.P.D.
WALLACE SARVER, L.A.P.D.

Police Technical Advisors
CALL THE COPS
RANDY WALKER
ED ARNESON
MICHAEL ALBANESE
JAMES DAHL
STEVEN STEAR

Cast Security
RONALD D. HUGHES

Weapons Master
HARRY LU

Weapons Specialist
TONY DIDIO

Functional Props
CAMAIR RESEARCH
MIKE CAMERON
VINCE CATLIN

Assistant to Mr. Cameron
ALEXANDRA DROBAC

Assistant to Ms. Austin
MARY LAMAR MAHLER

Assistant to
Mr. Schwarzenegger
ANNE MERREM

DGA Trainee
KELLY CANTLEY

First Aid
CINDY LASHER

Publicity
STEVE NEWMAN

International Publicity
DENNIS DAVIDSON
ASSOCIATES

Electronic Press Kit
ED W. MARSH
DAVID G. HUDSON

Assistant Casting Associate
EMILY SCHWEBER

Extras Casting
UNO CASTING

San Jose Extras Casting
ABRA EDELMAN

Extras Set Coordinator
ERIC SINDON

Projectionist
J. DOLAN PRODUCTION
UNITS

Second Unit

Second Unit Director
GARY DAVIS

Director of Photography
MICHAEL A. BENSON

Camera Operator
DON FAUNTLEROY

First Assistant Camera
TED HAWSER
BRUCE MANNING

Second Assistant Camera
BRUCE DeARAGON
TODD GAVIN

First Assistant Directors
GEORGE PARRA
RANDALL BADGER
BARRY THOMAS

Script Supervisor
KATHARYN JOYCE KING

Transportation Captain
PETE JOHNSON

Catering
SILVER SCREEN

Second Assistant Directors
GRANT GILMORE
DAVID FUDGE

Chief Lighting Technician
SALVATORE J. OREFICE

Key Grip
SCOTT ROBINSON

Costumers
COLLIN BOOTH
PATTIE MOON

Video Assist Operator
RICHARD J. DUNGAN

Post Production Supervisor
PAMELA EASLEY

Post Production Coordinator
CRYSTAL DOWD

First Assistant Editors
CAROLINE ROSS
JANE KASS

Supervising Music Editor
ALLAN K. ROSEN

Assistant to Mr. Fiedel
ROSS LEVINSON

Visual Effects Production
Supervisor
ALISON SAVITCH

Visual Effects Editor
MILLER DRAKE

Conceptual Artist
STEPHEN BURG

Supervising
First Assistant Editor
CLARINDA WONG

Second Assistant Editors
RON SOUTH
CLAY RAWLINS
KELLY TARTAN

Assistant Music Editor
DAN GARDE

Post Production Assistant
JOSEPH BERGER-DAVIS

Creative Supervisor/
Visual Effects Coordinator
VAN LING

Visual Effects Designer
JOHN BRUNO

Storyboard Artist
PHILLIP NORWOOD

Illustrator
GEORGE JENSEN

**Assistant Visual
Effects Editor**
JULIE J. WEBB

Special Projects
STEVEN QUALE

**Visual Effects
Lighting Consultant**
RICHARD MULA

Visual Effects Assistant
GEOFFREY BURDICK

Post Production Sound Services Provided By
SKYWALKER SOUND
A Division of LucasArts Entertainment Company
Marin County, California

Sound Designer
GARY RYDSTROM

Re-Recording Mixers
TOM JOHNSON
GARY RYDSTROM
GARY SUMMERS

Sound Supervisor
GLORIA S. BORDERS

Sound Effects Editors
ROBERT SHOUP
TIM HOLLAND
TERESA ECKTON
KEN FISCHER
RICHARD HYMNS
ETHAN VAN DER RYN
LARRY OATFIELD

Foley Editor
MARION WILDE
DIANA PELLEGRINI
SANDINA BAILO-LAPE

Re-Sync Editor
KATHLEEN KORTH

Dialogue Editors
PAIGE SATORIUS
STACEY FOILES
EWA SZTOMPKE
GWEN YATES-WHITTLE
SARA BOLDER

Sound Assistants
DIANE STIRPE
CLAIRE SANFILIPPO
VANESSA JAMES
KEVIN WILLIAMS
J.R. GRUBBS
PAM UZZELL
CLARE FREEMAN
PHIL OLBRANTZ
SAM HINCKLEY
HAEL KOBAYASHI
SUSAN SANFORD
JIM SEYMOUR
SUSAN POPOVIC

ADR Editors
C.J. APPEL
BARBARA McBANE
MICHAEL PERRONE

**Assistant
Sound Designers**
DAVID SLUSSER
TOM MYERS
SCOTT CHANDLER

Foley Artist
DENNIE THORPE

Foley Assistant
MARNIE MOORE

Foley Recordist
CHRISTOPHER BOYES

Computer Graphics Images By
INDUSTRIAL LIGHT & MAGIC
A Division of LucasArts Entertainment Company
Marin County, California

**Assistant Visual Effects
Supervisor**
MARK A.Z. DIPPÉ

**Computer Graphics
Shot Supervisors**
JAY RIDDLE
DOUG SMYTHE
LINCOLN HU
GEORGE H. JOBLOVE
SCOTT E. ANDERSON
THOMAS A. WILLIAMS
STEFEN M. FANGMEIER

**Computer Graphics
Software Developers**
ERIC ENDERTON
CARL NAI FREDERICK
MICHAEL J. NATKIN
ANGUS POON
JOHN F. SCHLAG
TIEN TRUONG

ILM Plate Photography
PATRICK McARDLE
CHUCK SCHUMANN
CARL MILLER

ILM Effects Photography
TERRY CHOSTNER
BOB HILL

**Plate Photography
Coordinator**
JACK GALLAGHER

**Computer Graphics
Animation Supervisor**
STEVE WILLIAMS

**Computer Graphics
Animators**
JOHN ANDREW BERTON, JR.
GEOFF CAMPBELL
RICHARD L. COHEN
JONATHAN FRENCH
CHRISTIAN HOGUE
ELIZABETH MAXWELL KEITH
JOHN NELSON
JOSEPH M. PASQUALE
STEPHEN ROSENBAUM
ANDREW SCHMIDT
ALEX SEIDEN
ANNABELLA SERRA

**Vice President and
General Manager**
SCOTT ROSS

**Executive in Charge
of Post Production**
ED JONES

**Executive In Charge
of Finance**
MARTY SHINDLER

**Computer Graphics
Coordinators**
JUDITH WEAVER
GINGER THEISEN

Visual Effects Producer
JANET HEALY

Visual Effects Art Director
DOUG CHIANG

Visual Effects Editor
MICHAEL GLEASON

Scanning Supervisor
JOSHUA FINES

**Optical Photography
Supervisor**
BRUCE VECCHITTO

**Visual Effects
Coordinator**
GAIL CURREY

Digital Supervisor
STUART ROBERTSON

Scanning Operators
RANDALL K. BEAN
GEORGE GAMBETTA
MICHAEL COOPER

Scanning Software
JEFF LIGHT

Negative Cutter
ROBERTO McGRATH

Scanning Coordinator
LISA VAUGHN

Digital Artists
BARBARA BRENNAN
JIM HAGEDORN
GORDON BAKER

Digital Transer Operator
GREG MALONEY

Digital Coordinator
SUSAN ADELE COLLETTA

Stage Technicians
CHUCK RAY
TIM MORGAN
PHIL HERON

Computer Graphics
Technical Assistants
JAMES D. MITCHELL
RACHEL FALK
DIANA ACE
ALICE ROSEN

Computer Graphics
System Support
JAY LENCI
KEN BEYER

Visual Effects
Assistant Editor
JIM MAY

Computer Graphics
Department Manager
DOUGLAS SCOTT KAY

Production Assistant
LESLIE SCHOR

Roto Supervisor
TOM BERTINO

Rotoscopers
TERRY MOLATORE
JACK MONOOVAN
JOANNE HAFNER
SANDY HOUSTON

Production Accountant
PAMELA KAYE

Special Makeup and Terminator Effects Created At
STAN WINSTON STUDIO

Art Department Coordinators
JOHN ROSENGRANT   SHANNON SHEA   SHANE MAHAN

Art Department

BILL BASSO
IAN STEVENSON
LEN BURGE
DAVID GRASSO
JOE READER
MIKE TRCIC
RICHARD DAVIDSON
GREG FIGIEL
KAREN MASON
ROB WATSON
MICHIKO TAGAWA
ALAN SCOTT
PAUL SCIACCA

DAN REBERT
SEAN ROGERS
GLEN EISNER
JOSEPH PATRICK TODD
MARK JURINKO
BRAD KRISKO
ROBERT BURMAN
MICHAEL SPATOLA
ANDY SCHONEBERG
CHRIS SWIFT
ADAM JONES
PAUL MEJIAS
DAVE BENEKE

MARK "CRASH" McCREERY
JEFF PERIERA
EILEEN KASTNER DELAGO
BETH HATHAWAY
J.C. MATALON
CURT MASSOF
BRUCE SPAULDING FULLER
BRENT BAKER
DAVID STINNETT
JOSEPH KELLEY

Artists' Assistant
MARK LOHFF

Assistant to Stan Winston
TARA MEANEY CROCITTO

Mechanical Department Coordinator
RICHARD LANDON

Mechanical Department

EVAN BRAINARD
CRAIG CATON
CHRISTIAN COWAN
MARK GOLDBERG

ARMANDO GONZALEZ
CHARLES LUTKUS
GREGORY MANION

HAL MILES II
JON C. PRICE
BROCK WINKLESS

Additional Digital Compositing
PACIFIC DATA IMAGES

Special Visual Effects By
FANTASY II FILM EFFECTS INC.

Visual Effects Supervisor
GENE WARRN, JR.

Model Makers
GARY RHODABACK
PETE GERARD
DENNIS SCHULTZ
DWIGHT SHOOK
MONTY SHOOK
STEVE PETRUZATES

Visual Consultant
JERRY POJAWA

Optical Engineers
BOB MICHELETTI
JIM MARTIN

Optical Supervisor
BETZY BROMBERG

Fire Shots
TONY ALDERSON

Ink and Paint Supervisor
MARY MULLEN

Visual Effects Producer
LESLIE HUNTLEY

Camera Operators
CHRISTOPHER WARREN
PAUL GENTRY
MICHAEL KARP

Illustrator
JOHN EAVES

Production Coordinator
BETH BLOC

Optical Camera
DON FERGUS
DAVID TUCKER
DAVE EMERSON

Head Animator
SEAN APPLEGATE

Sculptors
MAKE UP EFFECTS
UNLIMITED
BART MIXON
DAN FRYE
DAN PLATT

Pyrotechnic Supervisor
JOSEPH VISKOCIL

Model and Shop
Supervisor
MICHAEL JOYCE

Go Animation
PETER KLEINOW

Production Assistants
SCOTT BEVERLY
JAMES COOK
STEVE COHEN
TONY MOFFET
KIRBY JONES

Optical Line-Up
BRYAN COOKE

Roto Supervisor
BRET MIXON

Tesla Coil
THE ARTIFICIAL
LIGHTING COMPANY
ED ANGELL

Special Visual Effects Sequences
4-WARD PRODUCTIONS, INC.
ROBERT SKOTAK
ELAINE EDFORD

316

Visual Effects Supervisor ROBERT SKOTAK	Supervising Director of Photography DENNIS SKOTAK	Effects Coordinator JENNIFER BELL
Optical Effects Supervisor ROBERT COSTA/ GENESIS OPTICAL EFX	Production Designer MICHAEL NOVOTNY	Opticals HOLLYWOOD OPTICAL SYSTEMS, INC.
Directors of Photography JAMES BELKIN GEORGE D. DODGE	Editor W. PETER MILLER	Computer Imaging ELECTRIC IMAGE, INC.
Matte Painters RICK RISCHE RICHARD KILROY	Best Boy MARY SHELTON	Effects Lead Man EMMET KANE
Model Builders LOUIS ZUTAVERN BRIAN McFADDEN DANIEL CARTER WILLIAM STROMBERG JIM DAVIDSON DAVID ZEN MANSLEY ANTHONY STABLEY TIM CONRAD BRET ALEXANDER DOUG MOORE ANTHONY CHANEY JOSEPH THOMPSON	Gaffers MARK SHELTON GEORGE NEIL	Mliniature Set and Rig Supervisors RICC RUSKUSKI STEPHEN BRIEN
	Stage Manager JORGE FUENTES	Miniature Set Operator JOE STEINER
	Stage Assistants SAMANTHA STEVENS KEVIN BROWN SERGIO MORENO ANTHONY FORZAGLIA, JR.	Special Effects Technicians BOB AHMANSON THOMAS ZELL PHILLIP HARTMANN STEVE SANDERS
	Special Effects Supervisor JOSEPH VISKOCIL	Production Assistant PAULA PIROK

Terminator P.O.V., Video and Graphic Displays By
VIDEO IMAGE

RHONDA C. GUNNER
GREGORY L. McMURRY

RICHARD E. HOLLANDER
JOHN C. WASH

Crew

LARRY WEISS
ANTOINE DURR
JOHN DesJARDIN

SCOTT PETERSON
ANDY KOPRA

JOSEPH GOLDSTONE
CAROLINE ALLEN
SCOTT GIGIELER

"YOU COULD BE MINE" Performed by Guns N' Roses Written by Izzy Stradlin and W. Axl Rose Published by Guns N' Roses Music (ASCAP) Courtesy of Geffen Records	"BAD TO THE BONE" Performed by George Thorogood and The Destroyers Written by George Thorogood Published by Del Sound Music (BMI) Courtesy of EMI Records USA A division of Capital Records, Inc. By Arrangement with CEMA Special Markets	'GUITARS, CADILLACS" Written and Performed by Dwight Yoakam Published by Coal Dust West Music (BMI) Courtesy of Reprise Records By Arrangement with Warner Special Products

Soundtrack Available on Geffen Cassettes and Compact Discs.

Financial Services
FRANS J. AFMAN

Completion Bond Services Provided By
COMPLETE FILM CORPORATION

Production Insurance Provided By
ALBERT G. RUBEN & COMPANY, INC.

Cyberdyne Systems Corporation Building Courtesy
RENCO INVESTMENT COMPANY

The Producers wish to thank:
Advanced Computer Products; Atari Games Corporation;
Jon Bell; California Film Commission: California Steel Industries, Inc.;
CalTrans - Ray Baghshomali and Marc Duprey; Capt. Mike Lanam
and the Fremont Police Department; The City of Fremont, California;
Cinetica Giotto Bicycle Provided by Ochsner International;
The County of Los Angeles Economic Development Corporation
Film Office - Chandra Shah; Edge Innovations; ElectroCom Automation, Inc.;
Hero Cologne by Prince Matchabelli; The Hewltt-Packard Company;
Tom Hudson; The Los Angeles County Flood Control District;
Matte World; Midway Manufacturing Company; Miller Brewer Company;
Miller Electric Mfg. Co.; James Muro; National Drager;
Northgate Computer Systems; Pepsi-Cola Company
C.A. Robinson Company; Sega Enterprises, Inc.;
Southern California Prosthetic and Orthotics; Subway Sandwiches & Salads;
Williams Electronics Games, Inc; Yorba Systems.

Main Title Supervised By	Main Title Graphic Design By
ERNEST FARINO	PAUL OLSEN
Main Title Graphics By	Negative Cutting
LUMENI PRODUCTIONS INC.	MARY NELSON DUERRSTEIN
Color By	Color Timer
CFI	ART TOSTADO
Title and Opticals By	Process Compositing By
PACIFIC TITLE	HANSARD®

Prints by TECHNICOLOR® EASTMAN PRINT FILM

Lenses By ARRIFLEX® Camera by OTTO NEMENZ INTERNATIONAL

Cranes and Dollies
CHAPMAN

Lighting and Grip Equipment Supplied By
HOLLYWOOD RENTAL COMPANY, INC.

PLAY THE HIT NINTENDO GAMES FROM ACCLAIM/LIN ENTERTAINMENT

NOW READ THE BANTAM BOOK

T2™ and TERMINATOR™
are trademarks of Carolco Pictures Inc. and Carolco International N.V.

CAROLCO.

MPAA #31159
MOTION PICTURE ASSOCIATION OF AMERICA

THIS PICTURE MADE UNDER
THE JURISDICTION OF
AFFILIATED WITH
A.F.L. - C.I.O.

TRI
STAR
PICTURES

A TRI-STAR RELEASE

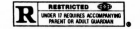

R | RESTRICTED
UNDER 17 REQUIRES ACCOMPANYING
PARENT OR ADULT GUARDIAN

TM and © 1991 Carolco.

TERMINATOR™ 2
JUDGMENT DAY

Official Fan Club Membership

Join the Official T-2 Fan Club today and take advantage of this special offer to obtain your own videocassette of "The Making of TERMINATOR 2 – Judgment Day."

Your T-2 Membership Package will include:

"THE MAKING OF TERMINATOR 2 – JUDGMENT DAY" Videocassette, not available in stores

Membership Welcome Letter

Plastic Wallet-Size Membership Card

Subscription Offer for T-2 Newsletter

Additional T-2 Authorized Products at Special Discounts for Members Only

Retail Value
$14.95

Yours for only
$9.95*

*Plus $3.95
Shipping &
Handling